Making the Modern South
DAVID GOLDFIELD, EDITOR

THOMAS DIXON JR.
and the Birth of Modern America

Edited by Michele K. Gillespie and Randal L. Hall

LOUISIANA STATE UNIVERSITY PRESS   BATON ROUGE

Published by Louisiana State University Press
Copyright © 2006 by Louisiana State University Press
All rights reserved
Manufactured in the United States of America
Louisiana Paperback Edition, 2009

Designer: Barbara Neely Bourgoyne
Typefaces: Clarendon BT, display; Adobe Minion Pro, text

LIBRARY OF CONGRESS CATALOGING-IN-PUBLICATION DATA

Thomas Dixon, Jr. and the birth of modern America / edited by Michele K. Gillespie and Randal L. Hall.

p. cm. — (Making the modern South)

Includes bibliographical references and index.

ISBN 0-8071-3130-X (hardcover : alk. paper)

1. Dixon, Thomas, 1864–1946—Criticism and interpretation. 2. Dixon, Thomas, 1864–1946—Knowledge—United States. 3. National characteristics, American, in literature. 4. Race relations in literature. 5. Racism in motion pictures. 6. Racism in literature. 7. Race in literature. I. Gillespie, Michele. II. Hall, Randal L., 1971– III. Series.

PS3507.I93Z87 2006

818'.5209—dc22

2005016977

ISBN-13: 978-0-8071-3532-7 (paper : alk. paper)

A portion of Louis Menand's essay appeared previously as "Do Movies Have Rights?" in *The New Gatekeepers: Emerging Challenges to Free Expression in the Arts,* eds. Christopher W. Hawthorne and others, 45–52 (New York: National Arts Journalism Program, 2004). Used by permission.

The paper in this book meets the guidelines for permanence and durability of the Committee on Production Guidelines for Book Longevity of the Council on Library Resources. ∞

For John B. Boles

Contents

1   Introduction

23 Thomas Dixon: American Proteus
    W. FITZHUGH BRUNDAGE

46 "My Books Are Hard Reading for a Negro": Tom Dixon
    and His African American Critics, 1905–1939
    JOHN DAVID SMITH

80 Gender and Race in Dixon's Religious Ideology
    CYNTHIA LYNN LYERLY

105 "Ours Is a Century of Light": Dixon's Strange Consistency
    DAVID STRICKLIN

124 Thomas Dixon and the Literary Production of Whiteness
    SCOTT ROMINE

151 Thomas Dixon and Race Melodrama
    JANE M. GAINES

164 The Cinematic Representation of Race in
    The Birth of a Nation: A Black Horror Film
    CHARLENE REGESTER

183 Do Movies Have Rights?
    LOUIS MENAND

203 Epilogue: The Enduring Worlds of Thomas Dixon
    WILLIAM A. LINK

211 *Appendix A: Thomas Dixon Jr.'s Selected Publications*
213 *Appendix B: Thomas Dixon Jr.'s Films*
215 *Contributors*
217 *Index*

Illustrations follow page 104

Thomas Dixon Jr. and the Birth of Modern America

Introduction

When Thomas Dixon Jr. wrote the screenplay for D. W. Griffith's epic, *The Birth of a Nation*, he produced searing, unforgettable images—racist portrayals of savage black men as sex-starved villains and lionhearted Ku Klux Klansmen as national heroes. Dixon did so, he explained, to invoke in his audience "a feeling of abhorrence in white people, especially white women, against colored men."[1] While *Birth of a Nation* is still appreciated for bringing the techniques of filmmaking into a new era, it is those horrific stereotypes, burned into the early twentieth-century white American consciousness, that have inflamed the hearts and minds of critics and racists alike over the course of nearly a century. Now, at the beginning of the twenty-first century and more than a generation after the civil rights movement, an African American artist and musician, Dj Spooky (Paul D. Miller), has decided to tackle head-on Dixon's most troubling legacy—the repellent racist imagery in this film. In performances in New York, Paris, Vienna, Charleston, and elsewhere, he has done so by actually remixing *Birth of a Nation*—reconfiguring the film's images and music and hence its message. Miller uses his project to show that images and ideas about race can be as mutable as film itself. While Dixon would never have acknowledged that race and racism are anything but God-given products of Nature, he would, ironically, appreciate Miller's insistence that *how* one communicates images and ideas, and in what forms, can profoundly influence how people think and act.[2]

Miller contends that in a world "dominated by broken treaties, ethnic oppression, raw power grabs and security threats, the time seems just right for revisiting . . . *Birth of a Nation*." For this conceptual artist, *Birth of a Nation*, "as a text of mythic proportions—of a nation occupied by foreign troops, of laws imposed without concern for the local populace, of exploitation and political corruption . . . still haunt[s] the world to this day—but in radically different forms" and therefore justifies his re-creation. *Rebirth of a Nation* conveys to viewers the extraordinary power of film to represent historical events. By remixing the visual, audio, and conceptual components of the original film, Miller seeks to tear apart the metaphorical bindings that hold past and present together "so that the future can leak through." Thus, for example, Miller replaces the Wagnerian score by Joseph Carl Breil, replete with its grandiose nationalistic throes, with a complex suite of hip hop and global music inspired by Robert Johnson's blues.

At the same time, Miller understands that while he wants his multimedia performance to challenge the ideas embedded in the original film, he is ironically treading the same creative path as D. W. Griffith. *Birth of a Nation* was the preeminent multimedia performance of its time because it mixed visual and narrative genres and techniques along with sound for a conceptual impact unique to its era. In this sense, Miller would argue that both Griffith and Dixon were not unlike DJs today who hijack contemporary images, sounds, and technologies to craft them into a powerful story of their own making. At the same time, Miller would insist that however similar the method of creative process, the product that results (whether that of Dixon the novelist, Griffith the filmmaker, or Miller the DJ) always remains open to interpretation by its audience, who is responsible not only for its reception, but also for its cultural and political uses.[3]

This volume invites readers to understand how and why Thomas Dixon's life work was received by Americans, as well as how and why he dedicated so much of his life specifically to shaping white Americans' conceptions of their history and culture. It places his ideas within the broader mainstream of American religiosity and progressivism, even as it recognizes how those ideas were fundamentally confined by his coming of age among rabidly conservative "Redeemers" who sought to restore the rule of white men in Reconstruction-era North Carolina. While it is easy to dismiss Thomas Dixon as a crackpot racist caught in a worn-out eddy of a beleaguered Confederate past, his ideas and his audience were all too often national in scope and impact, and his delivery of those ideas was far more modern than scholars have generally recognized. The repugnance of Dixon's racist imagination and its powerful impact on the American psyche do not excuse us from attempting to understand him or the many people who embraced his message.

By approaching Dixon through multiple disciplines and methods, including history, literature, film studies, music, and religion, and by employing gendered analysis and literary trope, we can begin to understand this man and his world in all their complexity and to grasp why race and racism were only two of several key points upon which Dixon's ever-evolving life and work turned. While now best known for authoring the novels and play that became *Birth of a Nation*, Dixon had an exceptionally long and varied career as an actor, lawyer, politician, minister, lecturer, writer, and filmmaker. He directed all his energy outward into the world, both to make a living and to feed his ego. Stimulated by the changing world around him, he wanted to reenvision and indeed reconcile the past he thought he knew with the increasingly complicated present he was living in. He learned to harness the new consumer culture and new forms of media and communication. He quickly grasped the social implications of urbanization and progressivism, and put them to work, too. He cultivated controversy on some of the most important issues facing the South and the nation in his time and in ours. This volume highlights the intellectual and cultural worlds of Thomas Dixon and their relationship to the processes and politics of modernization in the South and in America as a whole.

Dixon was born on January 11, 1864, to parents from prominent rural families in Cleveland County in the southwestern corner of the North Carolina piedmont. His family and their slaves had just returned from Arkansas, to which they had earlier fled in order to escape the Civil War, only to find their livelihood and property threatened anew. He grew up in Shelby, a politically influential piedmont town, hearing stories about his famed uncle, an academic star at the University of North Carolina, a colonel in the Confederacy, and an important leader in the Cleveland County Ku Klux Klan, who had died of tuberculosis before age thirty. Dixon worked hard as a child at farm labor, his father eking out a marginal existence from a combined career of mixed farming and Baptist ministry. Young Tom received only several years of formal schooling before his acceptance at a state Baptist institution, Wake Forest College, at the age of fifteen. He enrolled in the fall of 1879, following on the heels of his older brother A. C. (His siblings would lead illustrious lives of their own, though none would ever be as famous as Tom. Two of his brothers, including A. C., became respected Baptist ministers, and his sister joined the faculty of the Baptist University for Women in Raleigh and practiced medicine.)

Thomas Dixon won respect as a first-rate orator before the end of his first semester at Wake Forest and remained the top debater in the Euzelian Society throughout his college career. Classmates marveled at his silver tongue. Edwin M. Poteat, future president of Furman University, recalled, "I remember the first time Tom Dixon . . . took part in a debate. . . . The subject was Napoleon. No; I remember nothing that he said—only the zest with which he took hold." Dixon graduated in 1883 having won all the college prizes for oratory and many prizes for his scholarship as well, reportedly the most honors ever awarded a Wake Forest student up to that time. But Dixon chafed under the confines of his college education. Upon receiving his diploma, recalled Poteat, Dixon "was like a bird let out of a cage."[4] Although he would exercise his gift of oratory before crowds of thousands at the center of American intellectual life in Boston and New York only a few years later, this talented young man with his newly minted degree would have to try out a number of vocations before he found the right fit.

His stellar college career secured him a fellowship to study history and politics at Johns Hopkins University in 1883.[5] Working under Herbert Baxter Adams and attending seminars modeled after the German education system, Dixon read race-based arguments about the superiority of Teutonic peoples. During his time at Johns Hopkins, Dixon made many new friends who would support his career at later junctures in his life, among them future president Woodrow Wilson, who would screen *Birth of a Nation* in the White House on his old friend's behalf. Dixon's understanding of Adams's racialism returned with a vengeance in later writings about blacks and immigrants, and Dixon would henceforth seek to cloak all his ideas in academic respectability. However, the laborious life of the scholar did not suit this energetic youth.

Rejecting the life of the mind at Johns Hopkins, the nineteen year old preferred instead the worldliness of the stage, plying his new interest first as a critic and then as an actor. After only four months in graduate school, Dixon purchased a place in a traveling company, much to his family's embarrassment and chagrin. The zeal to perform and to bask in the warmth of a supportive audience never left Dixon, but the failure of his troupe, followed by his failure as an actor, propelled him home to Shelby and into another career. In the fall of 1884 he ran for a seat in the state legislature, using his oratorical and acting skills to wow Cleveland County voters. He defeated two well-known candidates to become a state representative before he was old enough to vote. His speech seeking relief for Confederate soldiers was highly regarded and earned him a statewide reputation, and he pressed for more backing for progressive education. Nonetheless, he was sickened by the vituperation of his fellow politicians and left office to study law in Greensboro. After passing the bar in 1885, he hung out his shingle in his hometown, where he practiced for little more than a year. During that time he also married Harriet Bussey, the daughter of a respected Georgia minister, whom he had met at Mardi Gras in New Orleans. The two lovers eloped to avoid the blatant disapproval of Dixon's future father-in-law. His experiences as a county lawyer disappointed Dixon as much as his time in the state legislature, and during a visit at Wrightsville Beach, while alone in the sand at the edge of the great Atlantic during a storm, he felt a calling from God that again set him veering dramatically and full-tilt in a new direction.

Ordained in 1886 as a Baptist minister, he was appointed to his first church in Goldsboro, North Carolina, but he was soon hopscotching from one pulpit to another in a quick rise to fame and influence. He was asked to move to the Second Baptist Church in Raleigh in 1887, where he exchanged ideas and beliefs with a relatively remarkable group of North Carolina intellectuals, before bouncing into the pulpit of the Dudley Street Church in Boston. It was while attending a talk criticizing the South at the Tremont Temple there that Dixon came to assume yet another vocation—vehement defender of the white man's South—which ironically only served to make him more attractive to northern congregations at a time when white Americans had begun to heal the wounds of the Civil War by closing ranks on racial matters.[6] When the Reverend Justin D. Fulton concluded his sermon by stating, "The only way to save this nation from hell is for northern mothers to rear more children than Southern mothers," Dixon could not help but laugh aloud, interrupting and ultimately ruining Fulton's lecture. It was at that moment, Dixon later claimed, that he determined to devote his life to conveying the "true" history of his region and its inhabitants.[7]

Dixon's subsequent contribution to the vigorous culture of faith in Boston did not escape notice. He was snapped up by the Twenty-Third Street Baptist Church in New York in 1889 at the tender age of twenty-five.

In New York—arriving at long last at the heart of modern American culture—Dixon stormed his way into popular opinion as a reformer. He attacked Tammany Hall and the festering social ills of urban America, and he attracted such crowds that the metropolitan dailies regularly covered his sermons. Usually overtly political, his messages ranged across a wide spectrum of contemporary concerns. As his popularity and effectiveness grew, he increasingly felt constrained by denominationalism, and in 1895 he broke away to form an independent, nondenominational congregation—a pioneering megachurch. He celebrated women's leadership in church and society. He embraced populist politicians and advocated Cuban independence, making clear that America needed to accept an imperialist role in guiding the world's less fortunate races. He made friends with John D. Rockefeller and championed Teddy Roosevelt. And eventually he found himself constricted even in his new church. He desired an even bigger audience to satisfy his ambition and drive to shape public opinion.

In 1899 Dixon left the ministry (though he remained religious) to become a national lecturer, drawing large crowds to his consistently engaging talks and earning several thousand dollars for each performance in the process. One of his contemporaries, while critical of the content of Dixon's speeches, painted an extraordinary picture of the charismatic North Carolinian at the peak of his oratorical power at the turn of the century. Dixon's intense physicality, at a lean six feet three inches, was striking. His luminous dark eyes and his aquiline nose conveyed "high emotion," as did his bell-like voice and his tendency to comb his fingers through his black hair, followed by a shake of his head to toss back the fringe of bangs across his forehead.[8] Dixon grasped the power of his words and of storytelling and studied the best ways to use his physical presence to convey them. He had also come to understand the reach and scope of the popular press, just as he would understand the power of film a little over a decade later. Now a highly popular and well-paid speaker, Dixon traveled through the Northeast and Midwest for a portion of every week but regularly returned to his wife and three children on the plantation estate he had purchased for them in the Chesapeake region of Virginia.

In his pleasant, nostalgic setting in the Old Dominion, Dixon took pen to paper with a new vengeance and wrote his first novel, *The Leopard's Spots*, in 1902. While his previous books had largely compiled sermons, Dixon now moved beyond the power of the spoken word to find in mass culture an even more efficient way to commune with a modern audience. At the urging of fellow Carolinian and publisher Walter Hines Page, the firm of Doubleday, Page, and Company put Dixon's manuscript into print. It was an immediate bestseller, touted as a rejoinder to Harriet Beecher Stowe's still-popular *Uncle Tom's Cabin*, which had been reincarnated as a widely produced play. Heavily autobiographical, Dixon's book lacked literary merit but told a vivid and violent story of the Civil War and Reconstruction from a white southern man's perspective. Steeped in nineteenth-century southern romantic fiction, Dixon's novel idealized the plantation, promulgated the myth of the happy slave, gave white women some measure of moral authority for safeguarding the hearth, and insisted on the dominance of white patriarchy.[9]

That book was followed by Dixon's *The One Woman*, which struck very different and intriguing ground by decrying the appeal of socialism (a topic to which Dixon would return). *The Clansman* followed in 1905 and was another bestseller, and then came *The Traitor* (1907), which lambasted those southern scalawags who supported the Republican Party and "Negro Rule" in the aftermath of the Civil War and whose treachery was ended only by "Clansmen [who] led a successful revolution out of defeat and ruin and tore the negro's hands from the throats of our women."[10] Together, *The Leopard's Spots*, *The Clansman*, and *The Traitor* composed Dixon's trilogy on the history of Reconstruction and its consequences. Like other writers of his era, including Joel Chandler Harris and his friend and colleague Thomas Nelson Page, Dixon borrowed imagery from the exceedingly popular tradition of the minstrel show to clothe his twin ambitions: the reconciliation of the nation and the condemnation of African Americans (for their alleged backwardness and savagery).[11]

The gendered dimensions of his imagery were critical to his success. Manhood, wrapped up in notions of race and class difference, was an American obsession at the turn of the century. Collective anxiety over manhood, from individual concerns over one's own masculinity to national concerns over the nation's manliness, dominated Americans' perceptions of their place and power within society and the world, an understanding Dixon grasped intuitively. Not only did this understanding exclude women, but it also depended on its corollary, that femininity and failure were linked. Dixon's novels borrowed heavily from southern romantic traditions, where white patriarchy always trumped white women's and African Americans' self-determination and male heroes often showed a more effeminate side. Although Dixon often gave his male heroes a dose of femininity, especially in terms of their sensitivity and allegiance to the white women in their lives, he veered from that tradition by ultimately investing them with powerful symbols of a racialized manhood, best conveyed by mounted Klu Klux Klan warriors racing to the rescue of aged parents, small children, virtuous women, and, symbolically, the nation as a whole.[12]

Drawing on the work of racist academics and rewriting history with mass appeal, Dixon presented the Civil War and Reconstruction as events wholly directed by misguided northerners, who unwittingly unleashed the bestial element in the newly freed male slaves and sent forth an animalistic Negro army that would rape the white daughters of the South and wreak havoc down through the generations with the miscegenation that must result. Southern white men, Dixon was implicitly extolling, were best equipped to rescue white manhood in America. The anarchy of the freed Negro shaped the entire social-sexual realm in Dixon's version of the recent past, and the chaos could be stopped only with the resurrection of the knightly Ku Klux Klan, which not only would bring racial order back to the South but would also knit the nation together once again.

Dixon's opinions mattered to whites and blacks alike. In January 1906, Mark Twain, Joseph H. Choate, and Robert C. Ogden, among others, joined Booker T. Washington in Carnegie Hall to raise funds for the Tuskegee Institute and its work in educating blacks. Dixon tried to disrupt the event by sending a note to Washington before the Tuskegee leader spoke "in which the writer said he would contribute $10,000 to Tuskegee if Mr. Washington would state at the meeting that he did not desire social equality for the negro, and that Tuskegee was opposed to the amalgamation of the races." Washington declined to comment, but Dixon felt compelled to rebut the praise for black accomplishments that the Carnegie Hall gathering delivered. Days later he joined several black ministers at the Baptist

Church of the Epiphany to debate "What Shall We Do With the Negro?" The resulting furor among the black audience members had "a good deal of the intensity of a riot," according to one reporter. Dixon's malevolent (but in some ways ironically prescient in light of widespread white opposition to the civil rights movement) comments epitomized the message he was delivering to national audiences:

> When Mr. Ogden or Mr. Choate say they would entertain negroes in their homes as social equals it is a humbug. They are fooling themselves and the public. Let the negro they seat at their tables dare to make love to their daughters and see how quickly they would kick him downstairs. And yet the right to love and wed one's love is the badge of human fellowship. . . . We must remove the negro or we will have to fight him. He will not submit long to the injustices with which we treat him both in the North and in the South. . . . And this thing, half devil and half child, is supposed to be your equal, and actually claims that equality. He does not get it now, but fifty years from now 60,000,000 negroes will claim those equal rights, and will take them if they are refused.

The Reverend M. W. Gilbert of Mount Olivet Baptist Church responded to Dixon's proposal to colonize blacks elsewhere, again presaging discussions to come in decades ahead:

> We know no other land than this. You brought us here 250 years ago against our will, and now those of us who are alive believe this to be our home. It is idle for Mr. Dixon to talk of peaceful colonization; there can be no peaceful colonization. He is right; we would fight to be put out. He tells us to go back to our home, the land we came from. All right; we'll agree to it if Mr. Dixon will go back to Germany, where he says his forefathers came from. Reasoning in that way he will give this land to the red men, to whom it actually belonged.[13]

Throughout Dixon's career, in fact, black intellectuals responded to his writings with ironclad critiques of his work and with impassioned calls for racial justice. Kelly Miller, a mathematician, public intellectual, and academic leader at Howard University, impugned Dixon as "the high priest of lawlessness, the prophet of anarchy" for his senseless but virulent propaganda.[14] W.E.B. Du Bois and the other leaders of the Niagara Movement defended black manhood and racial equality in the wake of Dixon's vitriolic books. But these and other voices, however compelling, were essentially unheard in the larger white culture.

By 1905 Dixon had adapted *The Leopard's Spots* and *The Clansman* into a play, which began its run in the South, moved on to northern cities that fall, and continued touring for five more years. Dixon often accompanied the performances of his play, took curtain calls with the actors, and on occasion even played a role, resurrecting his former short-lived acting career, much to the pleasure of the audience, who sometimes turned out more to see the famous minister-author-playwright than the play itself. Indeed, even Dixon's father, who saw the play in Shelby, commented that his son had "bore down a little too hard on the Negro. He wasn't to blame for the Reconstruction. Low vicious white men corrupted and misled him."[15] Dixon—the gifted speaker and famous preacher—cunningly combined his celebrity with his "redemptive" version of the white southern man's role in the Civil War and Reconstruction. The record crowds saw in him the very epitome of their modern America.[16]

Dixon was highly successful by 1905, and he and his family took advantage of their wealth, owning a Riverside Drive townhouse in New York and traveling at leisure when his schedule allowed. However, he suffered a series of personal setbacks, beginning with stock market investments that went bad in the panic of 1907, followed by the death of his father in 1909. Dixon's finances improved with royalties from *The Traitor*, and his interest in plays helped sustain him. His *Sins of the Father* opened in 1910, and following a freak accident in which the lead actor was killed in a shark attack, Dixon assumed the role, traveling for weeks at a time. He was also trying to complete his socialism trilogy, begun with *The One Woman* in 1903. *Comrades* appeared in 1909, and *The Root of Evil* in 1911. The former critiqued the leveling aspects of socialism, arguing that social hierarchies were implicit among human beings, while the latter attacked acquisitiveness and greed, favoring the golden rule as society's salvation instead. The unease of the time—symbolized by the potential for political radicalism—gave Dixon a new enemy to drive his plots and rally his readers.

Dixon relied on the recent wave of new "scientific" history to buttress his depictions of the past, just as he found in scientific racism, then at its height, modern authority on racial hierarchy to reinforce his deep-seated racial antipathy. But the times also introduced new threats to be countered. The unity of white Americans—achieved at a high cost and constantly under fire—could be endangered anew for him by the shiploads of uncouth immigrants arriving from eastern and southern Europe and, closer to his innermost fears, by a new generation of women aggressively taking a role outside the home. His novels featured the symbolic defeat of the first menace with the repeated failure of supporters of socialism and, later, communism, while his women characters constantly found themselves in need of rescue, no matter how intelligent or independent, whether from blacks or socialists. In these melodramatic plots, Dixon unwittingly dramatized the crisis of masculinity facing the inhabitants of a newly urbanized industrial nation—little wonder, then, that he found a large audience for many years.[17]

Over time, Dixon was no longer as great a draw as he had once been. In the years before the First World War, his plays and books were fading from the contemporary scene despite his continuing efforts to promote them. Dixon needed a new forum, and, always attuned to the audience, he discovered film and its incredible potential to breathe life into the past. Although he had attempted to bring *The Clansman* to the movie theater as early as 1911, raising venture capital had proved too daunting. He had met D. W Griffith and his wife, who had acted briefly in one of Dixon's plays, in 1907, but it was not until 1913 that the two men began to work together. Younger than Dixon, but from a similar southern background, the actor-turned-producer clearly grasped the emotional power that Dixon's race-based tragic version of the past could trigger in the viewer, especially when conveyed as an epic on the big screen. In turn, Dixon reportedly sought $25,000 for the rights to his work, but the Epoch Producing Corporation was such a shoestring operation that Dixon had to accept $2,000 and a 25 percent interest in the picture instead.

After another year and a half working closely together to write a screenplay based largely on *The Clansman* and then securing actors and music, Dixon and Griffith began marketing their effort. One of Dixon's most monumental decisions regarding the film was to change its title, originally the same as the novel and play, to *The Birth of a Nation* upon first hearing the powerful score by Joseph Carl Breil. Dixon then asked his old friend President Woodrow Wilson to see it. After Wilson, his daughter, and members of the president's cabinet and their families watched the film in its three-hour entirety in the White House, Wilson allegedly concluded, "It is like writing history with lightning. And my only regret is that it is all so terribly true."[18] Perhaps apocryphal, the comment nonetheless summarizes the malicious effect of combining a savage (though widely accepted) historical understanding with the flickering light of cutting-edge cinema.

The Clansman is set in the fictional town of Piedmont, South Carolina, modeled on Dixon's hometown of Shelby but moved to South Carolina because the Palmetto State had a larger African American population to further the sense of danger for the white characters. The Little Colonel, Ben Cameron, returns from the Civil War to find his family and their very way of life threatened by newly empowered black troops and politicians. While in a wartime hospital Ben had fallen in love with Elsie Stoneman, whose father, Austin Stoneman (a loosely disguised Thaddeus Stevens), is the Congress's strongest supporter of political rights for blacks. Stoneman and Elsie move to Piedmont to allow him to better coordinate his schemes, including the installation of his mulatto henchman George Lynch as governor. As turmoil grows, black men rape a white woman, Ben's neighbor. He and his father form a local Ku Klux Klan, and the masked riders arrive barely in time to save Elsie from a similar fate at the hands of Lynch. In the end, even Stoneman understands the plight of the South and sees the futility of Reconstruction. This plot (particularly in its iteration as a play by Dixon), along with some modifications and additional elements taken from *The Leopard's Spots,* served as the basis for *Birth of a Nation.*

The film opened in New York at the Liberty Theatre on March 3, 1915, and became the talk of the nation. Recalled Katharine Du Pre Lumpkin, who watched *Birth of a Nation* while at college in Gainesville, Georgia, "We poured out to the picture, everyone, students, townfolk. All around me people sighed and shivered, and now and then shouted or wept, in their intensity. . . . Southerners, I believe, had no doubt of what it said or what they read into it of the nobility of our history, the righteousness of our acts, the rightness of our beliefs . . . I felt old sentiments stir, and a haunting nostalgia, which told me that much that I thought had been left behind must still be ahead."[19]

Elsewhere in the nation, outrage at the film's degradation of African Americans occurred immediately. The New York Board of Censors after sustained debate continued to show the picture despite vigorous opposition. Crowds of thousands protested the showing of the film in Boston and New York. Harvard president Charles Eliot, social reformer and philanthropist Jane Addams, and educational leader Booker T. Washington publicly condemned the bigotry and intolerance the movie conveyed, as well as its false version of the American past. Despite the controversy, however, Dixon already understood the incredible force of film. The true capital of the world, he now contended, was not Geneva, where the politicians and diplomats struggled to bring peace, but Hollywood, California. Once again he had ridden the storms of modernizing America to new heights of prestige and cultural influence.

Following *Birth of a Nation,* which officially grossed over $18 million in the United States alone, Dixon's popularity and wealth suffered a number of reversals. Enthusiastic about the power of film, he formed his own production company. Despite some success with such films as *The Fall of a Nation,* which was an adaptation of one of his novels, he never matched the success of his collaboration with Griffith. Although he wrote nearly thirty books, nine plays, and several films in his lifetime and amassed personal earnings of over $1 million, his post–*Birth of a Nation* years became lean ones, especially after he lost most of his fortune in the late 1920s in a failed real estate venture in the mountains of North Carolina.[20] While Dixon lived in relative obscurity and diminished wealth during the last decades of his life, he remained as engaged as ever in analyzing the past and present. His embrace of jingoistic American nationalism never lagged. The reemergence of a modern Ku Klux Klan in the 1920s drew his wrath precisely because it undermined national unity. He condemned the secret organization for ignoring civilized government and encouraging riot, bloodshed, and anarchy. He explicitly lambasted clansmen for their foolish assault upon immigrants. "We are all foreigners, except the few Indians we haven't killed," he argued. "If this is 100 per cent Americanism, I for one spit on it."[21] Still, his racist beliefs did not waver, and the prospect of communism further tormented him, as evidenced in his vitriolic final novel, *The Flaming Sword* (1939).[22]

Thomas Dixon had mastered the art of gaining the public spotlight for most of his life, but his final years passed quietly. He returned to North Carolina during the Great Depression. In 1937, at the age of seventy-three, the same year his first wife, Harriet Bussey, died, he was appointed clerk of the federal court in eastern North Carolina, where he happily served until he resigned the post in 1943 because of ill health. He died in 1946 and was survived by his second wife, Madelyn Donovan Dixon, and a son and a daughter from his first marriage. At least one editor noted that the entire nation would notice his passing, for his name had become a household word.[23]

Dixon's ideas and writings have continually exercised influence in some circles since his death. In the late 1940s, a founder of a neo-Nazi group in Atlanta identified Dixon's work as a primary motivation for his organization. In the mid-1960s a reprint edition of *The Clansman* featured a flaming cross and KKK leader Robert Shelton on the cover. Another white supremacist introduced a reprint of the Reconstruction trilogy in the early 1980s, and even now websites of white supremacy organizations list the books as recommended reading. More subtly, *Birth of a Nation* also continues to influence cinematic representations of the Civil War era. Writing in *Cineaste,* one reviewer perceptively traced Dixon and Griffith's view of the war through *Gone with the Wind* and *The Outlaw Josey Wales* (itself from a book by white supremacist Asa Carter) to Ted Turner's trumpeted 2003 release *Gods and Generals,* with its cameo appearances by several conservative southern political leaders.[24] Unsurprisingly, scholars of film, literature, religion, and history seek to understand Dixon and his work, the context of his life in modernizing America, and his often malevolent impact then and now. It was in light of these recent realities, as well as important developments in southern and American history, that Wake Forest University held a symposium on its infamous alumnus—whose portrait still hangs in a little-used room in the Z. Smith Reynolds Library—and the influence of his ideas in April 2003. The essays that make up this volume were presented at the symposium on Thomas Dixon and the Making of Modern America, and they have been subsequently revised in light of those three days of brisk discussion and critical exchange.

W. Fitzhugh Brundage opens the collection with an overarching interpretation of how Dixon fluidly appropriated a variety of the important cultural trends of his day. Dixon took in the moral intensity of his Baptist background and of the broader culture of white Americans in the Victorian era but plied it in sometimes surprising ways. His popularity as he metamorphosed from lawyer to minister to novelist to playwright grew from his ability to manipulate with exceptional vigor the melodramatic form and to adapt its Manichaean racial message to novels, the stage, and the emerging forum of film. As Brundage points out, Dixon "could not cross the threshold of modernism, with its embrace of the sensual, the primitive, and the subconscious," but he helped to shape the culture of spectacle in its infancy.

At no point in Dixon's career as novelist and filmmaker did African American intellectuals fail to challenge his egregious racism. John David Smith sketches in bold outlines the shape and strength of black criticism of Dixon. For example, Sutton E. Griggs, a minister and novelist, wrote *The Hindered Hand* (1905) at the behest of the National Baptist Convention. In a plot as starkly formulaic as many by Dixon, Griggs captured the bleak alternatives open to black men who would try to overcome the heavy restraining hold of racism in the South. In a blistering epilogue, Griggs attacked *The Leopard's Spots* and singled out Dixon as a primary hand hindering black progress. The Howard University scholar Kelly Miller drafted a pamphlet in 1905 that exposed not only Dixon's false historical claims about African Americans' historical contributions, but also his distorted depiction of contemporary blacks. In turn, W.E.B. Du Bois criticized Dixon's violent fiction and later led opposition to *Birth of a Nation* by the National Association for the Advancement of Colored People (NAACP). For more than a generation, Dixon exchanged barbs with leading black intellectuals, and even in his bitter final novel, *The Flaming Sword*, he still sought to counter black thinkers, understanding rightly that a smart black writer embodied in living form a contradiction to Dixon's beliefs about black inferiority.

In complementary essays, David Stricklin and Cynthia Lynn Lyerly delve deeply into race, gender, and the Social Gospel. Examining Dixon's religious writings from the 1890s and some of his seldom-studied novels published in the first decades of the twentieth century, Lyerly underscores the complexity of the mix, identifying his fiction as combining Social Gospel theology and traditional gender assumptions. The love of women could redeem degenerate men caught in the urban melee, but only if the women assumed their traditional roles in ordering the home. Only white families could manage this righteous reclamation; blacks had sunk beneath hope in the novels. David Stricklin provides vital context for understanding the blending of social concern with racism in Dixon's religious thought. Imperialists justified U.S. expansion with expressions of concern for the dark-skinned people who stood to receive the apparent benefits of Christian and American values. Dixon's faith in the uplifting effect of American control abroad eased any inconsistencies or misgivings his supporters might have had about his ideology. Despite his ecumenical break from southern denominational identity, Dixon retained older racial assumptions while heralding the entry of the so-called New South into the mainstream of twentieth-century America.

Scott Romine and Jane M. Gaines further analyze Dixon's manipulation of melodramatic formulas. Romine applies literary theory to scrutinize the construction of whiteness in Dixon's novels, arguing that Dixon did not depict white identity as something unvarying and rigid. Rather, whites faced the challenge of constantly earning and defending (or alternately, betraying) their whiteness. The forms of romance and melodrama enable Dixon's heroes again and again to secure whiteness, with its many psychic and material benefits to reward their achievement. Gaines, in turn, gives a forceful reminder that one can hear—as well as read—melodrama. She analyzes the reception of Joseph Carl Breil's score for the New York City premier of *Birth of a Nation*. Dixon and others recorded their reactions, and Gaines probes the musical methods used to evoke such passionate hearings of the melodramatic score.

Charlene Regester reenvisions the controversial film from a different angle. To many audience members, the film illustrated the standards of an infant film genre: horror. Like future horror films, it pictured white women as victims, lingered on ape-like black monsters, and absolved white men for violence against the threat. Newspaper writers, Regester argues, added to the horror and fear through racist and sensational coverage of the movie's popularity. In not only showing (and enhancing) white fear, but also trying to frighten blacks, Griffith and Dixon manufactured an experience full of horror for both races. Technical innovations in filming and editing only enhanced the impact.

Commenting at the symposium, David M. Lubin laid out the film's rich potential for academic inquiry: "There would seem to be a contradiction here between Regester's paper and Gaines's, in that the movie can't be both a horror film and a domestic melodrama. Or can it? I'd say that the two papers together make us realize that *The Birth of a Nation* is a hybrid—the offspring of miscegenation, as it were, between two generic categories that normally are kept strictly quarantined from one another." The film did far more, though, in order to earn its status as a historically significant classic. Lubin went on, "Actually, more than two cinematic genres were given birth by Griffith's epic of apartheid, for *Birth of a Nation* is also a prototypical war movie, costume drama, action-suspense picture, and even comedy of manners. It's also a sort of documentary, or at least purports to be, with its 'you are there' facsimile recreations of quasi-historical illustrations and tableaux."

The NAACP recognized clearly the pathbreaking film's potential to incite violence against black Americans. In a conversational and wide-ranging essay, Louis Menand explains the young organization's coordination of boycotts and legal challenges to the movie. City and state officials restricted or closely regulated many attempts to show it. The officials could do so under a 1915 ruling by the Supreme Court that movies were not speech, and thus not protected by the First Amendment. Menand gracefully explores the irony that a group generally in favor of civil liberties would work to censor a film. Moving his story deftly forward to the early 1950s, he relates the contrasting fate of challenges to a film by Roberto Rossellini, *The Miracle,* that caused a furor among Catholics in New York City, many of whom regarded it as sacrilegious. The Supreme Court in 1952 reversed the earlier ruling and extended protection of free speech to film.

Even beyond the papers published in this volume, the symposium participants worked to clarify our understanding of Dixon's times, particularly the evolution of white racism at the turn of the century. One presenter concluded that in North Carolina in 1915 whites embraced the racist messages of *The Birth of a Nation* with less enthusiasm than they had demonstrated for a touring production of the play *The Clansman* only ten years earlier.[25] Commentator Richard H. King argued similarly, "If we follow the intellectual history of racism in America, the early part of the century sees a strong counterattack against racism, led by Franz Boas and Du Bois, Kelly Miller, William Monroe Trotter and other black intellectuals. This developed into a consensus among academic and intellectual elites in the inter-War years and was expressed most clearly in [Gunnar] Myrdal's *An America Dilemma* in 1944." On the other hand, commentator William A. Link questioned whether the waxing and waning strength of white racism really made any difference from the vantage point of black Americans who experienced unrelenting, if evolving, racial repression.

Smith and Menand explore discursive and legal responses by African Americans to Dixon's ideas, but scholars of the period also must not overlook an important cinematic counterpoint to *Birth of a Nation*. Charlene Regester ably introduced a screening of *Within Our Gates*, the second film in the career of African American director Oscar Micheaux. Released in January 1920, the work reflects Michaeux's recognition "that while cinema had been used by whites to *dis*-empower African Americans, this same cinema could be used to *empower* African Americans." *Within Our Gates* involves the lynching of a sharecropper couple, their adopted daughter's narrow escape from attempted rape by a white man, and her later work to raise funds in the North to support a black school in Mississippi. It survived "censorship difficulties" of its own, while serving as a black filmmaker's response to *The Birth of a Nation* (and an artistic accomplishment in its own right).

Discussion at the symposium again and again raised touchy issues of race, gender, and history, and in the finest tradition of intellectual exchange, the debate reached beyond the academy. The *Winston-Salem Journal* welcomed advance news of the symposium. It editorialized, "This symposium has the potential to be the study of history at its best: An understanding of Dixon and his popularity and influence in his day could yield insight into present-day problems, tensions and cultural influences." Not everyone agreed. In conjunction with an opening screening of *Birth of a Nation* (at the School of Filmmaking of the North Carolina School of the Arts), the symposium included an interracial discussion panel held at Winston-Salem State University. At the session (and in subsequent newspaper editorials), local minister and activist Carlton A. G. Eversley reminded everyone of the need to maintain a clear focus on racial injustice in the present, rather than devoting too much effort to understanding Dixon's context. He proclaimed, "Black people have a rightful paranoia when white people want to parse and nuance what is fundamentally evil."[26] Later, Joel Williamson anchored a spirited discussion that again included debates about the value of academic inquiry, the ongoing power of stereotypes, and the difficulty of achieving racial understanding—modern concerns all, with Dixon at the core of both their creation and their continuing complexity.

The energetic dialogue at the symposium and in the essays here accentuates the unavoidable vitality of the issues surrounding Dixon, particularly his relationship to historical memory. Biographer Raymond A. Cook joined Wake Forest faculty members J. Howell Smith, Sarah L. Watts, and Edwin G. Wilson in a discussion reflecting on Dixon's evolving meaning to his alma mater—from celebration to guarded avoidance of his legacy. Watts remarked, "It's clear that the memory of Dixon has not been incorporated into Wake Forest's sense of itself, though this symposium is the first step, just as the nation is still coming to terms with the legacy of the Civil War, or reconstruction, Jim Crow disfranchisement, segregation, and repression." The institution is not alone in its difficulty in coming to terms with memory and a troubled history: it is the problem of the entire region and, indeed, our nation. In his commentary, Samuel S. Hill considered Thomas Dixon vis-à-vis his brother Amzi Clarence Dixon. An internationally famous Baptist minister, A. C. exercised crucial leadership in the creation of fundamentalism in the early twentieth century. Hill imagined the two siblings "revising the old-time religion of the South, each of them in divergent ways, and riding the rails of a new America." Taking "sharply divergent routes, they were both with the times," but Thomas, at least, "got some of the worst of his regional culture without an abundance of the best."[27] Understanding that regional culture, Dixon's manipulation of it in the national spotlight, and his dance between the two in a rapidly modernizing national context occupies the contributors to this collection.

Dixon epitomizes many of the troubled currents of modern America.[28] The chapters in this volume recognize the complexity of the man and his context without diminishing his responsibility for accelerating and celebrating the most repressive racial and gender regimes in the America of his time. To conclude the book, William Link reprises the role of commentator with an epilogue considering more broadly some of the larger questions, still to be answered, that grow out of the symposium and the interdisciplinary perspectives in the vivid essays collected here.

NOTES

The editors wish to thank the following friends and colleagues for their generous assistance with this project: Julia Bradford, Walter Beeker, Vernon Burton, Rand Dotson, Sam Gladding, David Goldfield, Michael Hughes, Vicki Johnson, Meghan Mulder, Sylvia Frank Rodrigue, Derik Shelor, Sharon Snow, Jing Wei, and Ed Wilson.

1. Interview with Thomas Dixon by Role Cobleigh, May 26, 1915, in *The Movies in Our Midst: Documents in the Cultural History of Film in America*, ed. Gerald Mast (Chicago: Univ. of Chicago Press, 1982), 128–29.

2. *Winston-Salem (N.C.) Journal,* May 31, 2003, section A, p. 2; *Greensboro (N.C.) News and Record,* June 8, 2003, section D, p. 5.

3. Paul D. Miller, *Rhythm Science* (Cambridge, Mass.: MIT Press, 2004), 13, 32–33, 61; program notes for Paul D. Miller's *Rebirth of a Nation,* performed at The Stevens Centre, Winston-Salem, N.C., September 17, 2004.

4. *Winston-Salem Sunday Journal and Sentinel,* December 6, 1964, section D, p. 1; E. M. Poteat, "Thomas Dixon, Jr.," *Wake Forest Student* 28 (January 1909): 382.

5. For biographical background on Dixon, the best-known work remains Raymond Allen Cook, *Fire from the Flint: The Amazing Careers of Thomas Dixon* (Winston-Salem, N.C.: Blair, 1968), but another fine comprehensive study is James Zebulon Wright, "Thomas Dixon: The Mind of a Southern Apologist" (Ph.D. diss., George Peabody College for Teachers, 1966). Karen M. Crowe, "Southern Horizons: The Autobiography of Thomas Dixon, A Critical Edition" (Ph.D. diss., Columbia University, 1982), provides an edited version of Dixon's autobiography, the original version of which can no longer be located and which may have been heavily edited by Dixon's second wife shortly after his death. On Dixon's film career in particular, see Anthony Slide, *American Racist: The Life and Films of Thomas Dixon* (Lexington: Univ. Press of Kentucky, 2004). There are many additional secondary articles and book chapters on Dixon, but for more biographical information from contemporary sources, see also Poteat, "Thomas Dixon, Jr.," 382–85; and John Charles McNeill, "Thomas Dixon, Jr.," in *Biographical History of North Carolina,* vol. 7, ed. Samuel H. Ashe and Stephen B. Weeks (Greensboro, N.C.: C. V. Van Noppen, 1908), 88–93.

6. David Blight, *Race and Reunion: The Civil War in American Memory* (Cambridge, Mass.: Harvard Univ. Press, 2001).

7. *Charlotte (N.C.) Observer,* April 8, 1934, clipping from the Thomas Dixon File, University Archives, Wake Forest University, Winston-Salem, N.C.

8. McNeill, "Thomas Dixon," 92.

9. Lucinda H. MacKethan, "Domesticity in Dixon: The Plantation Novel and *Uncle Tom's Cabin,*" in *Haunted Bodies: Gender and Southern Texts,* ed. Anne Goodwyn Jones and Susan V. Donaldson (Charlottesville: Univ. Press of Virginia, 1997), 238–39.

10. Letter by Dixon quoted in Josephus Daniels, *Editor in Politics* (Chapel Hill: Univ. of North Carolina Press, 1941), 532.

11. Robert C. Toll, *Blacking Up: The Minstrel Show in Nineteenth-Century America* (New York: Oxford Univ. Press, 1974), 124–28.

12. Gail Bederman, *Manliness and Civilization: A Cultural History of Gender and Race in the United States, 1880–1917* (Chicago: Univ. of Chicago Press, 1995); E. Anthony Rotundo, *American Manhood: Transformations in Masculinity from the Revolution to the Modern Era* (New York: Basic Books, 1993); Tom Pendergast, *Creating the American Man: American Magazines and Consumer Culture, 1900–1950* (Columbia: Univ. of Missouri Press, 2000); Sarah Watts, *Rough Rider in the White House: Theodore Roosevelt and the Politics of Desire* (Chicago: Univ. of Chicago Press, 2003); Martin Summers, *Manliness and Its Discontents: The Black Middle Class and the Transformation of Masculinity, 1900–1930* (Chapel Hill: Univ. of North Carolina Press, 2004).

13. *New York Times,* January 23, 1906, pp. 1–2 (first quotation); and January 29, 1906, p. 4 (remaining quotations). See also *New York Age,* January 25, 1906, p. 1, and February 1, 1906, p. 1.

14. Kelly Miller, *Race Adjustment [and] The Everlasting Stain* (1908 and 1924; reprint, New York: Arno Press, 1968), 53.

15. Quoted in Cook, *Fire from the Flint,* 149.

16. John C. Inscoe, "*The Clansman* on Stage and Screen: North Carolina Reacts," *North Carolina Historical Review* 64 (April 1987): 139–61.

17. Watts, *Rough Rider in the White House,* chapter 1.

18. Quoted in Cook, *Fire from the Flint,* 170.

19. Katharine Du Pre Lumpkin, *The Making of a Southerner* (1946; reprint, Athens: Univ. of Georgia Press, 1981), 200.

20. Thomas Dixon obituary, *New York Herald Tribune,* April 4, 1946; and Thomas Dixon obituary, *Shelby (N.C.) Daily Star,* April 3, 1946, p. 4.

21. *Richmond News Leader,* January 25, 1923, p. 13.

22. *The Flaming Sword* is available from the University Press of Kentucky in a reprint edition edited by John David Smith.

23. *Shelby Daily Star,* April 3, 1946, p. 4.

24. Steven Weisenburger, "The Columbians, Inc.," *Journal of Southern History* 69 (November 2003): 821–60; Wright, "Thomas Dixon," 210; Christopher Sharrett, review of *Gods and Generals, Cineaste* 28 (summer 2003): 36–38; Jeff Roche, "Asa/Forrest Carter and Regional/Political Identity," in *The Southern Albatross: Race and Ethnicity in the American South,* ed. Philip D. Dillard and Randal L. Hall (Macon, Ga.: Mercer Univ. Press, 1999), 235–74.

25. See Inscoe, "*The Clansman* on Stage and Screen," 139–61.

26. *Winston-Salem Journal,* April 10, 2003, p. A18 (first quotation), April 11, 2003, p. B2 (second quotation).

27. The latest generation of Wake Forest students represented the university in a more positive light. Twelve undergraduates joined the organizers for a spring 2003 seminar on Dixon and his times. Taking an interdisciplinary approach, the seminar members produced research papers on literature, historical context, Dixon's religious development, and other topics. Jack Raffeto, Jamie Kidd, Meg Jongeward, Sean Lucas, and Katie Scott gave well-received papers at the symposium and benefited from the commentary of Catherine Clinton.

28. Nor can we ignore international intellectual currents. In an interview in 1907, Dixon discussed his work on a trilogy about socialism. He explained his intellectual development: "Years ago I was a rabid Socialist. One day I read a book by a Frenchman, Demolins, 'Anglo-Saxon Superiority.' That set me thinking in the other direction. Now I hate Socialism with an uncompromising fury. I would rather be an Anarchist than a collective Socialist, and I hope to make my new trilogy a complete glorification of individualism" (*New York Times Book Review,* August 10, 1907, p. 486). Beyond their common belief in Anglo-Saxon superiority, at times the phrasing of Demolins is similar to Dixon's wording. Demolins wrote, "The real question they ['lovers of Solidarity'] put is this: *Either the individual is to be subordinate to society, or society is to be subordinate to the individual*" (Edmond Demolins, *Anglo-Saxon Superiority: To What It Is Due,* trans. Louis Bert. Lavigne [London: Leadenhall Press, 1898],

305 [emphasis in original]). Compare Dixon's oft-quoted query in *The Leopard's Spots*: "Henceforth there could be but one issue, are you a White Man or a Negro? They declared there was but one question to be settled:—'Shall the future American be an Anglo-Saxon or a Mulatto?'" (See Thomas Dixon Jr., *The Leopard's Spots: A Romance of the White Man's Burden—1865–1900* [New York: Doubleday, Page, 1902], 159 [emphasis in original]).

Thomas Dixon: American Proteus

W. FITZHUGH BRUNDAGE

A man like Thomas Dixon, who wove stark moral imperatives so coarsely through his work, would seem at first glance easy to make sense of. After all, even passing familiarity with Dixon's corpus might lead one to conclude that his reliance on contrived plots and stereotypes and his embrace of strident racism signaled a one-dimensional personality that, like his work, lacked subtlety or contradiction. Is it not enough to depict him as a firebrand of white southern racism? As a case study of the cussedness of the human personality?

Several scholars, especially Joel Williamson, have looked to Dixon's psyche to make sense of the man. Readers of Williamson's *The Crucible of Race* will appreciate the enduring value of this approach. Dixon, Williamson writes, "is worthy of study because he offers some understanding of how the deeply personal and largely secret psychic needs of an individual might impel that person to extreme racism."[1] In Williamson's hands, Dixon's fixation on sexual violence may be traced to Dixon's belief that his mother had been the victim of rape while still a child.[2] In his novels and plays, Dixon obsessively worked through the deep trauma caused by his belief in his mother's alleged violation. Perhaps when Dixon becomes the subject of a scholarly biography that makes full use of all relevant sources Williamson's sketch of Dixon will be revised. In the meantime, I have no quibble with it.

We, however, need to recontextualize Dixon, resubmerge him, as it were, in his times in order to understand fully his influence over turn-of-the-century America. For all of the merits of Williamson's treatment of Dixon, it has comparatively little to offer as far as an explanation for Dixon's popularity. Is it enough to contend, as Williamson does, that "His grand themes" resonated at the dawn of the twentieth century because people "instinctively" and "passionately" knew them to be true?[3] Surely, the popularity of Dixon's work confirms this claim. Dixon himself boasted he felt the "heartbeat of eighteen million Southern people" and "gave voice to their faith."[4] But more problematic is the contention that Dixon's "psychic plight" was "representative of the psychic plight of several million contemporary white Southerners."[5] Just how, we might wonder, was Dixon's barely acknowledged but powerful guilt over his mother's traumatic youth shared by white southerners whose mothers presumably had various but undoubtedly different life experiences? That some of his harshest white critics were white southerners suggests that his "psychic plight" was not universal in the region. And are we to conclude that Dixon's popularity outside of the South demonstrates that Americans in general shared his "psychic plight"? Dixon undoubtedly appealed to and exploited the anxieties of his white audience. But any explanation of Dixon's popularity and influence should, I believe, acknowledge his virtuoso appropriation and use of melodrama, spectacle, and many other popular cultural forms of his day.

This essay, then, proceeds at the social rather than psychoanalytical level. Dixon's career and appeal will be analyzed not as a consequence of personality quirks, but in the context of his cultural milieu. His racial ideology, creative aspirations, and mode of expression, I suggest, exemplify what one scholar has called the "divided mind" of the late Victorian age.[6] Like Proteus, who possessed the gift of prophecy and an ability to change form at will, Dixon displayed a chameleon-like quality that singularly suited him to the opportunities and anxieties of his era. His successes as a minister, lecturer, novelist, playwright, and screenplay writer may be traced to his keen appreciation of contemporary appetites and tastes as much as to a contemporary sub-rosa psychic tick. To understand Dixon's appeal and influence, in short, we need to pay attention to his craft no less than his personal "baggage."

Essential to Dixon's broad appeal was his skill at invoking the language and ethos of the evangelical Protestantism that undergirded so much of nineteenth-century America's shared culture. From evangelical Protestantism Dixon gleaned values, language, and modes of expression, all of which resonated with his audiences. Indeed, it is tempting to explain Dixon by dwelling on the nineteenth-century southern Baptist Church in which he was nurtured. He, of course, was educated at Wake Forest, a Baptist institution, his father was a noted Baptist minister, and Amzi C. Dixon, his brother, became a renowned leader in the early fundamentalist movement. Dixon seems to have internalized many of the evangelical values that surrounded him, including an acute moral earnestness, even before he became a minister. While serving as a precociously young member of the North Carolina state legislature in 1885, he purportedly secured the passage of a bill suppressing the circulation of obscene literature. Henceforth, as minister, then lecturer, and finally as novelist and playwright, Dixon fixated on the moral extremes that he believed characterized worldly affairs—extremes of complete innocence and total depravity.[7]

His Manichaean worldview was consonant with nineteenth-century evangelical culture. For Dixon and many contemporaries, moral discipline was a crucial constituent of culture, of civilization. Such discipline was more than just polite manners or a code of personal conduct. Discipline elevated the individual; it enabled men and women to keep their baser instincts in check. Those who possessed restraint were civilized, those who lacked it savages. The latter were to be scorned because their behavior could only degrade, not elevate. In broadest terms, a relentless pursuit of moral purity and innocence stood at the heart of the evangelical Victorian culture that Dixon knew. This impulse led many late Victorians to strive for purity in all things and to repress unrestrained impulses. Dixon himself seems to have been fascinated by forbidden passions, if only so as to contrast and heighten the beauty of the pure. And even when such passions were acknowledged, they were condemned and punished.[8]

But it is a mistake to conclude that this moral orientation in Dixon's life and work reflected "an impassioned defense of conservative religious values."[9] Just as late nineteenth-century evangelicalism was beset by considerable sectarian and doctrinal turmoil, so too Dixon during his varied life deviated in surprising ways from the path his family anticipated for him (and which his brothers followed). Imagine how scandalized his family, friends, and teachers must have been when he pursued a career in theater during the early 1880s. To commit to a life on stage was to toy with blasphemy and to mingle with the debased. Lack of success rather than qualms about the probity of his chosen profession ended his first foray into theater. His subsequent flirtation with a legal career suggests confusion about his proper calling and the ongoing tug of respectability. Curiously, he recoiled from the corruption of lawyers more than he apparently ever did from the rumored moral license of actors. His law career ended quickly. Likewise, he ended his fleeting political career as a rising state legislator because, he claimed, he could not reconcile his Christian values with the exigencies of politics. That he eventually entered the ministry, however, did not mean that he had surrendered to convention.[10]

Dixon quickly strayed far from his Baptist moorings. His presence and manner of delivery conformed to evangelical conventions. Handsome, gifted with a deep, musical voice, and disposed to an "abrupt, militant, and uncompromising" manner of delivery, accentuated all the more by his tall and gaunt frame, Dixon delivered sermons like a latter-day Jeremiah.[11] He lashed out at the corrupt, immoral, and craven in fiery sermons. But he was no Billy Sunday, no end-of-the-century revivalist blasting modernity. Instead, he was a Social Gospel popularizer whose message of ecumenical Christian reform abandoned traditional denominational formulas and embraced, although not categorically, the future. During the late 1880s, when he briefly ministered at the Dudley Street Church in Boston before moving on to the Twenty-Third Street Baptist Church in New York, Dixon emerged as a leader in the burgeoning Social Gospel movement. An article in *Century Magazine* in 1896 that urged churches to embrace a "vigorous, robust, muscular Christianity . . . devoid of all the et. cetera of creed" succinctly described Dixon's inclinations.[12] Dixon scorned "all forms, ceremonies, rituals, places, paper creeds, and Church officialdom" as unsuited to the modern world. Rather than remain bound to the Baptist denomination, he resigned his ministry at the Twenty-Third Street Baptist Church and founded his own church in 1895.[13]

Dixon's spiritual trajectory was typical of other Social Gospelers. A heady mixture of Christian and communitarian millennialism inspired Dixon and like-minded others to envision the reconstruction of society along explicitly collective lines. By appealing to Christians to turn divine truths into practical terms and by equating the millennium with a complete reorganization of American institutions, Social Gospelers aligned themselves with the rich tradition of perfectionism in nineteenth-century America. In the pronouncements of Dixon and his fellow Social Gospelers, idealism and Christian theology became bound up in urgent and vivid forecasts of doom and redemption, social reform and spiritual regeneration. He set out to restate Protestantism "in the language of modern life, grateful for all of the light of science, philosophy, and criticism." In sermons, he refused to preach, as he put it, the "simple Gospel" or to meditate "on the number of feathers in the angel Gabriel's wings." He vowed instead to "proclaim the sacredness of the secular" so as to impel Christians to undertake immediate social reform.[14]

For Dixon, the impending and urgently needed millennial reordering of society awaited the spread of a "muscular Christianity," a term that had particular import for him. Perhaps as much as any Social Gospeler of his era, Dixon strove to reinvigorate Christianity by restoring its purported patriarchal identity. He shared with revivalist Dwight Moody a concern to draw men into church pews and to infuse the male workaday world with faith. For too long, Dixon complained, the church had been equated with the moral realm of the feminine private household. Protestantism, he insisted, needed to be reinfused with virility. Modern circumstances demanded "wrath and indignation" and that "the sword of Christianity" be wielded.[15] Only then could it inform the public realm completely.[16] The sentimental spirituality of traditional, feminine Protestantism must give way to a masculine faith propagated by manly preachers. Milquetoast ministers who catered to feminine sensibilities were particular targets of Dixon's ire. His contempt for the "effeminate vanity" of some ministers was manifest, for instance, when he sparred with Len Broughton, a leading Atlanta Baptist minister and early fundamentalist, over the morality and social value of modern theater. Distressed by the popularity of Dixon's play *The Clansman* when it opened in Atlanta in 1905, Broughton lashed out at the play, and theater in general, as sinful, corrupting diversion. After dismissing Broughton's attack as laughably old-fashioned, Dixon lampooned the Baptist evangelical as "a fairy masquerading in pantaloons" best known for his fastidiously maintained long locks of golden hair.[17] Such effeminacy was anathema to Dixon. His contempt flowed from his belief in the proliferation of "sexless monstrosities" and the erosion of patriarchy, evident in the surging woman's suffrage movement, an erosion that forecast the destruction of Christian civilization.[18]

Dixon's immersion in the Social Gospel complicates any portrait of him as an impassioned defender of conservative religious values. More important, the extroverted reform impulse that characterized the Social Gospel is essential to understanding Dixon's compulsion to escape the tranquility of the manse and enter into the arena of exhilarating activism. Following his adage that "Politics is religion in action," he became a reform gadfly in New York during the 1890s.[19] At his church he hosted prominent figures, ranging from noted reform ministers to radical activists. He also secured a place on the stage at seemingly every public reform meeting held in the city, from which he championed and impugned public figures and causes without restraint. Aligning himself with the urban reform movement, he launched the Civil Union, an organization for public-spirited young men. He endorsed reform politicians, especially Theodore Roosevelt, who was a paragon of the active, engaged, strenuous life that Dixon admired. (The future Rough Rider only grew in Dixon's estimation when he took up one of Dixon's pet causes, Cuban independence.) And Dixon was an outspoken champion of the need for expansive American leadership on the world stage.[20]

Dixon's chronic activism during the late 1880s and the 1890s took place against the backdrop of what one scholar calls "the golden age of the crank in America."[21] At a time when economic and social change undermined inherited beliefs and when intellectual discourse had not yet become the special preserve of academics sequestered in ivy-covered towers, amateur social engineers and political economists flourished. The era's freewheeling debates about American institutions and political economy interested equally the dilettante social visionary, the backwoods scholar, and the ambitious minister. Such circumstances encouraged Dixon and other reform-minded ministers to speak with urgency and unselfconscious authority. That Dixon had a penchant for intuitive rather than systematic thought and that he eschewed theory and never attempted a painstaking analysis of any issue in no way prevented him from holding a position on virtually every controversial topic. What may strike us as Dixon's extraordinary hubris and tendentiousness, in short, was a reflection of his age as much as his personality. The times in which he lived seemingly gave license to, even demanded such intellectual arrogance.

Nor was Dixon unusual in harboring conspicuously contradictory ideas. The chaotic times seemingly inhibited consistent positions. To take but one example, in 1900 Theodore Dreiser published *Sister Carrie*, a searing critique of modern capitalism and its corrosive impact on the individual. Yet Dreiser had previously written "Studies of Contemporary Celebrities" for *Success* magazine, in which he provided adulatory portraits of Philip D. Armour, Andrew Carnegie, and other buccaneering capitalists.[22] Likewise, Dixon could at once dine with John D. Rockefeller and consort with labor hero Eugene Debs, Populist Mary Elizabeth Lease, and Christian socialists without perceiving any contradictions in his behavior.[23] His flirtation with the Christian socialism of Edward Bellamy and W.D.P. Bliss implied not so much a rejection of capitalism as a rejection of laissez-faire economics.[24] He bridled at the corrosive effects of competition. Yet his beliefs did not preclude individualism; he later took to calling himself a "reactionary individualist."[25] On the contrary, the avowed purpose of the reforms he advocated was to enable all citizens to become more responsible and independent individuals. His stated reason for leaving the ministry—that he stood to make far more money as a lecturer than as a minister—displayed no apparent embarrassment over his monetary ambitions. Indeed, he ceaselessly publicized his subsequent sybaritic life as a Virginia estate owner and yachtsman.[26] These contradictions appear glaring to us, but they seemingly prompted little puzzlement from his contemporaries.[27]

So let us pause for a moment and take stock of this thirty-seven-year-old man at the outset of his literary career in 1901. What tendencies and convictions did he display at this point in his life? He exhibited the moral certainty characteristic of evangelicals. But he combined it with the reform ambitions and ecumenical sensibilities of the Social Gospel movement. Dixon's taste for the posh life did little to erode his disposition toward moral absolutism. Far from it. Dixon may have left the pulpit, but he had no intention to stop preaching. He remained deeply committed to his moral precepts as a writer and lecturer. "No man," he warned, "can write the truth and not preach."[28] This impulse in turn helped to fuel his unquenchable ambition to influence the public opinion of his day.

This ambition, perhaps as much as any inner turmoil, spurred on his serial change of careers. His genius for recognizing the most effective means to mold his generation's attitudes explains his easy and successful shift from minister to lecturer to author to playwright and film producer. Dixon recognized that the accelerating technological and cultural innovation of his age facilitated new forms of mass culture. Just as railroads made possible his hectic lecturing schedule during the 1890s, so too shifting theater tastes and newly awakened fascination with film would serve to spread his ideas in the new century. A son of the New South, where Henry Grady and his ilk tirelessly proselytized the gospel of modernization, Dixon was eager to exploit the wonders of his age. This inclination, stated simply, had as much to do with Dixon's success as the ideas that he expressed.[29]

Focusing on Dixon's pet subjects far more than on his favored forms of expression, scholars have cast Dixon's novels, plays, and screenplays as the epitome of extremist white racism during "the highest stage of white supremacy."[30] Dixon, admittedly, became fixated on race to a degree that was uncommon even for his age. In a 1905 review, W.E.B. Du Bois summarized the plots of Dixon's extant and future corpus with depressing accuracy: "There's a black man who thinks himself a man and is a man; kill him before he marries your daughter!"[31] Yet, without somehow excusing Dixon's lurid sectionalism and virulent racism, we nevertheless should acknowledge how commonplace novels of white supremacy were in turn-of-the-century America. The romanticization of the Ku Klux Klan, for example, was well under way before Dixon wrote *The Clansman*. His portrayal of the Klan was of a piece with the larger project of countless white southerners to "redeem" the region's honor after the Civil War. Dixon, however, hardly broke new ground in this regard. Almost two decades before he put pen to paper to write *The Leopard's Spots,* Albion Tourgée, a former abolitionist, grumbled that "our literature has become not only Southern in type but distinctly Confederate in sympathy."[32] Dixon repackaged tropes already commonplace in the sentimental local color fiction of Thomas Nelson Page and others. For instance, Page's *Red Rock,* published in 1898, recounted Reconstruction from a stridently southern perspective, complete with a heroic Ku Klux Klan. It even foreshadowed Dixon's preoccupation with black degeneracy. Lurking in Page's novel is the repellent and sinister figure Moses, a black politician who resembles a "beast" and a "reptile" and who harbors an uncontrollable lust for white women.[33]

Dixon's stridently hostile depiction of African Americans, tragically, was commonplace. That all races and peoples should be measured against a single criterion of development, or "civilization," and that western Europeans and Anglo-Americans stood at the apex of civilization was axiomatic in turn-of-the-century American fiction.[34] A case in point is Hamlin Garland's bestseller *The Captain of the Gray-Horse Troop,* published in 1902, the same year as Dixon's *The Leopard's Spots*. Garland's novel relates the efforts of a federal agent in Montana to uplift benighted Indians. Garland describes Indians as tragically backward; they need a protector because they cannot survive on their own, education has no impact on them, and citizenship has no meaning. It was up to Garland's white hero to be "their Moses." When Curtis, the novel's protagonist, gives his long-pursued love interest, Elsie, a tour of the reservation, she has an epiphany. "Here was a little kingdom over which Curtis reigned, a despotic monarch, and Elsie, if she did her duty, would reign by his side." A leading "realist" and popular novelist of the day, Garland offers a western version of the plantation novel, with the reservation and the Indian supplanting the plantation and Sambo. Garland may have mixed more compassion with his ethnocentrism than Dixon did, but otherwise the two authors were in agreement about the innate backwardness of primitive races. As Elsie comes to understand, with tears in her eyes, "They have so far to go, poor things! They can't realize how long the road to civilization is."[35]

In an age when white novelists pondered the future danger of a declining Anglo-Saxon birthrate, an exploding immigrant population, and escalating radical violence, what caught the attention of Dixon's contemporaries was less his unvarying subject matter—the problem of race in America—than his style, or, in other words, his mode of expression. It, at least as much as his subject matter, was the key to his ability to grip the imaginations and to shape the attitudes of his contemporaries.[36]

To emphasize the style of a writer who was criticized for his wooden characters, trite dialogue, and improbable plots at the height of his popularity may seem curious. Even white southerners cringed at his stylistic lapses. The editor of the *Columbia (S.C.) State* scolded him for his penchant for "tinsel setting" and "sensational drama."[37] A well-disposed reviewer characterized Dixon as "a yellow journalist busied with bookmaking."[38] Another reviewer dismissed Dixon's stories as an incoherent string of "scenes of a sentimental, sensational, moral or spectacular character."[39] He "writes like a madman," complained a letter writer to the *New York Times*. "His pile of wood is cut often with a dull axe and never sawed in a sharp saw."[40] An industrious reader calculated that Dixon must not edit his work, because no "novelist of long experience and high standing would bore the reader with three hundred and twenty-three references to the eyes of characters—an average of over one every two pages."⁴¹ Elegant, lapidary prose was not Dixon's metier.⁴²

Dixon's rough-hewn fiction did little to curb his popularity. A reader confessed that she herself accepted "without comment and with rapacious greed, his crudities and inaccuracies." She added, "there is no resisting him" and his "virile pictures of American life." Possessed of genius, which "may take its own way," Dixon, she judged, was one of the nation's "strongest" and "boldest" writers.⁴³

This reader's choice of words and repeated allusions to the virility of Dixon's prose is revealing. Dixon's moral compass may have been Victorian and his prose and plots may have reeked of cheap sentimentality, but the experiential intensity that he achieved tested the boundaries of genteel convention. As the letter writer to the *New York Times* recognized, there was an uncommon physicality to Dixon's fiction. For readers who tired of fiction characterized by "the overcivilized, the hyper-fastidious . . . the fragile, the trivial, the rarified, [and] the bloodless," Dixon's writings were an antidote.⁴⁴ Dixon, in this regard, contributed to the "reorientation of American culture" described by historians John Higham and Jackson Lears. This emerging culture was energetic and pleasure-oriented, befitting modern consumerism. The older sensibility of restraint was too pallid and tepid for Dixon and his readers. Victorian propriety coexisted with bursts of desire and excitement. Moralism and idealism retained a prominent place in this culture, but were now joined to heroic action. The pursuit of robust experience, of life in the fullest, and the cultivation of the strenuous self, these were the cultural aspirations that Dixon appealed to, first as a minister, then as a popular lecturer, and, above all, as a novelist and playwright. Not unlike his earlier efforts as minister and orator, Dixon's feverish prose, which pressed against inherited boundaries of control and restraint, was intended to reinvigorate Victorian culture.⁴⁵

That Dixon adopted the melodrama as his preferred literary, stage, and film form was well nigh inevitable. His use of and talent with this genre, which has gone largely unrecognized, enabled him to be heard over the cacophony of turn-of-the-century America, to reach, with unusual force, the divided minds of his generation. Melodrama's popularity, of course, predated both the eve of the twentieth century and Dixon's success. And it remains a pervasive cultural form to the present day. Yet, in fin de siècle

America, melodramatic spectacles reigned on the U.S. stage and would soon dominate the American screen. The popularity and pervasiveness of melodrama made possible the intertextuality that was a striking characteristic of Dixon's career; his use of the form facilitated his quick adaptation of his novel to the stage and then to the most revolutionary mass media of the age—film.

The appeal of melodrama to Dixon and his contemporaries was its moral transparency and urgency. Melodrama acquires particular appeal at times when moral verities seem threatened by headlong change. When "traditional imperatives of truth and ethics have been violently thrown into question," writes Peter Brooks, melodrama "becomes the principal mode for uncovering, demonstrating, and making operative the essential moral universe."[46] The melodramatic tradition was profoundly, inescapably moral. "The melodrama," explains Robert Lang, "does not simply stage a battle between good and evil (with good triumphing) but rather tries to establish that clear notions of good and evil prevail, that there are moral imperatives."[47]

Dixon's life-long propensity for moral absolutism almost certainly predisposed him to employ melodrama. Conventions of melodrama, whether in fiction, stage, or film, meshed easily with his Manichaean predisposition. The binary opposition essential to melodrama—good versus evil—allowed little scope for consideration of the "human dividedness" that figures so prominently in tragedy.[48] Instead, familiar opposites—primitive vs. civilized, rural vs. urban, moral vs. immoral—typified melodramas. Inevitably, stereotypes, especially ethnic and racial, gave human form to these binaries.[49] In print, on stage, and in film, melodrama characters necessarily were iconic figures with self-evident qualities and motivations. Heroic white fathers and brothers, virginal white mothers and daughters, bestial nihilistic black men—these were the characters who populated the melodramatic landscape. Well established in American stage melodrama, the exploitation of stereotypes quickly transferred to early silent film, in which the absence of dialogue complicated the conveying of meaning with clarity and force. A brief survey of some of the films that D. W. Griffith made before *Birth of a Nation,* for example, illustrates how central stereotypical characters were in early film. In Griffith's third film, *The Black Viper* (1908), a working-class "brute" stalks a virginal girl and attacks her. The climax of the movie involves the rescue of the girl and her sweetheart from the "viper" and his henchmen. In *The Fatal Hour* (1908), which depicts "a stirring incident in the Chinese White Slave Traffic," Griffith portrays the violent abductions of women by a Chinese villain and his lackeys. And in *The Chord of Life* (1909) a Sicilian "worthless good-for-nothing scoundrel" plots a devious revenge against a woman and her child. Dixon's characters, Dick and Gus, the animal-like black rapists in *The Leopard's Spots* and *The Clansman* respectively, easily fit within this tradition.[50]

Beyond imposing moral order on the chaos of turn-of-the-century life, melodrama whetted a popular appetite for valor and spectacle. By accentuating heroic feats and heightened sensation, melodramatic plotting and exposition contributed to the aesthetics of spectacle that was so pronounced in late nineteenth-century popular culture.[51] From rococo department store window displays to amusement rides at Coney Island and diversions at nickelodeons, "The thrill," film historian Ben Singer writes, "emerged as the keynote of modern diversion."[52] Audiences eager for exhilaration and suspense had little appetite for long-winded orations by embattled heroes and villains; they demanded spectacles of action and peril, often involving complex stagecraft. Thundering trains, swirling cyclones, roaring rapids, and, eventually, speeding automobiles came to grace the sets of stage melodramas. Early cinema carried this impulse yet further, such that fisticuffs, chases, escapes, battles, and other forms of visual sensation figured prominently, if not exclusively in early cinema.

That Dixon was immersed in and fascinated by the aesthetics of spectacle is clear. Even after his failed acting career in the 1880s, Dixon evidenced a keen interest in stagecraft. While ministering in New York City, he showed elaborate slide shows to illustrate his sermons.[53] When he turned to fiction, he wrote melodramas characterized by action, spectacle, dynamic narrative, and heightened emotions. Dixon's own prose shared some of the traits of silent film; the complaint of the reader who quantified Dixon's tiresome descriptions of his characters' eyes and facial expressions speaks to Dixon's reliance on exaggerated gestures and poses to convey mood and emotion. Dixon gave free rein to this tendency when he adapted *The Clansman* to theater. His elaborate staging, including somber gatherings of robed white men, flaming crosses, fights, black corpses, and charges of Klansmen on live horses, tested the limits of the era's stagecraft.[54] And years before

Dixon joined Griffith to make *Birth of a Nation* he recognized and yearned to exploit the illusionary potential and kinetic stimulation of film.[55]

Dixon's enthusiasm for spectacular illusion went hand in hand with his avowed commitment to realism. Dixon saw no contradiction between his contrived, far-fetched plot twists and his insistence on the verisimilitude of his work. In the introduction to *The Clansman* he proclaimed that he had not taken a single "liberty with any essential historical fact."[56] To a Columbia, South Carolina, audience he announced that his work "was a lighthouse of historic facts" and that he would unite the nation "in a knowledge of the truth." He then offered $1,000 to anyone who could disprove his "facts."[57] When challenged about his relentlessly hostile depiction of Congressman Thaddeus Stevens, Dixon roared back, "I dare my critic to come out . . . and put his finger on a single word, line, sentence, paragraph, page, or chapter of 'The Clansman' in which I have done Thad Stevens an injustice."[58] Dixon's concern for historical accuracy perhaps arose from his brief stint as a history graduate student at Johns Hopkins University in the 1880s. There historian Herbert Baxter Adams and others adapted German methods of instruction and research and instilled in a generation of students a commitment to the methodical, earnestly professional pursuit of "objective" historical truth. By claiming to have used the methods of "scientific" history when writing his fiction, Dixon coupled the century's ascendent source of authority—science—to his historical project.[59] And by insisting that the historical record supported his representation of the past, he moved his fiction and plays from the realm of polemic to that of unimpeachable truth.

More broadly, when Dixon boasted about his extensive historical research he aligned himself with the pursuit of verisimilitude that characterized so much of the age's popular culture. The goal (all of the claims of scientism notwithstanding) was not just verisimilitude and historical accuracy for their own sake, but so as to generate an intense, authentic atmosphere that in turn would augment the emotional intensity of the work. It was this quality that advertisements for *Birth of a Nation* dwelled on when they promised that viewers would see "whole pages torn from history and re-enacted before your eyes."[60] Likewise, the purported "tremendous realism" of the movie inspired audiences to become "almost hysterical," or as

James Weldon Johnson put it, to give vent to "the most dangerous human passions."[61] Similar passions drove some audience members of *The Clansman*, swept away by the play's perceived realism, to attack cast members, and some viewers of *The Birth of a Nation* to fire their revolvers at the screen during the film's climax. Whether in print, on the stage, or in film, Dixon's work drew upon and catered to the contemporary fascination with melodramatic spectacle, verisimilitude, and the authority of "facts."

Dixon's conspicuous participation in and contributions to the evolution of melodrama during the early twentieth century complicate our understanding of his influence. Raymond Williams's notions of "residual" and "emergent" cultures are useful in thinking about Dixon's popularity and cultural influence. "The residual, by definition, has been effectively formed in the past, but it is still active in the cultural process . . . as an effective element in the present," explains Williams. Dixon's ideas about and representations of civilization, race, and gender are a case in point. Dixon's thoughts on these topics were neither systematic nor unconventional; they were rooted in well-established nineteenth-century convictions. At the same time that Dixon was fashioning his fictional Armageddons, Charlotte Perkins Gilman and Franz Boas, among others, were imagining new conceptions of gender and race. Dixon rejected these new currents and instead drew upon inherited attitudes. In the process, he created works that had an enduring influence on the nation's ongoing dialogue over race and region. Whites in the southern hinterland would continue to attend showings of *Birth of a Nation* well into the 1930s. Yet, importantly, Dixon yoked his ideas to modern modes of cultural expression, which eventually would contribute to an emerging modernist ethos. Dixon's participation in the Social Gospel movement and, especially, his exploitation of the sensational melodramatic form represented an emergent, even "substantially alternative" culture.[62] As a Social Gospeler, Dixon expressed modern anxieties while simultaneously affirming inherited moral absolutes of virtue and villainy. Later his use of the melodramatic form to intensify the sensory experience of modern life created a dynamic aesthetic that could be applied to pressing contemporary concerns.

Dixon, however, could not cross the threshold of modernism, with its embrace of the sensual, the primitive, and the subconscious.[63] In this regard, Dixon may take his place beside Hamlin Garland, Ellen Glasgow, and other turn-of-the-century Americans who traced the boundaries of Victorianism without ever moving beyond them. Consequently, Dixon found it increasingly hard to attract audiences and readers as the twentieth century progressed. In the years after the war, the connections that Dixon drew between race, gender, and civilization lost some of their persuasive power at a time when psychology, consumerism, and modernist culture eroded nineteenth-century moral absolutes and fixed ideals of masculine and feminine behavior. Social scientists challenged assumptions of innate racial attributes and cultural potentials, and gradually, but unmistakably, the celebration of heroic Anglo-Saxon history lost both its urgency and the patina of modernity that it had once had. Despite the revival of the Ku Klux Klan in the 1920s (which Dixon condemned), his popularity waned.[64]

The insurgent Modernist culture, moreover, represented a deliberate repudiation of Victorian innocence and its perceived repression of human impulses. Modernists displayed a willingness, even eagerness, to dwell on the irrational in human life. Dixon may have depicted the irrational, but always so as to recoil from it. Now, Modernists treated the irrational as an essential part of humanity's unpredictable and turbulent nature. Perhaps most important, Modernists accepted tentative and relative moral standards rather than the absolutes of Dixon and his fellow Victorians. Dixon, with his unambiguous moral binaries, neither could nor wanted to embrace this modernist ethos. Consequently, his later films and fiction belabored tired themes and conventions and offered no aesthetic innovations.

Like an American Proteus, Dixon had been able to transform himself from actor into legislator, lawyer, minister, lecturer, novelist, playwright, movie producer, and finally real estate speculator. Along with such contemporaries as Booker T. Washington, Theodore Roosevelt, and Jane Addams, Dixon demonstrated an ability to align himself with some of the most powerful swirling currents of his era. In doing so he displayed the inventive elan so characteristic of the period. Dixon flirted with aesthetic innovation, displayed uncommon pessimism about the threats to the nation's future, and advocated adventurous engagement with social change. His discontents paralleled contemporary ferment in American thought and culture. His lamentable contribution to American life was to adapt the melodrama of white supremacy to new technologies of mass culture. In this regard, he arguably was as important as any of his contemporaries, including his collaborator D. W. Griffith.

But Dixon's transformations, like those of mythical Proteus, were of form, not of fundamental character. Dixon's imaginative spaciousness and transformative powers did not enable him to traverse the profound cleavages of his age, the conflict between tradition and innovation, order and liberation, expansive optimism and fearful pessimism. In the end, Dixon accommodated himself to many of his age's underlying desires and discontents, but tragically for his reputation and, more important, for American culture and people of color in the United States, his protean character and mind failed to enable him to develop a broad vision of humankind and therefore to overcome the conspicuous shortcomings of his work—dehumanizing racism, strident chauvinism, and reactionary politics. Yet even after the anxieties that fueled Dixon's popularity faded and popular tastes changed, the enduring appeal of the spectacles that Dixon created on the printed page, the stage, and the movie lot ensured that Dixon and his art continued to cast a shadow over American life.

NOTES

1. Joel Williamson, *Crucible of Race: Black-White Relations in the American South since Emancipation* (New York: Oxford Univ. Press, 1984), 151.

2. Dixon's mother, Amanda Dixon, was thirteen years old when she married Thomas Dixon Sr., who was twenty-seven. She suffered a number of miscarriages before her first child, Amzi Clarence, survived. Apparently Dixon perceived his mother's early experience with marriage and childbearing as the literal equivalent of rape. See Williamson, *Crucible of Race*, 158–65.

3. Ibid., 152.

4. Dixon went on to claim that "the number of Southern white people today who disagree with *The Leopard's Spots* could all be housed on a half-acre lot." *New York Times Book Review*, August 9, 1902, p. 10.

5. Williamson, *Crucible of Race*, 152.

6. Peter Conn, *The Divided Mind: Ideology and Imagination in America, 1898–1917* (Cambridge: Cambridge Univ. Press, 1983).

7. "Versatile Mr. Tom Dixon," *New York Times*, May 7, 1884, p. 3. The best account of Dixon's early life and career(s) is Raymond A. Cook, *Fire from the Flint: The Amazing Careers of Thomas Dixon* (Winston-Salem: Blair, 1968), 8–21, 35–49, 55–66. See also Williamson, *Crucible of Race*, 152–55.

8. For treatments of the Victorian nexus of culture, civility, and civilization, see Gail Bederman, *Manliness and Civilization: A Cultural History of Gender and Race in the United States, 1880–1917* (Chicago: Univ. of Chicago Press, 1995), especially chapter 1; John F. Kasson, *Rudeness and Civility: Manners in Nineteenth-Century Urban America* (New York: Hill and Wang, 1990); Daniel J. Singal, "Towards a Definition of American Modernism," in *Modernist Culture in America,* ed. Daniel J. Singal (Belmont, Calif.: Wadsworth, 1991).

9. James Kinney, "Thomas Dixon, Jr.," in *Encyclopedia of Southern Culture,* ed. Charles Reagan Wilson and William Ferris (Chapel Hill: Univ. of North Carolina Press, 1989), 881.

10. "Versatile Mr. Tom Dixon," *New York Times,* May 7, 1884, p. 3. For Dixon's own account of these years, see Thomas Dixon, *Southern Horizons: The Autobiography of Thomas Dixon* (Alexandria, Va.: IWV Publishing, 1984), 168–70, 173–91.

11. Cook, *Fire from the Flint,* 81.

12. Quoted in Anthony E. Rotundo, *American Manhood: Transformations in Masculinity from the Revolution to the Modern Era* (New York: Basic Books, 1993), 224.

13. "Rev. Thomas Dixon Resigns," *New York Times,* March 11, 1895, p. 8. Dixon's critique of modern Protestantism is summarized in Thomas Dixon Jr., *The Failure of Protestantism in New York and Its Causes* (New York: Victor O. A. Strauss, 1896). David Stricklin stresses how unorthodox Dixon's ecumenical orientation was for a white southern Protestant in "'Ours Is a Century of Light': Dixon's Strange Consistency," in this volume.

14. Dixon, *Failure of Protestantism*. Dixon's participation in the Social Gospel movement, at last, receives careful attention in Cynthia Lynn Lyerly, "Gender and Race in Dixon's Religious Ideology," and David Stricklin, "'Ours Is a Century of Light': Dixon's Strange Consistency," in this volume. I have also benefited from Eric Millin's "'The Scourge of Christ': The Social Gospel, Christian Manhood, and Thomas Dixon's Ku Klux Klan," unpublished essay, in the author's possession.

15. Dixon, *Failure of Protestantism,* 125, 129.

16. For an early call for "aggressive Christianity" as the mission of the modern Church, see Thomas Dixon Jr., *Living Problems in Religion and Social Science* (New York: Charles T. Dillingham, 1889), especially chapters 1 and 8. Also see Dixon, *Failure of Protestantism,* 61–79. For Dixon on the need to masculinize churches, see Dixon, *Failure of Protestantism,* 11–12, 18–19, 58, 59, 77, 124–25. Similar concerns emerged in Dixon's novel *The One Woman.* For a discussion of this theme and the novel, see Lyerly, "Gender and Race in Dixon's Religious Ideology." Dixon's masculine Social Gospel was in virtual opposition to an arguably even more important feminine Social Gospel. On this latter movement, see Wendy J. Deichmann Edwards and Carolyn De Swarte Gifford, eds., *Gender and the Social Gospel* (Urbana: Univ. of Illinois Press, 2003).

17. *Atlanta Journal,* November 6, 1905. For an extended account of the Dixon-Broughton contretemps, see Millin, "'The Scourge of Christ.'" For an excellent, concise biographical sketch of Leonard Broughton, see James Lutzweiler, *Fiche Fragments of Fundamentalism, Part I: The Works of Leonard Gaston Broughton (1865–1936)* (Greensboro, N.C.: Schnappsburg Univ. Press, 1993), 1–7. An early example of Dixon's penchant for impugning the masculinity of his critics is his response to a letter to the editor of the *New York Times,* "An

Old-Fashioned Clergyman," in which he nicknamed his critic a "Grannie" and castigated him for putting on "women's clothing" [Anglican robes] in pursuit of dignity on Sundays ("Mr. Dixon's Reply to Criticism," *New York Times*, January 14, 1895, p. 6).

18. Dixon's lament about the proliferation of "sexless monstrosities" and the resulting failure of Christian men to assume their proper role is repeated throughout *Failure of Protestantism* (see pp. 24, 104, 113). On his opposition to woman's suffrage, see "Mrs. Gougar Mr. Dixon's Equal," *New York Times*, July 13, 1896, p. 8. Dixon's patriarchal worldview is ably outlined in Cynthia Lynn Lyerly, "Gender and Race in Dixon's Religious Ideology," and Barbara Bennett, "Petticoats, Prejudice, and Patriarchy in the Novels of Thomas Dixon" (paper delivered at Wake Forest University Symposium, April 11, 2003).

19. Thomas Dixon Jr., *Dixon's Sermons, Delivered in the Grand Opera House, New York, 1898–1899* (New York: F. L. Bussey, n.d.), 103. Dixon also insisted that the "triumphant Church must be a social power" (Dixon, *Failure of Protestantism*, 150). For a small sampling of Dixon's early crusades, see *New York Times*, October 22, 1889, p. 8; "New York City's Shame," ibid., October 6, 1890, p. 1; and "What Reform Victory Really Means," ibid., November 5, 1894, p. 8.

20. Dixon's involvement in urban reform reached a fever pitch during the 1897 New York mayoral contest. See the following articles in the *New York Times*: "Seth Low as Candidate," September 6, 1897, p. 2; "Low Denounced by Dixon," September 13, 1897, p. 10; "The Woes of Tammany," September 20, 1897, p. 10; and "Dixon Assails Low Again," September 27, 1897, p. 3. For his recollections of his political activism, see Dixon, *Southern Horizons*, 231–38. Dixon's warmongering during the 1890s is displayed in Dixon, *Dixon's Sermons*, 1–48. See also "Would Have Cuba Free," *New York Times*, November 27, 1895, p. 5; "Pastors Preach Politics," ibid., September 21, 1896, p. 2; "In Behalf of Cuba Free," ibid., December 22, 1896, p. 2; "Cubans Honor Marti's Memory," ibid., May 17, 1897, p. 3; and Cook, *Fire from the Flint*, 91–95. Dixon's admiration of Roosevelt is explored in "Mr. Dixon and His Vote," *New York Times*, November 2, 1896, p. 16. See also *Dixon's Sermons*, 58–72, 89–90. Dixon's Anglo-Saxon imperialism is discussed by David Stricklin in "'Ours Is a Century of Light,'" in this volume. It also is treated in Eric Millin's "'The Scourge of Christ.'"

21. Carlos A. Schwantes, *Coxey's Army: An American Odyssey* (Lincoln: Univ. of Nebraska Press, 1985), 47.

22. Theodore Dreiser, "Studies of Contemporary Celebrities," *Success* 1 (October 1898): 3–4; ibid., 2 (June 1899): 453. Dreiser also wrote tributes to technology, such as "The Harlem River Speedway" for *Ainslee's* 2 (August 1898): 49–56, and "The Horseless Age," *Demorest's* 35 (May 1899): 153–55. These duties garnered him a comfortable lifestyle.

23. On Dixon, Debs, and Lease, see "Debs in Academy of Music," *New York Times*, February 21, 1898, p. 4; and "Mrs. Lease in the Pulpit," ibid., January 24, 1898, p. 10. Dixon continued to enthuse about Rockefeller later in life; see *Southern Horizons*, 207–11.

24. Dixon's vaguely socialist leanings are evident throughout *The Failure of Protestantism in New York*. He also acknowledged his earlier socialist tendencies in an interview in the *New York Times Book Review*, "A Romance of Money Madness," August 10, 1907, p. 486.

25. "Thomas Dixon Dies; Wrote *Clansman*," *New York Times*, April 4, 1946, p. 23.

26. "Thomas Dixon, Jr., Resigns," *New York Times*, March 11, 1895, p. 8. See also "Rev. Dixon's New Boat," ibid., December 6, 1897, p. 2; "The Dixie Probably Safe," ibid., February 18, 1899, p. 7; and Cook, *Fire from the Flint*, 95–97. Dixon waxed poetic about his country life in Thomas Dixon Jr., *The Life Worth Living: A Personal Experience* (New York: Doubleday, Page, 1905), especially chapters 2 and 10, and in *Southern Horizons*, 244–57.

27. Dixon describes his decision to leave the ministry in *Southern Horizons*, 258–62. David Stricklin makes the same point about the prevalence of contradictory ideas among prominent public figures during the early twentieth century in "'Ours Is a Century of Light.'"

28. "Mr Dixon's Literary Group," *New York Times*, December 31, 1894, p. 9. Dixon's compulsion to preach the truth led him, for instance, to reject Emile Zola's literary naturalism, because its principles were, he believed, fundamentally false. By leaving secret the "inner life" of his characters and instead describing only their behavior, Zola failed to achieve true realism, or so Dixon claimed. At this point in his life, Dixon insisted that the interior struggles of characters were the crux of literature, because it was in these struggles that morality became manifest (ibid.). Perversely, Dixon's criticism could be applied with far greater accuracy to his own later fictional characters.

29. Until recently, literary scholars and historians have displayed more interest in plot summaries of Dixon's best-known works than in either the conventions of the melodrama genre or Dixon's technique. For works that show welcome attention to Dixon's form, see Scott Romine, "Thomas Dixon and the Literary Production of Whiteness," in this volume, and Linda Williams, *Playing the Race Card: Melodramas of Black and White from Uncle Tom to O. J. Simpson* (Princeton: Princeton Univ. Press, 2001).

30. John W. Cell, *The Highest Stage of White Supremacy: The Origins of Segregation in South Africa and the American South* (Cambridge: Cambridge Univ. Press, 1982).

31. W.E.B. Du Bois, "The Problem of Tillman, Vardaman, and Thomas Dixon, Jr.," *Central Christian Advocate*, October 18, 1905, p. 1325. A white South Carolinian almost simultaneously offered a similar synopsis of Dixon's oeuvre: "Hate the Negro; he is a beast; his intention is to rob and murder and pollute; he should be transported or annihilated!" *Columbia (S.C.) State*, October 23, 1905, quoted in John Hammond Moore, "South Carolina's Reaction to the Photoplay, *The Birth of a Nation*," *Proceedings of the South Carolina Historical Association* 33 (1963): 33.

32. Albion Tourgée, "The South as a Field of Fiction," *Forum* 6 (December 1888): 405.

33. Thomas Nelson Page, *Red Rock: A Chronicle of Reconstruction* (New York: 1898), 356–58, 582. On fictional representations of the South, see David Blight, *Race and Reunion: The Civil War in American Memory* (Cambridge: Harvard Univ. Press, 2001), especially chapter 7; Jane Turner Censer, *The Reconstruction of White Southern Womanhood, 1865–1895* (Baton Rouge: Louisiana State Univ. Press, 2003); Sarah E. Gardner, *Blood and Irony: Southern White Women's Narratives of the Civil War, 1861–1937* (Chapel Hill: Univ. of North Carolina Press, 2003); and Nina Silber, *Romance of Reunion: Northerners and Southerners, 1865–1900* (Chapel Hill: Univ. of North Carolina Press, 1993).

34. On the civilizationist ideology, see Tunde Adeleke, *Unafrican Americans: Nineteenth-Century Black Nationalists and the Civilizing Mission* (Lexington: Univ. Press of Kentucky,

1998), especially chapter 1; Bederman, *Manliness and Civilization,* especially chapters 1 and 2; Louise Michele Newman, *White Women's Rights: The Racial Origins of Feminism in the United States* (New York: Oxford Univ. Press, 1999), especially chapter 1; Wilson Jeremiah Moses, *Afrotopia: The Roots of African American Popular History* (New York: Cambridge Univ. Press, 1998), chapters 4 and 6.

35. Hamlin Garland, *The Captain of the Gray-Horse Troop* (New York: Harper and Brothers, 1902), 56, 113, 121, 406–7, 414–15. Let me linger longer on the parallels between Garland and Dixon. Just as Dixon would have the ear of President Woodrow Wilson, so too did Garland have influence with President Theodore Roosevelt a decade earlier. As a member of Roosevelt's informal "cowboy cabinet," Garland offered advice to the president on western and Indian policy. Thus, the reach of Garland's ideas extended beyond the popular press to the corridors of power, just as Dixon's would during Wilson's presidency. Several recent works have delved into the fiction of white supremacy, including Cathy Broeckmann, *A Question of Character: Scientific Racism and the Genres of American Fiction, 1892–1912* (Tuscaloosa: Univ. of Alabama Press, 2000); Walter Benn Michaels, *Our America: Nativism, Modernism, and Pluralism* (Durham: Duke Univ. Press, 1995); and Mason Stokes, *The Color of Sex: Whiteness, Heterosexuality, and the Fictions of White Supremacy* (Durham: Duke Univ. Press, 2001).

36. Cynthia Lynn Lyerly makes the valuable point that Dixon did write popular novels that did not fixate on race. See "Gender and Race in Dixon's Religious Ideology."

37. *Columbia (S.C.) State,* October 9, 1905, quoted in Moore, "South Carolina's Reaction," 32. W. E. Gonzales, the *State's* editor, also wrote a blistering denunciation of Dixon in the "The Clansman Denounced," *New York Times,* January 2, 1906, p. 8.

38. "Mr. Dixon's Latest Ku Klux Novel," *New York Times Book Review,* August 3, 1907, p. 475.

39. "A Romance of Money Madness," *New York Times Book Review,* February 12, 1911, p. 70. The reviewer describes Dixon's work as a "cheap line of tawdry melodrama" and masterpieces of "claptrap." Another of Dixon's reviewers regretted Dixon's penchant for superlatives; "Everything is 'most' that does not even need to be 'more'" ("Upon a Blessed Isle," *New York Times Book Review,* February 6, 1909, p. 76).

40. (Mrs.) G. Vere Tyler, "The Southerner," *New York Times Book Review,* November 23, 1913, p. 647.

41. Lucile Armistead, "Views of Readers," *New York Times Book Review,* November 9, 1913, p. 616.

42. Some white South Carolinians were even more cool to the play. See Moore, "South Carolina's Reaction," 30–40.

43. (Mrs.) G. Vere Tyler, "The Southerner," *New York Times Book Review,* November 23, 1913, p. 647. Another letter writer resorted to similar adjectives—"vital," "throbbing," and "stirring"—to describe Dixon's prose (Mrs. Forest G. Hamrick, "Views of Readers," *New York Times Book Review,* August 10, 1913, p. 430).

44. James Lewis Allen, "Two Principles in Recent American Fiction," *Atlantic Monthly* 80 (October 1897): 438.

45. John Higham, "The Reorientation of American Culture in the 1890s," *Hanging Together: Unity and Diversity in American Culture* (New Haven: Yale Univ. Press, 2001), 173–99; T. Jackson Lears, *No Place of Grace* (New York: Pantheon, 1981). In a paper presented at the Wake Forest conference, Sean Lucas made a compelling argument that Dixon also pioneered a style of oratory that was distinctly "modern" and strikingly effective at holding the attention of his audiences (Sean Lucas, "Thomas Dixon and the Making of Modern Oratory," unpublished essay in the author's possession). Scott Romine makes a similar point about Dixon's appeal to white readers troubled by "experiential deprivation" (see Scott Romine, "Thomas Dixon and the Literary Production of Whiteness," in this volume).

46. Peter Brooks, *The Melodramatic Imagination: Balzac, Henry James, and the Mode of Excess* (New Haven: Yale Univ. Press, 1976), 14–15.

47. Robert Lang, *American Film Melodrama: Griffith, Vidor, Minnelli* (Princeton: Princeton Univ. Press, 1989), 18.

48. Robert Bechtold Heilman, *The Iceman, the Arsonist, and the Troubled Agent: Tragedy and Melodrama on the Modern Stage* (Seattle: Univ. of Washington Press, 1973), 9. Issues of race and racism were dealt with in the tragic form during the early twentieth century. The best example of a race tragedy is Edward Sheldon's *The Nigger* (1910). Sheldon's protagonist, an icon of the highest southern white culture, is trapped and destroyed by the racist stereotypes that he parrots after he learns that he is descended from a black woman.

49. Even the score for *Birth of a Nation*, as Jane M. Gaines demonstrates, mimicked the melodramatic binaries, with its contrasting primitive and refined musical motifs. See Gaines, "Thomas Dixon and Race Melodrama," in this volume. Linda Williams, in *Playing the Race Card*, contends that the melodrama has been the preferred genre used by Americans to ponder, debate, and evade the problem of race in the United States.

50. Indeed, Dixon's binaries were simplified when translated onto film. It is important to emphasize that Dixon and Griffith's *Birth of a Nation* was not simply a carbon copy of *The Clansman*. Significant elements of the play did not carry over to the screen version. In the stage version of *The Clansman*, the comic antics and verbal sparring of Nelse, described as "an old fashioned Negro," and Eve, his wife, provide periodic comic relief. Such comedic interludes, usually involving stereotypical ethnic humor, were commonplace in stage melodrama; they offered a respite from the intense drama of the plays and entertained audiences while sets were being shifted. The comedic elements of Dixon's play are conspicuously absent from the film. This absence was characteristic of the emerging film conventions, in which a consistent dramatic tenor ran throughout the narration. Whatever the reasons, when Dixon and Griffith cut these portions of the play they drastically narrowed their depiction of African Americans. However demeaning the minstrel-like scenes of jocular, bumbling, Sambo-like blacks were in the comedic interludes in *The Clansman*, at the very least they provided an alternative to the relentlessly threatening, violent, and primitive blacks who populate the film. Yet even the comedic interludes at best softened but never complicated Dixon's stark opposition of black and white, barbarism and civilization, immorality and morality. For a deft account of early film plot conventions, see Ben Singer, *Melodrama and Modernity: Early*

Sensational Cinema and Its Contexts (New York: Columbia Univ. Press, 2001), especially chapters 6 and 7.

51. Dixon's narrative strategies and their relationship to the melodramatic form are sensitively treated by Scott Romine in "Thomas Dixon and the Literary Production of Whiteness."

52. Singer, *Melodrama and Modernity,* 91.

53. For example, see "Passion Play Scenes," *New York Times,* February 28, 1898, p. 10.

54. The advertisements for the play dwelled on its large cast, elaborate scenery, and "small army of supernumeraries, horses, etc." The ads for *Birth of a Nation* similarly accentuated the size of the cast involved in the movie, as well as the orchestra that performed at each screening. See John C. Inscoe, "North Carolinians' Response to *The Clansman* on Stage (1905) and Screen (1915)" (paper delivered at Wake Forest University Symposium, April 11, 2003).

55. Dixon conveyed his enthusiasm for the power of cinema in *Southern Horizons*: "We can make them see things that happen before their eyes until they cry in anguish" (311). Ignoring his critics, Dixon insisted that he largely was responsible for elevating cinema plots from their crude, sensational origins (Dixon, *Southern Horizons,* 294–95, 310–11).

56. "Thomas Dixon on His New Book," *New York Times Book Review,* January 14, 1905, p. 29.

57. *Columbia (S.C.) State,* October 15, 1905, quoted in Moore, "South Carolina's Reaction," 33.

58. Quoted in John Hope Franklin, "Birth of a Nation—Propaganda as History," *Massachusetts Review* 20 (autumn 1979): 429. At least one of Dixon's readers compiled an extended survey of Dixon's "liberties" with fact. See Nancy Trevor, "Mr Dixon and History—Virginia Again," *New York Times Book Review,* August 24, 1913, p. 446.

59. For Dixon on his experience at Johns Hopkins, see *Southern Horizons,* 167. So, too, Hamlin Garland touted his research at the Tongue River Reservation as the basis of *The Captain of the Gray-Horse Troop.* Ellen Glasgow similarly bragged that she had studied contemporary politics for her novel *The Voice of the People* by secretly observing the Virginia state Democratic convention in 1898. Only a few years after the publication of *The Clansman,* Upton Sinclair would rile the American public with *The Jungle,* his graphic expose of the meatpacking industry derived from his experiences in Chicago feedlots and slaughterhouses. And on and on.

60. *Spartanburg Herald,* October 16, 1915, quoted in Moore, "South Carolina's Reaction," 37.

61. Quotations, in order, are from the *Charlotte Observer,* November 18, 1915, quoted in Moore, "South Carolina's Reaction," 37; and James Weldon Johnson, "The New York World Speaks," *New York Age,* April 1, 1915, quoted in Lawrence J. Oliver, "Writing from the Right during the 'Red Decade': Thomas Dixon's Attack on W. E. B. Du Bois and James Weldon Johnson in *The Flaming Sword,*" *American Literature* 70 (March 1998): 137.

62. Raymond Williams, *Marxism and Literature* (New York: Oxford Univ. Press, 1977), 122, 123.

63. John Inscoe, in "North Carolinians' Response," argues that Dixon's "message" in *Birth of a Nation* was already anachronistic by 1915 and that the film prompted far less debate in North Carolina than had Dixon's play *The Clansmen.* On the emergence of modernism in

the South, see Daniel Joseph Singal, *The War Within: From Victorian to Modernist Thought in the South, 1919-1945* (Chapel Hill : Univ. of North Carolina Press, 1982).

64. Bederman, *Manliness and Civilization,* 232-39.

"My Books Are Hard Reading for a Negro": Tom Dixon and His African American Critics, 1905–1939

JOHN DAVID SMITH

Tucked away in W.E.B. Du Bois's papers is a telling exchange between the great African American intellectual and Walter Hines Page, the North Carolina–born journalist who expatriated himself from the South to New York in 1885, frustrated by the unprogressive "Confederates" and "mummies" of the New South.[1] In late 1905, Page, now the influential New York publisher of Booker T. Washington's *Up From Slavery* (1901), expressed interest in also publishing Du Bois's work. Responding frankly, Du Bois wrote that he was hesitant to publish with "the exploiters of Tom Dixon." In response, Page reminded Du Bois that even Dixon, "who stands for what I regard as my enemies' doctrine," deserved "freedom of opinion." "Of course, you understand this principle as well as I," Page lectured Du Bois, "and it is for this reason that I am a little surprised that you should speak of us as 'exploiters' of Dixon. We are simply his publishers."[2]

Page's disingenuous remark about "freedom of opinion" angered Du Bois. Page published Dixon's viciously anti-Negro romantic novels *The Leopard's Spots: A Romance of the White Man's Burden, 1865–1900* (1902) and *The Clansman: An Historical Romance of the Ku Klux Klan* (1905). Both books portrayed African American men as servile, bestial, or as sexual threats; they sold extraordinarily well. (*The Leopard's Spots* sold more than 1 million copies.)[3] Dixon's biographer Raymond A. Cook correctly observes that in *The Leopard's Spots* "the primary goal of the emancipated Negro, as portrayed by Dixon, is sexual union with any convenient white woman. The immediate popularity of the novel indicated the deep-seated fear and widespread ignorance of the Negro as a human entity."[4]

A reviewer of *The Leopard's Spots* described the book as both "crude" and timely—appearing "when our unfortunate experiment in the Philippines has so generally deadened the public conscience toward any appeal to that finer regard for the rights of man simply as man."[5] Another critic charged that "Mr. Dixon creates monsters that he may make war upon them." The end product, the reviewer said, was "to accentuate the bitterness between the races."[6] Jim Crow–era white southerners in truth had a seemingly insatiable appetite for Dixon's anti-Negro, white supremacist literature. Historian Francis Butler Simkins observed that *The Clansman* appealed to "millions of Southerners ordinarily unimpressed by fiction."[7] "In the first decade of the new century," added historian C. Vann Woodward, "the extremists of Southern racism probably reached a wider audience, both within their own region and in the nation, than ever before."[8]

Du Bois understood that whites at the fin de siècle were infected with racial anxieties and had a rage for racial control. It was the feared and hated Negro, he explained to readers of Kansas City's *Central Christian Advocate*, that transformed the race-baiting Dixon into an author "more widely read than Henry James." Mocking Dixon and his cruel and incendiary novels, Du Bois summarized the North Carolina writer's simple solution for uppity Negroes who demanded full political and social equality: "There's a black man who thinks himself a man and is a man; kill him before he marries your daughter!" One way or another, whites sought to rid themselves of the "Negro problem." But, Du Bois argued, the Negro would not go away.[9]

Since emancipation, he explained, African Americans had proven themselves "one of the great human races." They could not and would not be returned to Africa. Granting blacks full citizenship strengthened, not weakened, America. "Lecherous whites," not Negroes, were responsible for the South's mulatto population. "I was born here [in the United States], my father was born here and my forefathers were honest, hard-working Americans 200 years before the Dixons were dime-novelists," Du Bois wrote. "If Mr. Dixon is allowed the protection of the flag he fought against, surely I may claim the protection of that same flag which my fathers gave their blood to preserve in every war of the Republic except, thank God, the last [the Spanish-American War]."[10]

Du Bois and other African Americans had every reason to fear Dixon and what historian Rayford W. Logan has characterized as his "hate-mongering writings." According to Logan, *The Leopard's Spots* "surpassed in bigotry and vituperation" even Dixon's *The Clansman*, which literary critic Robert A. Bone considers "the apex of Negrophobia in American literary history."[11] Historian Joel Williamson judges *The Leopard's Spots* "the one work nearest to a codification of the Radical dogma"—"an encyclopedia of Radicalism." Racial radicals decried the purported retrogression of Negroes toward savagery and bestiality since emancipation, the threat of miscegenation that hovered over America like a miasma, and the incompatibility of the two races to live harmoniously together.[12] Premising his books on the essential inferiority of the Negro, Dixon identified three possible scenarios for future race relations in America. Blacks could accept Caucasian superiority; they could separate; or they could be annihilated.

Early in *The Leopard's Spots* Dixon established his retrogressionist theme, asserting that the Negro was "transformed by the exigency of war from a Chattel to be bought and sold into a possible Beast to be feared and guarded. Around this dusky figure every white man's soul was keeping its grim vigil." In a later passage, one that recurs several times in the novel, Dixon's character the Reverend John Durham, the Baptist minister of Hambright, North Carolina, explains that "in a Democracy you can not build a nation inside of a nation of two antagonistic races, and therefore the future American must either be an Anglo Saxon or a Mulatto. And if a Mulatto, will the future be worth discussing?" As long as the two races lived together, Dixon wrote again and again, the "Negro problem" could never be solved. In his chapter "The Black Peril" he said that "amalgamation simply meant Africanisation. The big nostrils, flat nose, massive jaw, protruding lip and kinky hair will register their animal marks over the proudest intellect and the rarest beauty of any other race. The rule that had no exception was that one drop of Negro blood makes a negro." "If a man really believes in equality, let him prove it by giving his daughter to a negro in marriage. That is the test. When she sinks with her mulatto children into the black abyss of a Negroid life, then ask him!"[13]

In *The Clansman,* Dr. Richard Cameron complains that "a thick-lipped, flat-nosed, spindle-shanked negro, exuding his nauseating animal odour, to shout in derision, over the hearths and homes of white men and women is an atrocity too monstrous for belief." Cameron later explains, "Education, sir, is the development of that which *is.* Since the dawn of history the Negro has owned the Continent of Africa—rich beyond the dream of poet's fancy, crunching acres of diamonds beneath his bare black feet. Yet he never picked one up from the dust until a white man showed to him its glittering light."[14] Variants of this passage occurred throughout Dixon's fiction and nonfiction to justify the author's belief that just as one could not change the Leopard's spots, one could not change the Negro by educating him. Though in his novels Dixon altered slightly his characters, plots, and subplots, each work contained essentially the same Radical racial ideology that Dixon espoused from *The Leopard's Spots* through the publication of his last novel, *The Flaming Sword* (1939).

The idea of "racial conflict as an epic struggle, with the future of civilization at stake," ran through Dixon's books like a leitmotif.[15] Writing in 1905 in the *Saturday Evening Post,* he set forth his basic premises. America's "race problem," Dixon said, was quite literally the "Negro problem." African Americans were inherently inferior to whites and "no scheme of education or religion" could solve it. Dixon considered efforts to elevate the Negro even by conservative reformers, including Booker T. Washington, problematical. According to Dixon, "no amount of education of any kind, industrial, classical or religious, can make a Negro a white man or bridge the chasm of the centuries which separate him from the white man in the evolution of human civilization." The races were separated by "the gulf of thousands of years of inherited progress which separates the child of the Aryan from the child of the African."[16] Dixon found Washington's goal of "broadening horizons and expanding minds" too radical.[17]

Dixon also believed that virtually all blacks ("ninety-nine Negroes out of every hundred") were determined to bridge the gap between the races by what he termed "assimilation"—intermarriage—which Dixon considered "the greatest calamity which could possibly befall this Republic." He cited three black intellectuals, Du Bois, the novelist Charles W. Chesnutt, and the mathematician Kelly Miller, who reportedly favored the "fusion" of blacks and whites into a "new race." According to Dixon, even Washington, ever cautious, diplomatic, and guarded, favored "amalgamation" once blacks had made whites economically dependent upon them. But whites, Dixon insisted, would tolerate neither the competition of black labor nor the fusion of the races. They would do anything necessary to preserve the superiority of their race. Unless, as Abraham Lincoln and African Methodist Episcopal bishop Henry McNeal Turner had warned, black Americans separated and colonized Liberia, "bloodshed" would ensue. Dixon predicted race war— "the most fiery and brutal of all its forms." White Americans owed the Negro "a square deal," Dixon said, but "we will never give it to him on this Continent."[18]

Dixon thus blamed the victims—African Americans—for racial tensions in twentieth-century America. "Somehow," notes Williamson, in Dixon's mind "the Negro had caused the Civil War, and the failure of the North during Reconstruction to recognize the rising reversion of free blacks to bestiality had continued to divide the nation. But Southern Anglo-Saxon blood had mustered its will to dominance and had redeemed itself from Reconstruction." By 1900, white southerners had convinced northerners of the degeneracy of the freedpeople. "Thus tested and tempered by the awful fires of civil war and Reconstruction," Williamson adds, "North and South were reuniting, joining together the material genius of the North and the spiritual genius of the South to realize the promise that God had given his chosen people, white Americans."[19]

Black Americans, however, challenged Dixon's Radical racist ideology, his retrogressionst view of blacks, his gross insults, and his lurid depictions of black men lurking after and raping white women. In 1902, William Monroe Trotter, the fiery editor of the *Boston Guardian,* referred to Dixon as "slippery Tom," "the ranting, wandering divine," the "unasylumed maniac" who vented his sick ideas in "terms of sound and fury only."[20] Three years later William A. Sinclair, an ex-slave who received his medical degree from Meharry Medical College in Nashville, found unconscionable Dixon's characterization of the Negro as "a human donkey." "You can train him, but you can't make him a horse," Dixon wrote in *The Leopard's Spots.* "Mate him with a horse, you lose the horse, and get a larger donkey called a mule, incapable of preserving his species."[21] "The moral obliquity, the want of charity, the absence of dignity indicated by these words," Sinclair charged in *The Aftermath of Slavery* (1905), "mark off their author as seriously beneath the standards of thousands of educated colored men, whose life, words, and conduct shame these critics into insignificance."[22] Ironically, in his personal copy of Sinclair's book Dixon wrote "*imitation*" in response to Sinclair's description of Meharry's 1915 graduation ceremony.[23] Though he publicly radiated bravado and self-confidence, Dixon privately monitored closely the actions and comments of African American critics such as Sinclair.

Dixon was obsessed, for example, with proving that Booker T. Washington sought "social equality" with whites, once charging in newspapers that Washington and white philanthropist Robert C. Ogden had hugged each other publicly.[24] In 1906, on the day Washington delivered a fund-raising speech at New York's Carnegie Hall, Dixon fired off a letter offering to donate $10,000 from the proceeds of *The Clansman* to the Tuskegee Institute if Washington would give "complete and satisfactory proof that you do not desire Social Equality for the Negro and that your School is opposed to the Amalgamation of the races." The next day Dixon invited Washington "to debate with me in the largest Hall available in New York the question of 'The Future of the Negro in America.'" He insisted that they discuss "Social Equality and Race Amalgamation"—topics, according to Dixon, "which the American people will demand that you face squarely sooner or later."[25] In 1905, Dixon noted that "every large convention of Negroes since the appearance of my first historical novel on the race problem has gone out of its way to denounce me and declare my books caricatures and libels on their people. Their mistake is a natural one," Dixon added. "My books are hard reading for a Negro, and yet the Negroes in denouncing them, are unwittingly denouncing one of their best friends."[26]

Blacks, however, considered Dixon their worst enemy.[27] Upon Dixon's death in 1946, columnist Lucius C. Harper of the *Chicago Defender* remarked that "every black man takes particular pride at this hour on reading his obituary.... America would have been blessed had he died in infancy."[28] Robert A. Bone observed that in response to the likes of Dixon, "the early Negro novelist traded blow for blow with his traducers, answering stereotype with counter stereotype in an effort to stem the tide of anti-Negro propaganda."[29] "The Negro novelists answered the white racists with political arguments and with a succession of characters of spotless virtue and outstanding intelligence," explains Judith R. Berzon.[30]

For example, in Thomas H. B. Walker's *J. Johnson or "The Unknown Man,"* his 1915 sentimental novel about an African American's determination to prove his racial identity and find himself, Jim Johnson, the hero, proclaims that "'the Negro is not trying to get away from his race; there is no woman under the sun that holds the charms for him as is found in his own women."' Susie Smith, who refuses to marry Jim until he can prove that he is a black man, declares that "no Negro woman desires inter-marriage of any kind, legal or illegal, with a white man. To the women of my race such a thought is odious." Walker's message was clear if not subtle. Blacks had no desire to mix sexually with whites. The Negro, unlike the beasts Dixon portrayed, was proud of his race and despite all odds was "a Good Samaritan"—"he will feed even the slayer of his brother and those who revile, maltreat and abuse him." Walker subtitled his book *An Answer to Mr. Thos. Dixon's "Sins of the Fathers."*[31]

According to historian Glenda Elizabeth Gilmore, in *The Sins of the Father* (1912) Dixon had blamed seductive black women for miscegenation. That book, she notes, "is Dixon's answer to his African-American critics, and it attempts to explain and excuse white men's part in miscegenation." Gilmore argues that by blaming African American women for miscegenation, Dixon freed white men—including his father, rumored within the black community to have conceived a child, Tom Dixon's half-brother, with his slave cook—from responsibility for the South's biracial population.[32]

While few readers read either Walker's or Dixon's later obscure books, black intellectuals Kelly Miller and Sutton E. Griggs gained national attention by assaulting Dixon, focusing closely on *The Leopard's Spots* and exposing its base ugliness. Their expressions of moral outrage, their defense of their race's honor, and their sense of the unfair treatment accorded them by Dixon represented well African Americans' collective response to the novelist's vile and wretched slander.

Miller (1863–1939) descended from a free black father and a slave mother and grew up on a farm in rural north central South Carolina. He attended Howard University on a scholarship and studied mathematics, physics, and astronomy at The Johns Hopkins University, where he was the first African American student and, according to Du Bois, was "politely unwelcomed."[33] Miller later served as dean at Howard. Though a renowned mathematician, in 1895 he introduced sociology to the curriculum, convinced that the new field would develop scientific analyses of American race relations. In frequent newspaper columns, essays, and pamphlets, Miller challenged white notions of black inferiority, while straddling the ideological fence between Booker T. Washington's conservatism and Du Bois's radicalism. Too moderate for black militants, too capitalist for black unionists, Miller also was too much a traditionalist for the "New" Negroes of post–World War I America.[34] In 1919 he informed readers of the *American Journal of Sociology* that "the great vice of American slavery was that it strove to identify the color line with the cultural level. This is the crowning evil of the prevailing method of dealing with the race question today."[35]

Years before, Miller had gained national attention by refuting statistician Frederick L. Hoffman's "scientific" argument that since emancipation African Americans were retrogressing and were destined to extinction. With the skill of a surgeon, Miller dissected Hoffman's work by exposing flaws in his logic, his mathematics, and his racial assumptions.[36] In 1905, Miller assumed a similar task, publishing *As to the Leopard's Spots: An Open Letter to Thomas Dixon, Jr.* In this pamphlet Miller blasted Dixon as a rank propagandist, "the chief priest of those who worship at the shrine of race hatred and wrath." Responding to Dixon's arguments about the alleged degeneration of the freedpeople, Miller argued that races matured over time at different speeds and that African Americans had consistently proven their aptitude for "civilization." Miller flatly denied Dixon's allegation in the *Saturday Evening Post* that he favored racial amalgamation and charged that Dixon possessed a "frantic dread of amalgamation." Was it not Dixon, Miller asked, who was "probably the foremost promoter of amalgamation between the two oceans?" "I know of no colored man who advocates amalgamation as a feasible policy of solution," Miller insisted. "This would be self-stultification with a vengeance."[37] According to theology processor Samuel K. Roberts, in the *Saturday Evening Post* "either deliberately or unwittingly, Dixon misrepresented Miller's position" regarding racial mixing. "If anything, Miller was as much a purist in terms of preserving distinct racial traits as Dixon."[38] In fact, in his article Dixon quoted nonconsecutive passages without an ellipsis and thereby distorted Miller's meaning.[39] In 1926, Miller blamed the white man, who "defeats by his lustful indulgences by night all of his finely spun theories of race purity elaborated by day," for miscegenation.[40]

Sutton E. Griggs (1872–1933) was the son of a Baptist minister and was from Navarro County, Texas. He graduated from Bishop College in Marshall, Texas, in 1890, from Richmond Theological Seminary (today's Virginia Union University) in 1893, and then held Baptist pastorates in Virginia,

Tennessee, and Texas. Griggs published five novels, most notably *Imperium in Imperio* (1899) and *The Hindered Hand: or, The Reign of the Repressionist* (1905), and a large corpus of generally unanalyzed nonfiction.[41] The critic Hugh M. Gloster credits Griggs with writing the first openly political Negro fiction and pronounces him "the most neglected Negro writer of the period between the Spanish-American War and World War I." He adds that "though virtually unknown to white Americans of his time," because Griggs published, promoted, and sold his own books among African Americans, his novels "were probably more widely circulated among Negroes than the works of Charles W. Chesnutt and Paul Laurence Dunbar."[42] According to literary historian Mason Stokes, like other early African American authors, Griggs "wanted not only to sell books but to wrest away from Dixon the terms of racial discourse."[43] Ironically, literary scholar Susan Gillman identifies many similarities between Griggs and Dixon. While hardly "procrustean bedfellows," the two authors nonetheless shared similar worldviews and literary philosophies.[44]

Griggs, however, unlike Dixon, used his fiction to expose slavery's legacies in the Jim Crow South, to denounce segregation, to extol black pride and accomplishment, to underscore the tragedy of miscegenation, and to argue for civil and political rights for blacks. Griggs underscored the difficult conditions African Americans experienced, the threats of lynching and mob violence they endured, and the complex social relations miscegenation bred.[45] He credited Miller for inspiration and received Du Bois's thanks for representing black writers at the second Niagara conference in 1906, a meeting that Chesnutt chose not to attend.[46] In his works Griggs advocated both American imperialism abroad and the establishment of a black empire at home, lacing his rhetoric of empire with images of ultra-black masculinity.[47] An electrifying platform speaker, Griggs promised blacks that if they attended school, patronized black businesses, and stoked "the fires of hope, that all of the Negroes' enemies could not keep him down."[48]

In *Imperium in Imperio* Griggs lamented that "in the South to-day a race that dreams of freedom, equality, and empire, far more than is imagined, is put down as a race of chicken thieves." Yet he was cheered by the thought that "the cringing, fawning, sniffling cowardly Negro which slavery left, had disappeared, and a new Negro, self-respecting, fearless, and determined in the assertion of his rights was at hand."⁴⁹ In the third revised edition of *The Hindered Hand*, Griggs appended an essay entitled "A Hindering Hand: A Review of the Anti-Negro Crusade of Mr. Thomas Dixon, Jr." Griggs considered "Mr. Dixon . . . the ultra radical element of Southern whites."⁵⁰ This, according to critic Gloster, represents "the most elaborate attack upon Thomas Dixon in American Negro fiction."⁵¹

In a pamphlet, *The One Great Question: A Study of Southern Conditions at Close Range*, published five years after *The Hindered Hand*, Griggs identified Dixon as North Carolina's best representative of what he termed the "repressionist regime." According to Griggs, "where repression reigns . . . you will find oozing therefore helplessness on the part of the Negro in the face of aggression, unrestrained maltreatment on the part of the mean of heart, cruel indifference, paralyzing self-interest and sometimes wanton oppression on the part of the chosen governing agencies—chosen with the distinct understanding that the Negroes, having no voice in their making, are to be utterly ignored as a factor in determining their policies." He went on to declare that "the better element of the white South spews the Rev. Thomas Dixon, Jr., and his grossly misleading productions, out of its mouth, but his adroit groupings of half-truths which make abominable untruths are but the legitimate fruit of a system of repression, a system repugnant to the moral sense of civilization. It is a case of a father committing a crime, a son committing perjury to shield the father and the father chastising the boy for his sin."⁵²

In their criticism, Griggs and Miller contextualized Dixon's racist venom. Repeatedly Dixon misrepresented and misstated facts to diminish and distort blacks' positive contributions to American life. Griggs judged Dixon a product of the southern lower class, "where hatred of the Negro was a part of the legacy handed down from parent to child." Dixon's views mirrored those of the white masses who remained "thoroughly committed . . . to the doctrine of the *ineffaceable, inherent* inferiority of the Negro."⁵³ Miller connected Dixon's racist rhetoric to the discredited "pro-slaver scientists" who espoused theories of Negro inferiority. Since emancipation, however, African Americans had overcome many obstacles and garnered numerous accomplishments, Miller said. "There is not a single intellectual, moral or spiritual excellence attained by the white race to which the Negro does not yield an appreciative response."⁵⁴

Miller and Griggs attributed the comparative backwardness of African Americans not to innate racial inferiority, but to environmental forces, specifically African isolation, American slavery, and white racism. According to Miller, "The Negro has never, during the whole course of history, been surrounded by those influences which tend to strengthen and develop the mind."[55] Griggs agreed. "With isolation and lack of contact the Negroes have been compelled to rely upon their own narrow set of ideas," he argued, "while the progress of other peoples has been the result of the union of what they begot with what strangers brought them."[56] Miller insisted that alleged notions of Anglo-Saxon superiority and African American inferiority were at best fluid, relative, and transitory. Given their environments and histories, the two races advanced differently but on a similar trajectory. Responding to Dixon's across-the-board condemnation of blacks, Miller found "no hard and fast line dividing the two races on the scale of capacity. There is the widest possible range of variation within the limits of each."[57]

Both black critics rejected Dixon's allegations that black men were obsessed with sexual relations with white women, what Miller termed Dixon's "frantic dread of amalgamation."[58] Griggs charged that during slavery whites inflicted "mulattoism" upon blacks and since emancipation "Negroes have gone on developing race pride and visiting their supreme disfavor upon all who signify inability to find thorough contentment within the race." He challenged Dixon's characterization of black men as rapists, noting that "in order to attain his end he picks up the degenerates within the Negro race and exploits them as the normal type." "Nowhere in the world," Griggs added, "does woman get more respect from men than what Negro men render to the white women of the South."[59] Miller blamed "the bleaching breath of Saxon civilization" for America's mixed-race population and, echoing novelist Charles W. Chesnutt's ideas, remarked that because of miscegenation "the Afro-American is hardly a Negro at all, but a new creature." Miller implored Dixon not to lecture blacks about "race purity." "The most effective service you can render to check the evil of amalgamation," he wrote, "is to do missionary work among the males of your own race."[60]

Miller and Griggs agreed that Dixon's influential writings intensified and aggravated contemporary racial tensions. Miller charged Dixon with inciting white southerners to hate and slaughter innocent blacks. "You poison the mind and pollute the imagination through the subtle influence of literature," he wrote. "You preside at every crossroad lynching of a helpless victim; wherever the midnight murderer rides with rope and torch in quest of the blood of his black brother, you ride by his side; wherever the cries of the crucified victim go up to God from the crackling flame, behold, you are there; when women and children, drunk with ghoulish glee, dance around the funeral pyre and mock the death groans of their fellow-man and fight for ghastly souvenirs, you have your part in the inspiration of it all." Ironically, Miller explained, Dixon's racist invective proved more harmful for whites than for blacks. "Those who become inoculated with the virus of race hatred are more unfortunate than the victims of it." Race hatred paralyzes the mind, freezing creativity and chilling the soul. "You are a greater enemy to your own race," Miller warned Dixon, "than you are to mine."[61]

Griggs diagnosed Dixon as suffering from "the virus of race prejudice." His "lurid and grossly misleading pictures" of blacks, Griggs wrote, blurred "the contribution of the Negro to the coming composite Americanism" and ignored "the slumbering Negro mind that must ere long awake to power." Despite Dixon's literary demagoguery and Anglo-Saxon rant, Griggs identified a silver lining in his racist cloud. "The coming of this radical of radicals before the bar of public opinion, clothed in his garb of avowed prejudice of the rankest sort, means that the self-satisfied isolation of the past is over, that even the radicals desire or see the need of sympathetic consideration from other portions of the human family—decidedly a step forward for them."[62]

Notwithstanding Griggs's magnanimous comment, in "A Hindering Hand" he took a parting shot at Dixon, one that Miller, Du Bois, and other early twentieth-century African Americans would have universally applauded. Griggs proposed that upon Dixon's tombstone should be carved: "This misguided soul ignored all of the good in the aspiring Negro; made every vicious offshoot that he pictured typical of the entire race; presented all mistakes independent of their environments and provocations; ignored or minimized all the evil in the more vicious element of whites; said and did all things which he deemed necessary to leave behind him the greatest heritage of hatred the world has ever known. Humanity claims him not as one of her children."[63]

Though in his review Griggs "lynched" Dixon symbolically,[64] "the exploiters of Tom Dixon" paid Griggs's epitaph little heed. Dixon remained an influential national figure; his racist creed remained available—in print, on stage, and on screen—in the years before and long after World War I. Years later Dixon recalled how much pleasure he gained from the success of *The Leopard's Spots*. "I had given the tortured South a hearing in the forum of the world," he explained.[65] Dubbing Dixon a "professional southerner," Du Bois in 1915 charged in *The Crisis* that in David Wark Griffith's *The Birth of a Nation* (1915), the immensely popular film adaptation of Dixon's book and touring stage play *The Clansman* (1905–1906), Griffith and Dixon portrayed the Negro "either as an ignorant fool, a vicious rapist, a venal and unscrupulous politician or a faithful but doddering idiot." Du Bois dismissed the original play, which many blacks and some whites had also demonstrated against, "as a sordid and lurid melodrama."[66]

The Survey, a reform journal edited in Chicago by whites, agreed, describing Dixon's film as showing "Negroes perpetrating one outrage against decency after another, from chasing white girls to voting with both hands on election day." Even though African Americans and their liberal white friends formed a phalanx to ban *The Birth of a Nation*, they ultimately failed.[67] Years later Du Bois denounced the long-term damage to race relations occasioned by Griffith's and Dixon's racist film. "There was fed to the youth of the nation and to the unthinking masses as well as to the world a story which twisted the emancipation and enfranchisement of the slave in a great effort toward universal democracy, into an orgy of theft and degradation and wide rape of white women."[68] According to historian David Levering Lewis, *The Birth of a Nation* "was uniquely responsible for encoding the white South's version of Reconstruction on the DNA of several generations of Americans."[69]

"Small wonder," Du Bois wrote, referring to Dixon, "that a man who can thus brutally falsify history has never been able to do a single piece of literary work that has brought the slightest attention, except when he seeks to capitalize burning race antagonisms."[70] During the Harlem Renaissance of the 1920s, the distinguished black writer and critic William Stanley Braithwaite remarked that the publication of Dixon's *The Leopard's Spots* signified "a distinct stage in the treatment of the Negro in fiction. The portraiture here descends from caricature to libel." According to Braithwaite, "only occasionally during the next twenty years" were blacks "sincerely treated in fiction by white authors."[71] Walter White, who in 1931 became executive secretary of the National Association for the Advancement of Colored

People (NAACP), noted the persistence of Dixon's baleful perception "of what the Negro is and does and thinks."[72] Like Miller and Griggs, Du Bois, Braithwaite, White, and other African Americans recognized that during his long literary life Dixon had won the hearts and minds of whites. He also earned the everlasting opprobrium of blacks.

Through Dixon's varied career as a lawyer, state legislator, minister, platform speaker, essayist, and writer (he published over two dozen books), he routinely deflected the criticisms of blacks and whites alike. Responding to Miller, for example, he described his black critic as "an over-educated Negro; a danger and menace to America . . . just what I'm trying to call to the attention of the American whites in my novel [*The Leopard's Spots*]. We must check the progress of this sort of Negro before he ruins the white race."[73] Dixon also openly defended the accuracy and authenticity of his work and taunted critics—commonly offering to pay them if they could prove him wrong. In the case of *The Clansman*, Dixon went so far as to offer to endow a professorship in Greek at a Negro college if a critic could prove that he in any way had misrepresented Thaddeus Stevens.[74] Incapable of grasping why the NAACP found *The Birth of a Nation* so offensive, Dixon believed that the organization was urging "its members to arm themselves to fight the whites."[75] Fiercely independent, self-righteous, and convinced of his apocalyptic vision of race relations in America throughout the 1920s and 1930s, Dixon was, according to Moorfield Storey, first president of the NAACP, "substantially insane on the subject" of white supremacy.[76]

Dixon, for example, enthusiastically supported Marcus Garvey's "Back-to-Africa" movement, his opposition to racial mixing, and his Universal Negro Improvement Association.[77] In 1938, Dixon agreed with white supremacist Earnest Sevier Cox's description of Garvey as "'the greatest advocate of race progress, race integrity and race nationality that the Negro has produced.'" Dixon endorsed congressional and state legislation to repatriate blacks. "We owe the Negro Race," he explained, "the establishment of a great free republic. We should appropriate hundreds of millions for this voluntary movement and give the new nation our love and sympathy and protection."[78] Dixon informed Cox that he had "carefully read and studied and used in my [forthcoming] novel extracts from his [Garvey's] wife's book which I am sure are authentic." He asked Cox if he had "first hand information on any acts of the National Association for the Advancement of Colored People in the fight to destroy Garvey's movement?" "I know that all the amalgamationists were against him," he added.[79] Dixon later accused Du Bois of orchestrating the suppression of Garvey's writings and his legal prosecution.[80]

Garvey, not surprisingly, was familiar with Dixon's work, especially *The Clansman* and *The Birth of a Nation*.[81] Writing from London in 1938, he explained that "Mr. Dixon's presentations up to the present have been regarded by a large number of Negroes as being doubtful as far as their interests are concerned. Another number of us have not given sufficient thought to the work to place it in any particular category, and still there are some of us who regard his work as being expressive of the white man's desire to make plain what he sees to be a dangerous matter." Garvey added that he was "very much interested in Mr. Dixon's new work and more so when he has stated that his desire is to work in behalf of the repatriation of Negroes to Africa—that is, that section of them who would willingly leave for such a domicile. I wish Mr. Dixon all that is good and do hope to be able to correspond with him leading toward that object."[82]

The following year, in his "new work," *The Flaming Sword*, Dixon lauded Garvey as "a man of striking personality, a coal black whose face bore the lines of a born fighter" (415). In Du Bois's opinion, however, "not even Tom Dixon or Ben Tillman or the hatefulest [sic] enemies of the Negro have ever stooped to a more vicious campaign tha[n] Marcus Garvey, sane or insane, is carrying on."[83] In writing *The Flaming Sword*, Dixon, then near penniless and sick, was a man on a mission to evangelize the colonization of Negroes and to save the New South from the triple threats of racial mixing, Socialism, and Communism.

In *The Flaming Sword*, Dixon also responded to his critics, mostly blacks, by using them as characters in the book. "I have tried in this story," Dixon explained in the preface, "to give an authoritative record of the Conflict of Color in America from 1900 to 1938. To do this I have been compelled to use living men and women as important characters." Aware of the risk he was taking in imbedding real persons in his fiction, Dixon added confidently: "If I have been unfair in treatment they have their remedy under the law of libel" (prefatory page). In doing so Dixon, the old lawyer, brazenly threw down the gauntlet to his early black critics, including Miller, Du Bois, and the novelist and poet James Weldon Johnson. Dixon obviously took the opinions of these writers seriously and he felt compelled to respond to them.

The Flaming Sword remains among Dixon's most obscure, least analyzed, yet most interesting works, especially for students of southern race relations. This grim, neglected text brought Dixon's saga of interracial conflict in America from the Progressive Era up to the age of Franklin D. Roosevelt and gave him an opportunity to underscore what he considered the cancer of Communism infecting American life and the apathy of white Americans to that threat. Though The Flaming Sword was more reactionary than his earlier novels, the work's graphic, pathological ugliness offers an extraordinary window into how Dixon's racial ideology remained essentially constant from 1902 to 1939.[84] In the book, Dixon responded to what he considered the role of blacks in a subversive Socialist-Communist-criminal threat. The Flaming Sword also provided the feisty seventy-five-year-old author with a venue to answer his black critics of more than three decades.

Though Dixon had supported Roosevelt in 1932 and spoke throughout the nation in 1934 on behalf of the National Recovery Act, by 1936 he had abandoned the Democrats, having become increasingly uncomfortable with Roosevelt's liberal agenda and convinced that Communist subversives were infiltrating the New Deal.[85] In 1938 Dixon informed the white supremacist and emigrationist Earnest Sevier Cox, a fellow Garveyite, that the NAACP was "all powerful at the White House through Mrs. Roosevelt."[86] In The Flaming Sword "the wife of the President" appears at an Alabama meeting of a Communist front group established "to stir in the deep South the ugliest phase of the Negro Problem by a brazen demand for social equality" (503). Here Dixon referred to Eleanor Roosevelt's 1938 attendance at the Birmingham, Alabama, meeting of the Southern Conference for Human Welfare in which she defied the state's segregation laws.[87]

Years earlier, Dixon had published a trilogy of books—*The One Woman* (1903), *Comrades* (1909), and *The Root of Evil* (1911)—outlining what he considered the evils of Socialism. Dixon spoke of Socialism and Communism interchangeably—never distinguishing between the two—convinced that the systems "were signs of racial degeneracy."[88] Responding in 1919 to Dixon's diatribes against Socialism, Wilfred A. Domingo, a Jamaican Socialist who served as an early editor of Garvey's weekly *Negro World*, reminded African Americans "that the very men like Thomas Dixon . . . who are fighting Socialism or as they maliciously call it Bolshevism, are the same men who exhaust every unfair means to vilify, oppress and oppose Negroes."[89] After abandoning the Democrats over what he considered their sympathy to Communists and blacks, Dixon broke with the New Dealers and campaigned for Republican nominee Alfred M. Landon in 1936. "The increasing influence of Communistic advisers around" President Franklin D. Roosevelt, Dixon railed, "has steered Roosevelt more and more into radical channels. I have no use for them—the devil take them!"[90] Isaac M. Meekins, a Republican judge, rewarded Dixon for his new political allegiance by appointing him clerk of the Federal Court for the Eastern District of North Carolina.[91]

Dixon's new day job supported his real work—the writing of *The Flaming Sword*—a book that he informed Edward Young Clarke, the former imperial kleagle of the Ku Klux Klan, was "the most important thing I have ever done." It was to be "bigger and far more sensational" than his previous works, Dixon said, predicting that it "will certainly sell a million, if pushed with faith and enthusiasm."[92] To do his part, Dixon spent as much as sixteen hours a day researching and writing the book.[93] He charged that Doubleday Doran, the press that had published *The Clansman*, rejected the manuscript, "afraid to antagonize the Negroes." Dixon feared contracting with one of the major presses because "they could lie down before a savage Negro attack and crucify me." Instead, Dixon sought "a daring young house, fearing neither man or the Devil, who will DRIVE the thing for all it is worth." He sought publishers "who believe as I believe on the Race Problem." Ultimately Atlanta's Monarch Publishing Company brought out the book.[94]

Raleigh's *News and Observer* announced that *The Flaming Sword* was a sequel to *The Clansman*, drawing for its inspiration upon "the Scottsboro case, the rise of Red Communism among Negroes and scores of interracial incidents blazed across 20th century newspapers." The newspaper predicted that Dixon's new book would have all the power of *The Birth of a Nation*. Dixon explained that his new book would begin where *The Leopard's Spots* ended "and bring the romance of the South from Reconstruction Days down to 1937." He promised to include "strong, dramatic characters" and to portray contemporary race relations, especially the spread of Communism among Negroes under Du Bois, whom Dixon characterized as a "Red radical preaching dictatorship of the proletariat."[95] Dixon stated that his book title came from a passage in Du Bois's *Black Reconstruction in America* (1935),[96] a text he branded "a blazing manifesto of Communism"[97] and "the Negro Bible of Communism."[98] Dixon assured readers that in his book he would depict the Costigan-Wagner Antilynching Bill (designed "to put the South back under bayonets as in Reconstruction") as the work of Du Bois's "Negro Communist Society" and the NAACP.[99] In fact, though in the late 1920s and early 1930s Du Bois admired Soviet Russia, both he and the organization opposed American Communists. Du Bois left the editorship of the NAACP's *Crisis* in June 1934.[100]

Dixon's 562-page *The Flaming Sword* appeared in mid 1939, soon after he had succumbed to a crippling cerebral hemorrhage and as war was breaking out in Europe. Dixon would die seven years later.[101] The novel, according to literary critic James Kinney, "combines the threats of socialism and racial equality, presenting blacks as communist dupes attempting the overthrow of the United States."[102] Literary historian Lawrence J. Oliver explains that in the work Dixon "dramatized, for the final time, the recurring theme of his fiction and nonfiction: that Reconstruction had let loose upon the land a savage black beast who would, if unchecked, 'Africanize' the United States and destroy the greatest civilization that the world has ever known."[103]

While *The Flaming Sword* builds upon many of the themes and set characters introduced in *The Leopard's Spots* and *The Clansman,* in 1939 Dixon updated them to reflect his obsessions with miscegenation, Communist-inspired black revolt, and race war in the South. Like Margaret Mitchell in *Gone with the Wind* (1936), in *The Flaming Sword* Dixon revived the race melodrama. But whereas Mitchell situated her book in the nineteenth century, Dixon set his in the recent past and present—"allowing him to make a full-scale assault on Reds as well as Blacks." The book, Oliver concludes, "reflects in dramatic fashion the virulent racism and right-wing 'Americanism' that pervaded the 'Red Decade.'"[104] It also signifies, according to Stephen Joseph Karina, the closest student of Dixon's last novel, Dixon's last-ditch, reactionary warning to Americans—"his surrealistic view of history since 1900, which condemned the entire black race for individual criminal offenses and supposed that all blacks waved red flags because a handful of their leaders turned to Communism."[105]

The Flaming Sword begins in idyllic Piedmont, South Carolina, early in the new century.[106] Though hardworking whites are transforming the New

South into an industrialized society "without violating the community's natural innocence,"[107] racial tension hovers over the land. Almost on cue, Dan Hose (presumably the brother of Sam Hose, the Negro lynched in Georgia in 1899), a sex-craved, beast-like Negro, savagely murders Dave Henry, an upwardly mobile yeoman, and his infant son, David; Hose also rapes Dave's sister-in-law, Marie Cameron.[108] Hose was inspired to rape Marie by reading James Weldon Johnson's 1915 poem "The White Witch," published originally in the NAACP's magazine *The Crisis*, edited by Du Bois and, according to Dixon, "a vile bundle of poison" (154).[109] "'A nigger in Harlem,' Dan says after raping Marie, 'sent me a little book dat say I got de right ter marry a white gal ef I kin git her. Can't marry her down here, but by God, I got her'" (172). Upon learning that Hose had a copy of Johnson's poem in his coat pocket, John Lovelace, one of Dave's friends, remarks: "That's the sort of damned stuff given to Niggers to read. There's the match that fired the powder." Marie's rape, Dixon adds, "was a blow of race." It was "a challenge to the existence of the white man and his people" (179).

Unquestionably, by 1939 standards the detailed rape scene was obscene. After Dan threatens to kill baby David, Marie agrees to succumb to his lust if the baby's life is spared. "He gripped her wrist," Dixon wrote, "and dragged her unresisting into the large bed room, crushed his naked sweating body against hers, and pressed his bulging thick lips into her mouth until she gasped for breath. For half an hour he played with her as a cat a mouse, raped her with brutal violence and ordered her to get up, while he stretched his huge black body full length on the bed, his mud covered wool socks staining the white linen." After Dan orders Marie to sit in a chair, she began to slouch. "'Straighten up—damn ye! he grunted. 'I want ter see all of ye. Jist like the devil made ye ter lead men ter hell and damnation. Straighten all the way against the wall, and put yer hans behin' yer head and keep 'em thar till I tell ye ter come back ter me.'" When Marie begins to slump again, Dan whips her (172–73). "For another half hour he subjected her to the agony and shame of indescribable sex atrocities until she sank unconscious to the floor" (174).

Commenting on Dixon's rape scene in 1966, historian James Zebulon Wright remarked that "no more lewd picture can be found in inexpensive paperback novels today."[110] Karina correctly notes that Dixon's "preoccupation with black sexuality assumed almost pathological proportions" and raises "questions [about] his very sanity."[111] "Reverend Dixon in fact spends three pages describing the rape and degradation of Marie," writes Oliver, "and he is not squeamish about providing prurient details capable of inflaming racial passions. . . . Of course, Dixon himself had to imagine the scene in order to depict it. His graphic account suggests that the lustful, violent brute is a projection of his own suppressed impulses." Dixon's assertion that Johnson's poem "idealiz[ed] the Negro's passion for white women" (266), according to Oliver, "is absurd. The poem in fact explicitly warns black males to *avoid* the snares of the white temptress."[112] Dixon also has one of his characters cite the notorious African American Negrophobe William Hannibal Thomas as an authority on the male Negro's "imperious sexual impulse, which, aroused at the slightest incentive, sweeps aside all restraint" (196).[113] Dixon's gruesome and violent post-rape lynching scene—including details of Hose's emasculation and incineration—served as the author's transitionary device to the second part of the book.

This occurs in New York City, where Angela Cameron Henry, Dave's wife and Marie's sister, relocates after overcoming the trauma of their deaths. She is committed to studying Negroes anthropologically in Harlem in order to help solve the race problem. Phil Stephens, a lawyer, racial liberal, and Angela's rejected beau from Piedmont, joins her in New York and works first with the Inter-Racial Commission and then the NAACP to promote racial harmony. But gradually Angela and Phil come to see the "Negro problem" more clearly. It was, she explains, "an unsolved and insolvable tragedy" (105). Blacks are inherently inferior and degenerate; education only exacerbates, not ameliorates, their condition. Blacks are obsessed with the idea of full "social equality," making them especially susceptible to New York's radical "Negro Junta" (Dixon's term for the NAACP), their white liberal supporters, and Communists who promise black men sex with white women in exchange for their support. Dixon included Oswald Garrison Villard, Joel E. Spingarn, Albert E. Pillsbury, and Moorfield Storey among white supporters of Du Bois's "Negro Junta."[114] According to one of Dixon's characters, every member of the NAACP is "a goddam racial imbecile who thinks that a Negro is better than a white man" (241).

As she ponders the complexities of the race problem, Angela concludes that racial purity can only be achieved by separation—colonizing the blacks to Africa. Influenced by a prorepatriation speech delivered by the white supremacist John Temple Graves in 1900, and the colonizationist ideas of black leaders Henry McNeal Turner, Lucius Holsey, and William H. Councill,[115] she endorses repatriation. "We have the ships—we have the millions. It only remains to develop the plan of a peaceful friendly separation" (234). Angela next devotes herself to studying Communism. "The thing is in the air," she says (400). Angela fears that American Communists are plotting to use the vast army of unemployed and disgruntled Negroes to topple the U.S. government.

Observing blacks in Harlem, Angela sees the "New Negro" for the first time and listens to jazz (277). "Whether worth while or not," Dixon wrote, black music "was certainly a direct growth of the African jungle. As their dancing is an expression of sex impulses straight from the tropical forests. As is their low resistance to the poison of syphilis and alcohol, and their easy surrender to the sway of superstition which they call religion" (273). In Harlem, Angela feels "for the first time the threat of a nation inside a nation under the teachings of radicals whose hatred of whites had become an obsession. Certainly the days of 'Mammies,' 'Aunties,' and 'Uncles' had gone forever" (276–77). She cringes at the seemingly ubiquitous sight of black men arm in arm with white women, usually blondes, practicing "the oldest profession known to woman" (275).

While in New York, Angela, Phil, and Tony Murino, a reformed bootlegger also committed to destroying the Communist threat, establish the Patriot Union—a secret national army of whites devoted to protecting America from the Communists. According to Tony, "Communism is the collapse of the human mind under the pressure of modern life. It is a malignant, contagious, mental disease now sweeping the world as the Black Death swept Europe in the middle ages. Its victims can see but one way to safety. A return to the herd life out of which an intelligent humanity grew. This impulse to touch shoulders with the herd, to sink back into the mass for food and shelter, means the end of all progress and the death of civilization itself" (500). Convinced that Soviet-inspired Communists had infiltrated America's schools and churches, its labor unions, its communication and transportation networks, the postal service, and even its military and navy, Angela goes undercover and enters the party's Inner Circle.

Determined to learn the date of the imminent revolution, Angela and Phil desperately but unsuccessfully try to prevent the overthrow of American democracy by radical blacks and Communists. The Negro-Communist insurrection begins during one of Roosevelt's fireside chats in 1940. In the South, members of the all-black Nat Turner Legion rise up in "a reign of terror—burning, murdering and raping" (561). "Negro criminals have been detailed to fire every Southern city, rape every white woman who can be taken, and blow up the armories" (550). After a violent coup the totalitarian Soviet Republic of the United States triumphs and rules North America.

Dixon blamed the nightmarish demise of Anglo-Saxon civilization on Communists and the "Negro Junta," especially the writings of his old black critics Du Bois, Johnson, and Miller—whom he charged with challenging racial segregation, demanding intermarriage of blacks and whites, and rejecting repatriation in order to enlist the black masses in the revolution.[116] Dixon believed that Depression-era blacks were ripe for what he considered the cheap and dangerous rhetoric of black intellectuals, their white neoabolitionist friends, and Communists. He judged their agenda—antilynching legislation, equal access to education and employment, and the end of Jim Crow laws—as radical steps prone to usher in the demise of white society.

Early in *The Flaming Sword*, for example, Captain Tom Collier, the conservative superintendent of Piedmont's school system, quotes Miller as saying that whites are "arrogant and rapacious, the most exclusive and intolerant race in history." This may be so, Collier explains, but he insists that one must answer the "cold blooded question: Can you change the color of a Negro, the swell of his lip or the beat of his heart with a spelling book or the use of a gang plow?" (41). Collier next alleges that "social equality with the great white race has become the passionate faith of ninety-nine out of every hundred educated Negroes in America. It is the soul of Du Bois' teachings. Charles W. Chestnut [sic], your Mulatto Cleveland novelist, believes it and proclaims it. Professor Kelly Miller, your distinguished Negro teacher in Washington, believes it" (42). Later, following Marie's rape, Angela's friend Ann Lovelace quotes Johnson as saying that "in the cone of the heart of the African race problem the sex factor is rooted." Ann, however, informs Angela that "the physical contact of two such races is a constant violation of God's law. We pay the price of that violation. We must obey the law or pay the penalty" (196–97).

Dixon, however, reserved his special disdain for Du Bois, whom he described as "the greatest Negro leader the race has yet produced in America," "the bold champion of the Dictatorship of the Proletariat" (477, 481). Dixon transformed Du Bois, his long-standing critic, into *The Flaming Sword*'s "Black villain."[117] According to Wright, Dixon owned most of Du Bois's books, and his marginal comments in them "reveal a genuine disgust with the Negro professor." For example, "when Du Bois wrote of the Negro's love of liberty, Dixon wrote '*Rats!*' Of Du Bois' mention of 'ancient African chastity' Dixon wrote '*Fool or Liar—.*' Du Bois' statement that race prejudice was 'deplorable in its intensity, unfortunate in results, and dangerous for the future, but nevertheless a hard fact which only time can efface' evinced an exclamatory '*Race Imbecile!*' from Dixon."[118] In *The Flaming Sword* Dixon referred to Du Bois as "the Mulatto," "this Mulatto," or "a Mulatto Professor in Atlanta University" (24, 18). Du Bois served as the lightning rod for Dixon's most personal, racist, slanderous, and vicious attacks. Dixon blamed him for trying to censor *The Birth of a Nation* (281) and named Du Bois as an "agitator" fomenting a bloody John Brown–like "Negro insurrection" and a Communist leader with direct ties to Moscow (336). Unlike white historian Avery O. Craven, who dismissed *Black Reconstruction in America* as "not history but only a half-baked Marxian interpretation of the labor side of Reconstruction and a badly distorted picture of the Negroes' part in Southern life," Dixon recognized the book's polemical brilliance. For him *Black Reconstruction in America* became "the central text of the revolutionaries."[119]

Near the start of *The Flaming Sword,* Angela's grandfather, Dr. Richard Cameron, the father of Ben Cameron, Dixon's hero in *The Clansman,* denounces Du Bois's *The Souls of Black Folk* (1903) as "a little black book" published "with the deliberate purpose of stirring the worst passions—a firebrand thrown into the imaginations of ten million Negroes" (18).[120] Dr. Cameron next questions Du Bois's credibility as an authority on the "Negro problem." "Professor W. E. B. Du Bois," he said, "was born in Massachusetts. His people never knew slavery.... All he knows of the history of our states and our people he drew from the imagination of Abolition fanatics who caused the Civil War." Du Bois's knowledge of slavery was second- and third-hand—"from sources of ignorance and prejudice," Dixon explained, and "his reference to ancient African Chastity ... stamps the writer an ignoramus on the history of the Africa from which our Negroes came" (20).

Cameron later compares Du Bois with "the scoundrels who first sowed hate" among the black man during "the black days of Reconstruction when Negroes, Carpetbaggers and Scalawags ruled this country" (26, 55). Captain Collier believes that Du Bois's flaws were most readily identifiable "in his glorification of Frederick Douglass, the Negro orator, whose final triumph was his marriage to a white woman." Collier charges that, like Douglass, Du Bois's solution to America's race problem was "'assimilation by self-assertion and by no other means.' That is to say the making of American Mulatto [sic] by the self assertion of the Negro" (39).

Though Dixon openly criticized Booker T. Washington, he nevertheless considered him more qualified to lead the race than Du Bois, whose ideas he judged "daring and dangerous" (400). "There was no trace of the Negro in him," Phil observes of Du Bois, "except the light tinge of brown in his skin, and that was not marked. A pointed beard, dark melancholy eyes, a quiet man of culture, French looking rather than American, he gave no impression of an African.... It was easy to believe that he had taken degrees at Harvard and in Germany.... It was difficult to believe that such a man, with a bare trace of a Negro in his makeup, should be so fiercely, passionately, and insistently African as to lead a crusade of violence against the white race" (248–49). Phil finds Du Bois's *Black Reconstruction in America* so radical that he severs ties with the NAACP when the organization's leaders refuse to censure its author. Du Bois's treatment of economic issues, he remarks, was "a specious plea for the philosophy of Karl Marx" (478).

Black Reconstruction in America, Phil explains, contradicted all previous interpretations of Reconstruction. It audaciously championed the rule of blacks over whites in this period "in terms that will not bear discussion." Phil judges Du Bois's book "so bitterly partisan" that it was worthless "as an historical document. His theme is that the Negro made in the tragic fiasco of Reconstruction a noble record. That his white rivals of the South were his inferiors" (478). Though Du Bois was a scientifically trained scholar, in *Black Reconstruction in America* he exposed himself as a doctrinaire Marxist; his book was a "firebrand." "It is in no sense a history," Phil concludes, "in spite of its jumble of irrelevant and worthless quotations. It is a call to race riot by a man who has become a monomaniac in his hatred of whites. In every line one feels the passionate desire of the author to slit the throat of every white man in the world. His theme is merely the platform from which he rises to harangue the mob and excite them to violence" (479).

Later in the story Dixon explained Du Bois's shift to the Left—into the Communists' ranks—as a pragmatic move designed to retain influence among his people. According to Dixon, "the struggle of the Red leaders for control of the race threw the amalgamation Junta in New York into a panic of fear for their future. Du Bois met the situation by a sharp turn to the left in his writing and speeches. The Russian Government was praised, our own denounced. Atheism was applauded. Denunciation of the white race increased in violence. Every device of insinuation and direct attack was now used to stir the hate of Negroes against the Southern people" (466–67). On the eve of the revolution, a member of the Communist Inner Circle informs Russia's ambassador to the United States that thanks to Du Bois's influence, 550,000 armed blacks would fight for the Red cause. "Du Bois is the greatest leader we have ever produced in America," he says. "His book advocating the Dictatorship of the Proletariat has become what he designed it to be, the Bible of the Negro. We'll give the Southerners the biggest surprise of all" (523).

In the end, however, it was Dixon who was surprised by the negative and/or indifferent response to *The Flaming Sword*. As war loomed in Europe, Depression-era Americans found little interest in Dixon's sexual fantasies and his rant against miscegenation and Negro Communists. Writing in the *Raleigh News and Observer*, Frank Smethurst, managing editor of the newspaper, remarked that the book more appropriately deserved "news treatment rather than literary criticism." Dixon's novel, Smethurst explained, "gathers up the loose threads of the race problem . . . and weaves them into the pattern of a new national menace, Communism." He dismissed *The Flaming Sword* as generally gratuitous—"a preachment of conservative patriotism and an indictment of the liberal concept in race relations which the author scores as an invitation to the radicalism he seems to fear with something like hysteria."[121] Similarly, the critic in the *New York Times* brushed off the book as a manifestation of Dixon's paranoia, predicting that the public would judge it as "nightmare melodrama," "the expression of a panic fear."[122] Though the *New York Herald Tribune* paid *The Flaming Sword* short shrift, the proximity of the book's appearance to the signing of the August 23, 1939, Molotov-Ribbentrop Pact and Adolf

Hitler's invasion of Poland nine days later inclined the reviewer to remark that Dixon's "vehement melodrama . . . is not as wildly incredible today as it might have seemed a few short weeks ago."[123]

While Americans watched with horror the war that would quickly envelop Europe, they ignored Dixon's lurid fears of miscegenation, his pathetic and wildly inaccurate accusations of a Negro Communist conspiracy, and his erroneous forecasts of race war at home. His last novel was an utter failure. Just as Du Bois never responded to Dixon's libelous and malicious attacks in *The Flaming Sword*,[124] Americans rejected his hysterical, dog-eared recitations of black degeneracy, black retrogression, and pending racial doom. But African Americans had always found Dixon's books "hard reading." Early in the twentieth century, blacks had good reason to fear the harmful backlash of Dixon's malicious lies on members of their race. They understood too well the racial phobias and venomous race hatred that lay at their core.

By 1939, however, blacks considered Dixon's final warnings to be the sick fantasies of a bitter, desperate, and isolated man. As Americans braced for a second world war, the author of *The Flaming Sword* stood dramatically out of touch with the accomplishments, achievements, and self-determination of modern black Americans.[125] Shortly before that book appeared, Dixon informed Earnest Sevier Cox that "some . . . people may find sentences in my books that are hard reading on the surface. I have simply tried in all my writing to develop Lincoln's and Jefferson's views through the characters which I have created showing that separation is the only sane solution. Personally I have always loved the Negro race, and for that very reason have savagely opposed amalgamation."[126] The "Negro problem" as Dixon defined it thus had become quite literally *his* problem. African Americans long before had disproven the rabidly racist misrepresentations and predictions of Tom Dixon.

NOTES

Thomas H. Appleton Jr., Jeffery J. Crow, John C. Inscoe, Glenda E. Gilmore, Randall M. Miller, Steven Weisenburger, and William L. Van Deburg generously commented on earlier versions of this essay. I received research assistance from Daire Roebuck, Mimi Riggs, Marihelen Stringham, Ann Rothe (North Carolina State University), Elizabeth Dunn (Duke University), Randal Hall (Rice University), Alexander Andrusyszyn (Yale University), and Jane Ruffin (*Raleigh News and Observer*).

1. For an analysis of Page's decision to exile himself, see John Milton Cooper, *Walter Hines Page: The Southerner as American, 1855-1918* (Chapel Hill: Univ. of North Carolina Press, 1977), 79–81.
2. Walter H. Page to W.E.B. Du Bois, November 22, 1905; Du Bois to Page, n.d.; Page to Du Bois, November 27, 1905, in *The Correspondence of W. E. B. Du Bois*, vol. 1, *Selections 1877–1934*, ed. Herbert Aptheker (Amherst: Univ. of Massachusetts Press, 1973), 113–14.
3. Cooper notes how "commercialism undermined Page's principles" and that in the case of publishing Dixon, Page "recognized how badly he had compromised his literary and social views." See Cooper, *Walter Hines Page*, 168, 169.
4. Raymond A. Cook, *Thomas Dixon* (New York: Twayne Publishers, 1974), 68.
5. W. H. Johnson, "The Case of the Negro," *Dial* 34 (May 1, 1903): 301.
6. "Mr. Dixon's 'The Leopard's Spots,'" *New York Times Saturday Review of Books and Art*, April 5, 1902, p. 234.
7. Francis Butler Simkins, *The South Old and New* (New York: Knopf, 1947), 352.
8. C. Vann Woodward, *Origins of the New South, 1877–1913* (Baton Rouge: Louisiana State Univ. Press, 1951), 352.
9. W.E.B. Du Bois, "The Problem of Tillman, Vardaman and Thomas Dixon, Jr.," *Central Christian Advocate* 49 (October 18, 1905): 1324–25, in *Writings by W. E. B. Du Bois in Periodicals Edited by Others*, vol. 1, *1891–1909*, ed. Herbert Aptheker (Millwood, N.Y.: Kraus-Thomson Organization Limited, 1982), 263, 265.
10. Ibid., 265–66.
11. Rayford W. Logan, *The Betrayal of the Negro: From Rutherford B. Hayes to Woodrow Wilson* (new, enlarged edition of *The Negro in American Life and Thought: The Nadir, 1877–1901* [New York: Dial Press, 1954]; New York: Collier Books, 1965), 351, 354; Robert A. Bone, *Down Home: Origins of the Afro-American Short Story* (1975; reprint, New York: Columbia Univ. Press, 1988), 125. For an analysis of *The Leopard's Spots* and "race," see Maxwell Bloomfield, "Dixon's *The Leopard's Spots*: A Study in Popular Racism," *American Quarterly* 16 (fall 1964): 387–402. For an especially insightful early study, see Max Frank Harris, "The Ideas of Thomas Dixon on Race Relations" (master's thesis, University of North Carolina, 1948).
12. Joel Williamson, *The Crucible of Race: Black-White Relations in the American South since Emancipation* (New York: Oxford Univ. Press, 1984), 6, 140–41. In 1902, Dixon was so convinced of the broad acceptance of his arguments that he unabashedly sent an advance copy of *The Leopard's Spots* to Booker T. Washington, confident that Washington would review it favorably. Walter Hines Page reportedly sent a copy of *The Clansman* to Charles W. Chesnutt. See Dixon to Washington, March 4, 1902, in *The Booker T. Washington Papers*, 14 vols., ed. Louis R. Harlan (Urbana: Univ. of Illinois Press, 1972–1989), 6:413, and Dean McWilliams, *Charles W. Chesnutt and the Fictions of Race* (Athens: Univ. of Georgia Press, 2002), 181.
13. Thomas Dixon Jr., *The Leopard's Spots: A Romance of the White Man's Burden—1865–1900* (New York: Doubleday, Page, 1902), 5, 242, 333, 382, 460.
14. Thomas Dixon Jr., *The Clansman: An Historical Romance of the Ku Klux Klan* (1905; reprint, Lexington: Univ. Press of Kentucky, 1970), 290, 292.

15. James Kinney, "Dixon, Thomas, Jr.," in *Encyclopedia of Southern Culture,* ed. Charles Reagan Wilson and William Ferris (Chapel Hill: Univ. of North Carolina Press, 1989), 880.

16. Thomas Dixon Jr., "Booker T. Washington and the Negro," *Saturday Evening Post* 178 (August 19, 1905): 1. On Dixon's relationship with Washington, see Mark Bauerlein, "The Tactical Life of Booker T. Washington," *Chronicle of Higher Education,* November 28, 2003, pp. B12–13, and Robert J. Norrell, "Understanding the Wizard: Another Look at the Age of Booker T. Washington," in *Booker T. Washington and Black Progress: "Up From Slavery" 100 Years Later,* ed. W. Fitzhugh Brundage (Gainesville: Univ. Press of Florida, 2003), 71.

17. Wilson Jeremiah Moses, *Afrotopia: The Roots of African American Popular History* (Cambridge: Cambridge Univ. Press, 1998), 183.

18. Dixon, "Booker T. Washington and the Negro," 2.

19. Williamson, *Crucible of Race,* 140.

20. William Monroe Trotter in *Boston Guardian,* November 29, 1902, quoted in Stephen R. Fox, *The Guardian of Boston: William Monroe Trotter* (1970; reprint, New York: Atheneum, 1971), 189.

21. Dixon, *Leopard's Spots,* 460.

22. William A. Sinclair, *The Aftermath of Slavery: A Study of the Condition and Environment of the American Negro* (Boston: Small, Maynard and Company, 1905), 222.

23. James Zebulon Wright, "Thomas Dixon: The Mind of a Southern Apologist" (Ph.D. diss., George Peabody College for Teachers, 1966), 282 (emphasis added).

24. See Hugh C. Bailey, *Liberalism in the New South: Southern Social Reformers and the Progressive Movement* (Coral Gables: Univ. of Miami Press, 1969), 90.

25. Thomas Dixon Jr. to Booker T. Washington, January 22, 23, 1906, in Harlan, ed., *Booker T. Washington Papers,* 8:508.

26. Dixon, "Booker T. Washington and the Negro," 1.

27. For an overview of the black literary response to Dixon's writings, see Cook, *Thomas Dixon,* 133–38.

28. Lucius C. Harper, "What Reward Has God for Thomas Dixon, the Hater?" *Chicago Defender,* April 13, 1946, p. 6.

29. Robert A. Bone, *The Negro Novel in America* (New Haven: Yale Univ. Press, 1958), 22.

30. Judith R. Berzon, *Neither White Nor Black: The Mulatto Character in American Fiction* (New York: New York Univ. Press, 1978), 61.

31. Thomas H. B. Walker, *J. Johnson or "The Unknown Man": An Answer to Mr. Thos. Dixon's "Sins of the Fathers"* (De Land, Fla.: E. O. Painter, 1915), 57, 155, 7.

32. Glenda Elizabeth Gilmore, "'One of the Meanest Books': Thomas Dixon, Jr. and *The Leopard's Spots,*" *North Carolina Literary Review* 2 (July 1994): 97–98.

33. W. E. Burghardt Du Bois, "Possibilities of the Negro—The Advance Guard of the Race," *Booklover's Magazine* 2 (July 1903): 11.

34. See August Meier, "The Racial and Educational Philosophy of Kelly Miller, 1895–1915," *Journal of Negro Education* 29 (spring 1960): 121–27, and Bernard Eisenberg, "Kelly Miller: The Negro as a Marginal Man," *Journal of Negro History* 45 (July 1960): 182–97.

35. Kelly Miller, review of *The Mulatto in the United States*, by Edward Byron Reuter, *American Journal of Sociology* 25 (September 1919): 223.

36. Kelly Miller, *A Review of Hoffman's Race Traits and Tendencies of The American Negro*, The American Negro Academy Occasional Papers, No. 1 (Washington, D.C.: The Academy, 1897); Alfred A. Moss Jr., *The American Negro Academy: Voice of the Talented Tenth* (Baton Rouge: Louisiana State Univ. Press, 1981), 51, 53, 93–95.

37. Kelly Miller, *As to the Leopard's Spots: An Open Letter to Thomas Dixon, Jr.* (Washington, D.C.: Howard University, [1905]), 3, 15, 16.

38. Samuel K. Roberts, "Kelly Miller and Thomas Dixon, Jr. on Blacks in American Civilization," *Phylon* 41 (2nd quarter, 1980): 205 n.

39. Compare Dixon, "Booker T. Washington and the Negro," 2, with Kelly Miller, "The Anglo-Saxon and the African," *Arena* 28 (December 1902): 582, 583.

40. Kelly Miller, "Is the American Negro to Remain Black or Become Bleached?" *South Atlantic Quarterly* 25 (July 1926): 243.

41. For two useful recent studies on Griggs, see Randolph Meade Walker, *The Metamorphosis of Sutton E. Griggs: The Transition from Black Radical to Conservative, 1913-1933* (Memphis: Walker Publishing, 1991), and Finnie Delarry Coleman, "The Archaeology of African American Literature: [Re]Introducing the Works of Reverend Sutton E. Griggs" (Ph.D. diss., University of Virginia, 1999).

42. Hugh M. Gloster, "Sutton E. Griggs, Novelist of the New Negro," *Phylon* 4 (4th quarter, 1943): 337; Hugh M. Gloster, "New Preface," in Sutton Griggs, *Imperium in Imperio* (1899; reprint, New York: Arno Press, 1969), iii–iv.

43. Mason Stokes, *The Color of Sex: Whiteness, Heterosexuality, and the Fictions of White Supremacy* (Durham: Duke Univ. Press, 2001), 12.

44. Susan Gillman, *Blood Talk: American Race Melodrama and the Culture of the Occult* (Chicago: Univ. of Chicago Press, 2003), chapter 3.

45. Robert E. Fleming, "Sutton E. Griggs: Militant Black Novelist," *Phylon* 34 (1st quarter, 1973): 73–77; Arlene A. Elder, *The "Hindered Hand": Cultural Implications of Early African-American Fiction* (Westport: Greenwood Press, 1978), 69–103; Wilson Jeremiah Moses, *The Golden Age of Black Nationalism, 1850–1925* (New York: Oxford Univ. Press, 1978), chapter 9; Wilson Jeremiah Moses, "Literary Garveyism: The Novels of Reverend Sutton E. Griggs," *Phylon* 40 (3rd quarter 1979): 203–16; and Hanna Wallinger, "Secret Societies and Dark Empire: Sutton E. Griggs's *Imperium in Imperio* and W. E. B. Du Bois's *Dark Princess*," in *Empire—American Studies*, Swiss Papers in English Language and Literature, vol. 10, ed. John G. Blair and Reinhold Wagnleitner (Tübingen: Gunter Narr Verlag, 1997), 197–208.

46. Coleman, "Archaeology of African American Literature," 108, 204, 210.

47. Michele Mitchell, "'The Black Man's Burden': African Americans, Imperialism, and Notions of Racial Manhood, 1890–1910," *International Review of Social History* 44 (Supplement, 1999): 91–92.

48. Lee L. Brown, "Rev. Dr. Sutton E. Griggs Delivers Address at Fifth Street Church," *Indianapolis Freeman*, September 9, 1911, Hampton University Newspaper Clipping File, Hampton University Library, Hampton, Virginia.

49. Griggs, *Imperium in Imperio*, 57, 62. Literary scholar Eric J. Sundquist notes that Griggs was one of the earliest to employ the discourse of the "New Negro"—long before the Harlem Renaissance. See Eric J. Sundquist, *To Wake the Nations: Race in the Making of American Literature* (Cambridge: Belknap Press of Harvard Univ. Press, 1993), 335.

50. Sutton E. Griggs, "A Hindering Hand: A Review of the Anti-Negro Crusade of Mr. Thomas Dixon, Jr.," in *The Hindered Hand: or, The Reign of the Repressionist*, 3rd ed., revised (1905; reprint, New York: AMS Press, 1969), 332. Coleman explains that in 1903 Griggs was commissioned to publish his "stern Tractarian response to Thomas Dixon" by the Baptist National Convention, but the church group ultimately failed to provide financial support. See "Archaeology of African American Literature," 104, 107, 122.

51. Gloster, "Sutton E. Griggs, Novelist of the New Negro," 343. Commenting on Griggs's review of Dixon's book, Arlene A. Elder writes that "unfortunately . . . this essay does not increase the artistic unity of the book, but adds yet another element of propaganda to a work already weakened by racial theorizing, political debate, and lengthy proposals for social action." See Elder, *The "Hindered Hand*," 32.

52. Sutton E. Griggs, *The One Great Question: A Study of Southern Conditions at Close Range* (Philadelphia: Orion Publishing Company, 1907), 32, 38, 52.

53. Griggs, "Hindering Hand," 304–5, 309.

54. Miller, *As to the Leopard's Spots*, 5, 18.

55. Ibid., 11.

56. Griggs, "Hindering Hand," 314–15.

57. Miller, *As to the Leopard's Spots*, 6, 7.

58. Ibid., 16.

59. Griggs, "Hindering Hand," 313, 311.

60. Miller, *As to the Leopard's Spots*, 17, 18. On Chesnutt and "assimilationism," see Dickson D. Bruce Jr., *Black American Writing from the Nadir: The Evolution of a Literary Tradition, 1877–1915* (Baton Rouge: Louisiana State Univ. Press, 1989), 173–74.

61. Miller, *As to the Leopard's Spots*, 19, 20.

62. Griggs, "Hindering Hand," 328, 317, 331, 332.

63. Ibid., 332–33.

64. Sabine Sielke, *Reading Rape: The Rhetoric of Sexual Violence in American Literature and Culture, 1790–1990* (Princeton: Princeton Univ. Press, 2002), 55, 58–59.

65. Thomas Dixon, *Southern Horizons: The Autobiography of Thomas Dixon* (Alexandria, Va.: IWV Publishing, 1984), 267.

66. Dickson D. Bruce Jr., *Archibald Grimké: Portrait of a Black Independent* (Baton Rouge: Louisiana State Univ. Press, 1993), 211; Deborah Gray White, *Too Heavy a Load: Black Women in Defense of Themselves, 1894–1994* (New York: Norton, 1999), 84; [unsigned editorial], "The Clansman," *Crisis* 10 (May 1915): 33, in *Writings in Periodicals Edited by W. E. B. Du Bois: Selections from THE CRISIS*, vol. 1, *1911–1925*, ed. Herbert Aptheker (Millwood, N.Y.: Kraus-Thomson Organization Limited, 1983), 98.

67. See "Progressive Protest Against Anti-Negro Film," *Survey* 34 (June 5, 1915): 209–10; "'The Birth of a Nation,'" *Crisis* 10 (June 1915): 69–71; and Thomas R. Cripps, "The Reaction

of the Negro to the Motion Picture 'Birth of a Nation,'" *Historian* 25 (May 1963): 344–62. For a careful analysis of the different reception to the play and the film in one state, see John C. Inscoe, "*The Clansman* on Stage and Screen: North Carolina Reacts," *North Carolina Historical Review* 64 (April 1987): 139–62.

68. W. E. Burghardt Du Bois, *Dusk of Dawn: An Essay Toward an Autobiography of a Race Concept* (1940; reprint, New York: Schocken Books, 1968), 240.

69. David Levering Lewis, *W. E. B. Du Bois: The Fight for Equality and the American Century, 1919–1963* (New York: Henry Holt, 2000), 87.

70. [unsigned editorial], "The Clansman," 99.

71. William Stanley Braithwaite, "The Negro in American Literature," in *The New Negro*, ed. Alain Locke (1925; reprint, New York: Atheneum, 1968), 33.

72. Walter White, "The Negro and American Tradition," in ibid., 364.

73. Dixon quoted in Harper, "What Reward Has God for Thomas Dixon, the Hater?" p. 6.

74. See Cook, *Thomas Dixon*, 67, 71.

75. Thomas Dixon to Rolfe Cobleigh, March 27, 1915 (copy), National Association for the Advancement of Colored People Records, Manuscript Division, Library of Congress.

76. Storey quoted in William B. Hixson Jr., *Moorfield Storey and the Abolitionist Tradition* (New York: Oxford Univ. Press, 1972), 132.

77. On Dixon's enthusiasm for Garvey, see Tony Martin, *Race First: The Ideological and Organizational Struggles of Marcus Garvey and the Universal Negro Improvement Association* (1976; reprint, Dover, Mass.: Majority Press, 1986), 352–54. On Garvey on repatriation and race mixing, see Lawrence W. Levine, "Marcus Garvey and the Politics of Revitalization," in *Black Leaders of the Twentieth Century*, ed. John Hope Franklin and August Meier (Urbana: Univ. of Illinois Press, 1982), 130–31.

78. Dixon to Cox, September 17, December 11, 1938, Earnest Sevier Cox Papers, Duke University.

79. Dixon to Cox, September 21, 1938, Cox Papers. In 1923 Garvey's wife, Amy Jacques Garvey, compiled a collection of his sayings and speeches, *Philosophy and Opinions of Marcus Garvey*.

80. Dixon to Cox, December 11, 1938, Cox Papers; Thomas Dixon, *The Flaming Sword* (Atlanta: Monarch Publishing Company, 1939), 422–23. All future page references to this work will be parenthetical.

81. See "Speech by Marcus Garvey" [September 25, 1921], in *The Marcus Garvey and Universal Negro Improvement Association Papers*, 9 vols., ed. Robert A. Hill (Berkeley: Univ. of California Press, 1983–1995), 4:89.

82. Marcus Garvey to Earnest S. Cox, October 6, 1938, in ibid., 7:892–93.

83. W.E.B. Du Bois, "A Lunatic or a Traitor," *Crisis* 27 (May 1924), quoted in ibid., 5:583. For a valuable, perceptive study that argues persuasively that Dixon and Garvey shared little ideologically, see Stephen Joseph Karina, "With Flaming Sword: The Reactionary Rhetoric of Thomas Dixon" (Ph.D. diss., University of Georgia, 1978), 243–44, 289.

84. For a recent overview of the relation between *The Flaming Sword* and Dixon's earlier texts, see Anthony Slide, *American Racist: The Life and Films of Thomas Dixon* (Lexington: Univ. Press of Kentucky, 2004), 8, 14, 24, 99–100, 135, 186–89, 193.

85. Karina, "With Flaming Sword," 128–29.

86. Dixon to Cox, December 11, 1938, Cox Papers. On Cox's ties to Garvey, see Earnest Sevier Cox, *Let My People Go* (Richmond: White America Society, 1925), [4].

87. See Thomas A. Krueger, *And Promises to Keep: The Southern Conference for Human Welfare, 1938–1948* (Nashville: Vanderbilt Univ. Press, 1967).

88. William David Harrison, "The Thoughts of Thomas Dixon on Black and White Race Relations in American Society" (master's thesis, University of South Carolina, 1970), 25. On Dixon's fears of Marxism, Socialism, Communism, and feminism, see Cook, *Thomas Dixon*, 80–88. These aspects of Dixon's thought cry out for systematic scholarly attention.

89. W. A. Domingo, "Socialism: The Negroes' Hope," *Messenger* 2 (July 1919), quoted in *A Documentary History of the Negro People in the United States*, 6 vols., ed. Herbert Aptheker (Secaucus, N.J.: Citadel Press, 1951–1993), 3:262.

90. "Dixon Gets Post in Federal Court," *Raleigh News and Observer*, May 2, 1937, p. 1.

91. Raymond Rohauer, "Postscript," in Dixon, *Southern Horizons*, 322; Cary D. Wintz, "Introduction," in Thomas Dixon Jr., *The Clansman: An Historical Romance of the Ku Klux Klan*, ed. and abridged by Cary D. Wintz (Armonk, N.Y.: M. E. Sharpe, 2001), xvi; Wright, "Thomas Dixon," 288–89. Dixon held the clerkship until 1943. See "Dixon's Funeral to Be Held Today," *Raleigh News and Observer*, April 4, 1946, p. 1.

92. Thomas Dixon to Edward Y. Clarke, August 11, 1938, Thomas Dixon Papers, Duke University.

93. Wright, "Thomas Dixon," 288.

94. Thomas Dixon to Oscar, August 18, 1938, Dixon Papers.

95. "'Birth of Nation' Will Have Sequel," *Raleigh News and Observer*, October 22, 1937, p. 8.

96. Lawrence J. Oliver, "Writing from the Right during the 'Red Decade': Thomas Dixon's Attack on W. E. B. Du Bois and James Weldon Johnson in *The Flaming Sword*," *American Literature* 70 (March 1998): 135, pinpoints the quotation in W.E.B. Du Bois, *Black Reconstruction in America: An Essay toward a History of the Part Which Black Folk Played in the Attempt to Reconstruct Democracy in America, 1860–1880* (1935; reprint, New York: Atheneum, 1973), 707. Du Bois wrote: "A clear vision of a world without inordinate individual wealth, of capital without profit, and of income based on work alone, is the path out, not only for America but for all men. Across this path stands the South with flaming sword" (706–7).

97. "'Birth of Nation' Will Have Sequel," *Raleigh News and Observer*, October 22, 1937, p. 8.

98. Thomas Dixon to Earnest Sevier Cox, November 22, 1939, Cox Papers.

99. "'Birth of Nation' Will Have Sequel," *Raleigh News and Observer*, October 22, 1937, p. 8. This bill, proposed unsuccessfully in 1934 by Democrats Edward Costigan and Robert Wagner on behalf of the NAACP, would have imposed a $10,000 fine on counties where lynchings occurred. See George C. Rable, "The South and the Politics of Antilynching Legislation, 1920–1940," *Journal of Southern History* 51 (May 1985): 201–20.

100. Elliott M. Rudwick, *W. E. B. Du Bois: Propagandist of the Negro Protest* (New York: Atheneum, 1972), 256–57, 283.

101. Raymond Allen Cook, *Fire from the Flint: The Amazing Career of Thomas Dixon* (Winston-Salem, N.C.: Blair, 1968), 223.

102. Kinney, "Dixon, Thomas, Jr.," 881.

103. Oliver, "Writing from the Right during the 'Red Decade,'" 132–34.

104. Ibid.

105. Karina, "With Flaming Sword," 273–74.

106. For a useful summary of the characters and plot of *The Flaming Sword*, see Daniel W. Jolley, "Thomas Dixon's Literary Crusade for Racial Purity" (Honors Essay, Department of History, University of North Carolina at Chapel Hill, 1992), 159–87.

107. F. Garvin Davenport Jr., "Thomas Dixon's Mythology of Southern History," *Journal of Southern History* 36 (August 1970): 361.

108. On Dixon's repeated use of Hose in his psychosexual dramas, see Stokes, *The Color of Sex*, 218 n. 21.

109. James Weldon Johnson, "The White Witch," *Crisis* 10 (March 1915): 239.

110. Wright, "Thomas Dixon," 277n.

111. Karina, "With Flaming Sword," 270.

112. Oliver, "Writing from the Right during the 'Red Decade,'" 140, 142 (emphasis in original). Oliver adds (p. 142) that "on the symbolic level the 'white witch' that lures and destroys African Americans is not a woman at all but materialistic 'white' culture."

113. For Thomas's comment, see William Hannibal Thomas, *The American Negro: What He Was, What He Is, and What He May Become* (New York: Macmillan, 1901), 176–77. On Thomas, see John David Smith, *Black Judas: William Hannibal Thomas and "The American Negro"* (Athens: Univ. of Georgia Press, 2000).

114. On Villard, Spingarn, Pillsbury, and Storey in these years, see Richard B. Sherman, *The Republican Party and Black America from McKinley to Hoover, 1896–1933* (Charlottesville: Univ. Press of Virginia, 1973).

115. On Graves and his speech cited by Dixon favoring repatriation, see John David Smith, "'No Negro is upon the program': Blacks and the Montgomery Race Conference of 1900," in *A Mythic Land Apart: Reassessing Southerners and Their History*, ed. John David Smith and Thomas H. Appleton Jr. (Westport: Greenwood Press, 1997), 125–50, and John David Smith, ed., *Anti-Black Thought, 1863–1925: "The Negro Problem,"* 11 vols. (New York: Garland, 1993), 2:48–57. On Turner, Holsey, and Council, respectively, see Stephen Ward Angell, *Bishop Henry McNeal Turner and African-American Religion in the South* (Knoxville: Univ. of Tennessee Press, 1992); Glenn T. Eskew, "Black Elitism and the Failure of Paternalism in Postbellum Georgia: The Case of Bishop Lucius Henry Holsey," *Journal of Southern History* 58 (November 1992): 637–66; and John David Smith, "William Hooper Councill," in *American National Biography*, 24 vols., ed. John A. Garraty and Mark C. Carnes (New York: Oxford Univ. Press, 1999), 5:586–88.

116. Oliver devotes considerable attention to Dixon's response to Johnson in "Writing from the Right during the 'Red Decade,'" 136–37, 141, 144.

117. Roy Stanley Flewelling Jr., "Three Voices on Race: Thomas Dixon, Marcus Garvey and Lothrop Stoddard on the Future of the American Stock" (master's thesis, University of North Carolina at Chapel Hill, 1971), 29.

118. Wright, "Thomas Dixon," 283 (emphasis added).

119. Avery O. Craven, review of W.E.B. Du Bois, *Black Reconstruction in America: An Essay toward a History of the Part Which Black Folk Played in the Attempt to Reconstruct Democracy in America, 1860–1880*, in *American Journal of Sociology* 41 (January 1936): 535; Mark Emory Elliott, "Albion W. Tourgée and the Fate of Democratic Individualism" (Ph.D. diss., New York University, 2002), 92.

120. In 1905, Dixon had remarked that in *The Souls of Black Folk* "we see the naked soul of a Negro beating itself to death against the bars in which Aryan society has caged him! No white man with a soul can read this book without a tear." See Dixon, "Booker T. Washington and the Negro," 2.

121. Frank Smethurst, "Americans in Black, White and Red," *Raleigh News and Observer*, August 6, 1939, p. 5.

122. K. W., "A Novel of Conflict," *New York Times*, August 20, 1939, section 6, p. 18.

123. George Conrad, review of *The Flaming Sword*, by Thomas Dixon, *New York Herald Tribune Books* 16 (September 17, 1939): 12.

124. Du Bois left no record of his response to *The Flaming Sword*. When in 1940 a correspondent asked for his opinion of the book, Du Bois failed to address the question. See Mrs. J. G. Cockrane to Du Bois, November 10, 1940, and Du Bois to My dear Madam, November 18, 1940, in *The Correspondence of W. E. B. Du Bois*, vol. 2, *Selections 1834–1944*, ed. Herbert Aptheker (Amherst: Univ. of Massachusetts Press, 1976), 239–41.

125. On the context of black modernism, see Houston A. Baker Jr., *Modernism and the Harlem Renaissance* (Chicago: Univ. of Chicago Press, 1987).

126. Dixon to Cox, September 21, 1938, Cox Papers. On Dixon's frequent use of Lincoln as an "archsegregationist" symbol, see Michael Davis, *The Image of Lincoln in the South* (Knoxville: Univ. of Tennessee Press, 1971), 148–52, 170.

Gender and Race in Dixon's Religious Ideology

CYNTHIA LYNN LYERLY

The first of Thomas Dixon's novels to be among the top ten bestsellers in America was not *The Leopard's Spots* or *The Clansman*, but the book he wrote and sold in between these two Reconstruction novels, *The One Woman*. The ninth best-selling book of 1903, it tells the story of a New York minister who, after being seduced by dangerous socialist doctrines, leaves his wife and children for another woman. And surprise of surprises, there are no racist speeches, indeed no black people, in this book. Dixon's interests outside of race-baiting are little known, but since he published many books (and produced plays and movies from them)[1] on other subjects, we would do well to understand this side of Dixon if we are to evaluate his impact on modern America.

Thomas Dixon had firm ideas about economics, society, politics, blacks, women, love, family, and the place of religion in modern life. The bundle of ideas that he endlessly promoted is best viewed, I would argue, as a religious ideology. Dixon had contempt for creeds and doctrines. He believed that denominationalism hurt the cause of Christ, for it engulfed Christians in endless disputes over nonessentials. Creeds, too, did not suit the age; actions, not "the platitudes of dead traditions," were needed.[2] Yet Dixon's beliefs were remarkably rigid and systematic, and religion informed them at every turn. Historian Michael Hunt astutely defines ideology as "an interrelated set of convictions or assumptions that reduces the complexities of a particular slice of reality to easily comprehensible terms and suggests appropriate ways of dealing with that reality."[3] Dixon's worldview and agenda dovetail neatly with Hunt's definition. Especially in terms of race and gender relations, Dixon saw the world in schematic and limited ways.[4]

Nurtured by bitter ex-masters in the crucible of radical Reconstruction, Dixon's racism was part of his intellectual and familial heritage. His father and uncle were Ku Klux Klansmen who taught him that for blacks to vote, hold office, and bear arms was a horror to be resisted with force. Dixon was not, however, persuaded by every tenet of Lost Cause nostalgia, as he had no yearning to re-create the Old South. Slavery had been, per Dixon, a benevolent institution for blacks, but it had also brought the African to American shores. For Dixon, any good done African Americans by the peculiar institution was far outweighed by the evil of black-white proximity. Throughout his adult life, Dixon would maintain that black and white could not and should not peacefully coexist. The only solution to the "race question" was returning American blacks to Africa.[5]

Outside of his upbringing, Dixon's most formative experience was his ministry in turn-of-the-century New York City, where he embraced Social Gospel Christianity. Attracted to the metropolis because it offered him a wide audience, he was appalled by urban poverty, overcrowding, and squalor. New York presented a host of temptations for young men, and Dixon came to believe that only radical reform could transform the city and help the masses. The tenets of the Social Gospel remained central to Dixon's worldview long after he left the ministry; he continued to sermonize in lectures and novels against the evils he first encountered in New York.

For those in the Social Gospel movement, one served God by serving humankind—their bodies as well as souls.[6] For Dixon, one *came to know* God intimately through romantic love. Dixon sacralized romantic love between white men and women, linking experience of the divine with the feelings of attachment to a lover or spouse. Once a man and woman had a child together, God bonded them together forever in a mystical and physical union that could not be dissolved except at great peril to the soul. Woman inspired the loftiest and most admirable in man and could redeem him. Dixon's dedication of his first book reads like a summary of many of his views: "Dedicated To My Wife, In whose dear person the day-dreams and ideals of my boyhood live as the sweetest realities of manhood, the inspiration of whose love, as the voice of God, CALLED ME from the valley of the world's ambitions to the heights of nobler aims, unto her, with tenderest love, this book I bring, a sheaf from the first fruits of that better life."[7] As a Social Gospeler, Dixon came to argue that "politics . . . is but religion in action."[8] His writings indicate that he saw romantic love as religion in practice.

Dixon's interest in Social Gospel Christianity dates at least as early as his ministry in New York City and is, on its surface, difficult to reconcile with his virulent racism. As a pastor there from 1889 to 1899, Dixon could scarcely avoid the problems of the city.[9] He came to New York from Boston, where his attacks on the Catholic influence over public schools garnered him modest acclaim.[10] In less than a year after his arrival in New York, Dixon's congregations at the Twenty-Third Street Baptist Church were so large that Sunday services were moved to the Young Men's Christian Association Hall.[11] By September of 1890, the *New York Times* referred to him as "one of the most eloquent of New-York pulpit orators."[12]

Dixon initially won sustained notice in the press by his persistent attacks on the corruption of Tammany Hall.[13] The first glimmerings of Dixon's Progressivism seem to date from his growing involvement in anti-Tammany reform groups.[14] Like many other ministers of the era, Dixon came to believe that the churches were losing their relevance and influence in the modern city. In an 1890 sermon, he contrasted the typical clergyman, who was "somewhere writing an essay on the number of feathers in the angel Gabriel's wings" with the newspaper editor, who "exposed corruption in high places."[15] Soon thereafter, he made it a practice to give a brief prelude on a pertinent issue of the day before Sunday morning services. Topics he addressed included "Who Is Responsible for Tammany's Misrule,"[16] "The Future of Tammany,"[17] "Shall We Have Free Rum?"[18] "The Eight-Hour Movement,"[19] "The Saloon and the School,"[20] and "Sectionalism and the Farmer's Alliance."[21] As the mixture of political and moral topics indicates, Dixon was striving to be more like the typical editor than like a theologian.

In these years, Dixon began to develop a religious ideology that would remain, with slight modifications, largely intact. He was only twenty-five when he took over the New York pastorate, and his decade preaching in the city profoundly influenced him. His gradual abandonment of doctrinal nuance is evident in the titles of sermons he gave in these years: "Our Churchless Millions," "The City's Heathen," "Dead Preachers," "Dead Theology," and "Dead Churches."[22] In 1895, Dixon resigned from Twenty-Third Street

Baptist and left the church of his father to found a nondenominational "People's Church" because he believed it was time to "insist upon the non-essentiality to true religion of all forms, ceremonies, rituals, places, paper creeds, and Church officialism." His mission was to the "non-churchgoing masses" and to promote the idea that "politics is religion in action."[23]

Free from his "denominational baggage," as he termed it, Dixon fully embraced the Social Gospel and its concerns. He condemned both prostitution and the theater.[24] Dixon called the saloon "a wild beast, that still prowls with blood-stained claws and teeth along the highways. . . . It has no mission save to murder and destroy that which is good, true, and beautiful in our life."[25] In typical Progressive fashion, he urged "the reigning sovereign of polite society," by which he meant woman, to exhort against drinking "in the parlor and the dining room," and "especially . . . at the marriage altar" (*LP* 172). Young girls who would never knowingly marry a criminal would marry a good-looking drunkard "to reform him. O climax of idiocy!" (*LP* 172). He declaimed against gambling, and included stock-market trading as one form of this sin (*LP* 38). Profoundly disturbed by greed and monopoly, Dixon often invoked the maxim that "a man cannot serve God and Mammon" (*LP* 130). He liked to shock by noting that there was one family on Fifth Avenue whose wealth was "greater than the entire valuation of the State of North Carolina."[26]

Echoing Jacob Riis and other Progressive authors, Dixon drew dismal pictures of poverty in New York. "The poor," he wrote, "are . . . crowded in dark and dingy tenements . . . until it seems as if the filthy foundations of the buildings would groan at the burden of the woe they bear" (*FP* 24). He bemoaned the problem of homelessness, the "army of 50,000 that do not know where they will lay their heads to night" (*FP* 32). In his quest for solutions, Dixon flirted for a brief time with ideas he would later identify as socialist.[27] In *The Failure of Protestantism in New York,* for example, he declared: "A man is certainly entitled to existence. He is entitled to enough clothes to keep him from freezing. He is entitled to a house to cover his head, and he has a right to work" (*FP* 29).

Two urban problems that especially concerned Dixon bear on the central themes of this essay: the plight of working women and the feminization of Protestant churches. That women would work for wages at all bothered Dixon. As one of his characters would put it later, "I don't believe that God ever meant us for work when He made us women. He made us women for something more wonderful."[28] The only positive portrayals of working women in Dixon's writings are of women with careers in teaching, journalism, or the arts who abandon them once married. Yet his concern for New York's working women was inspired by the horror of their situation as much as by his views about woman's place. As "the mother of civilization," if woman were degraded, then, Dixon argued, "life is degraded" (*FP* 30). Too many of the working women in New York (he gave the number of 250,000 in 1896) were employed in low-skilled jobs, none of which "paid a just return for their labor" (*FP* 30). Needlewomen earned a paltry seven cents for each pair of pants they made, this at sewing machines they provided and tended fourteen hours a day. Their "life," said the preacher, "is being ground out at a pace that makes the thing little short of murder" (*FP* 31). Others worked sixteen hours a day "unrelieved by a single gleam of light or hope or cheer" for $3.50 a week, "half of which goes to pay rent" (*FP* 30). "Many of the women who work in this underworld of horror," he warned, "are dying to hope" (*FP* 31).

The fact that Protestant churches were composed mostly of women in Progressive-era America was deemed a problem by many preachers of the day. Dixon loved to recall his first Sunday at the Twenty-Third Street Baptist Church in New York. The building could seat between fifteen hundred and sixteen hundred persons, yet only eighty showed up that Sabbath, and those were "prim elderly women and a few fidgety old men."[29] Why were young men staying away? The churches themselves were to blame. New York Protestantism catered to the bourgeoisie and disdained workingmen. Preachers were obsessed with "dead theologies" (*FP* 58). Men thus "leave [religion] to the women and children and go about the more serious work of life—that life whose activities involve the progress of the human race, that life of reality in which deeds are the only creeds worthy of notice" (*FP* 59). To attract men, Protestantism must be radical. It must invite in the "unwashed, abandoned people" and be a "social power" instead of preaching a "merely individual gospel." Men would come hear a "vital gospel": one that touched on business, labor, capital, and politics (*FP* 124–25).

Dixon's analysis echoed that of other Social Gospel ministers, who in turn were influenced by larger cultural anxieties about masculinity.[30] Intellectuals and political leaders alike worried that men were becoming overcivilized and effeminate. The era was one that witnessed Teddy Roosevelt's call for a "strenuous life" for American men and the nation; America needed men with "those virile qualities necessary to win in the stern strife of actual life."[31] In an effort to attract men to Christianity, Social Gospelers such as Walter Rauschenbusch depicted Jesus as a "man's man" with nothing "mushy, nothing sweetly effeminate" about him.[32] Dixon likewise protested those who saw only one aspect of Jesus's character: "He is gentle, He is loving, He is tender, He weeps, and yet deliberately makes a scourge of cords and with physical violence drives from the Temple those who were desecrating his Father's house and with physical violence overturns their tables" (*FP* 104). Christians must remember, Dixon concluded, that "[t]here is an hour for Christianity to wield the lash and use the knife" (*FP* 104).

In keeping with Social Gospel ministers' desire to reclaim Christianity for virile men, Dixon presented himself as a manly warrior. He spoke of his battles with corruption and vice in New York as if they were duels, several times, for example, stressing that "from the Devil I ask no quarter nor do I give him any."[33] Historian Anthony Rotundo identifies a "growing sense of opposition between action and thought" in the late nineteenth century, with the former being perceived as masculine and the latter as feminine.[34] Dixon's self-presentation as heroic and his stress on "deeds," not "creeds," exemplifies this trend. By offering the men of New York a way to translate piety into social and political reform, he promoted Christianity as a dynamic force for change in modern life and thus an acceptable outlet for manly men. Women had stifled social activism in churches, Dixon argued: "the feminine temperament is essentially conservative. Woman is the conservator of the race. All radicalism is essentially masculine, all conservation essentially feminine" (*FP* 119). Christian warfare and social reform were the work of men. Once, when Dixon publicly debated the issue of woman suffrage, he argued that women were not "physically strong enough to take part in life's battles, and are not strong enough to stand the strain of voting."[35] Though he would come to modify his views of women's weakness later on, he continued to insist that men be forceful, active, and heroic in righteous causes.

Yet Dixon avoided the extremes of the Muscular Christianity movement. When he organized the People's Church, he announced that half of the members of the Board of Deacons would be women, which the *New*

York Times reported was "loudly applauded by the women present."[36] Most surprising is that in 1896 Dixon opened his pulpit to Dr. Anna Howard Shaw, one of the first women to be ordained to preach in the mainline denominations, and a prominent suffragist and reformer.[37] Dixon's church joined the Liberal Congress of Religion, which included several churches with women pastors.[38] Women's church and volunteer work would feature positively in many of his novels. For Dixon, the problem was not the presence of women, but the absence of men and the failure of churches to advocate radical reform.

Social Gospel concerns and gender relations among whites would surface time and again in Dixon's novels. Although the plot of *The Clansman* is well known, Dixon's other novels are far less so. It is thus useful to explore in depth some of these novels before returning to how they bear on his racial views. In *The One Woman*, an idealistic pastor, Frank Gordon, "champion of the people" and "friend of the weak,"[39] dreams of building a "temple . . . of Christian Democracy . . . that would flash its glory from the sky above the sordid materialism that is crushing the lives and hearts of men" (*OW* 15). Pastor Gordon alienates "one of the richest men" in his congregation by preaching in support of the women shirt-makers' strike. When a deacon tells him that this rich man has left the church, Gordon, like the real-life Dixon before him, is defiant: "Yes; I saw him jump up and go out during the service. The women were making shirts for his house at thirty-five cents a dozen, finding their own thread and using their own machines. I said if I found one of those shirts in my house I'd put it in the fire with a pair of tongs, and I would. I'd be afraid to touch a seam lest I felt the throb of a woman's bruised fingers in it" (*OW* 46).[40] Gordon and a beautiful parishioner, Kate Ransom, organize kindergartens, a night school to teach girls "domestic science," and a reading room. To help working men and women find wholesome places to eat, they establish a coffeehouse and a free lunch counter (*OW* 101). All of these efforts put Gordon and his ministry squarely within the urban Social Gospel tradition.

Yet Gordon is drawn to Christian Socialism as he watches a mayor who ran on a reform platform become as corrupt as the politicians who preceded him. In despair, Gordon concludes that "Greed, commercialism, competition and the monopolistic instincts are the cause of all this crime and misery and confusion" (*OW* 103). The first voice of caution in the novel is that of Gordon's friend, Mark Overman, a Wall Street banker and multimillionaire. "Socialism takes the temper out of the steel fiber of character" and "makes a man flabby," Overman warns (*OW* 33). Worst of all, "Socialism will destroy the monogamic family" (*OW* 35). "Destroy the integrity of the family and the salt of the earth is lost," he predicts. "The whole thing will rot" (*OW* 167). Overman proves right. Gordon decides to leave his wife (and the mother of his two children) for Kate Ransom and an open marriage, for "Love bound by chains is not love at all" (*OW* 185). Gordon's father rushes to New York to dissuade his son from abandoning "The One Woman God had meant for the mother of your children." In a message that would resurface many times in Dixon's novels, Gordon's father reminds his son that "the man and woman whom God hath made one in the beat of a child's heart cannot get hopelessly apart" (*OW* 192). The family, Gordon's father argues, is "the basis of civilisation itself. To destroy it is to return to the beast of the field" (*OW* 194).

Gordon's first wife, Ruth, refuses to remarry and continues to wait for her one true love to come to his senses and return to her. Ruth's love is pure: "a love that suffereth long and is kind, vaunteth not itself, is not puffed up, seeketh not its own, believeth all things, endureth all things—[a] love that never faileth" (*OW* 142). Echoing Gordon's father, Ruth tells her wandering man that "our very flesh became one in Nature's miracle of love," their first child (*OW* 153). Even when Ruth is pursued by an old flame, who becomes the governor of New York State, she waits for Frank to return. Ruth believes that "What God hath joined together man cannot put asunder" (*OW* 260).[41]

Gordon's Temple of Man becomes a secular church for radicals of all stripes, who soon begin bickering among themselves. Kate Ransom falls in love with the Wall Street banker Overman. Pastor Gordon, in an animalistic rage, refuses to let Kate leave him. As was predicted by his father, once the family is destroyed, man becomes a beast. Gordon, before attacking Overman, shouts: "I feel throbbing in my veins to-day the blood of a thousand savage ancestors who made love to their women with a club and dragged them to their caves by the hair—yes, and more, the beat of impulses that surged there with wild power before man became a man" (*OW* 302). Frank brutally kills Overman with his bare hands.

Ruth stands by Frank as he is tried, convicted of murder, and sentenced to death. Like her Old Testament namesake, she is selflessly loyal. She visits him every day in prison, trying to comfort him and keep his spirits up. After Frank loses his appeal, Ruth throws herself at the governor's feet (we should recall that he is conveniently in unrequited love with her) and begs shamelessly for the life of her former husband. The governor cannot deny Ruth her wish, and after pardoning Frank, he arranges for the two to remarry. The governor declares, in awe of Ruth's faithfulness: "In the presence of a love so pure, so divine as that which hallows your life, I uncover my head. I am on holy ground—I am in the presence of the living God" (*OW* 349). Dixon would continue, in his fiction, to stress that white romantic love was sacred.

This novel sold ninety thousand copies within five months of its release.[42] The fact that it is Dixon's *second* work of fiction ought to give us pause. Dixon wrote nine novels in which race was never or rarely mentioned. With the exception of his three fictional biographies (of Abraham Lincoln, Jefferson Davis, and Robert E. Lee), his novels have white heterosexual love and families as a central element to their plots.[43] In many of his works, white gender and family relations are the *sole* theme. Dixon loved to boast that he did not write for the critics and did not attempt to write "Literature." "I never write a book unless I have something to say," he told the readers of the *New York Times Book Review*.[44] In his autobiography, he was more direct: "My sole purpose in writing was to reach and influence with my argument the mind of millions. I had a message and wrote it as vividly and simple as I know how."[45] Dixon was, it seems, as determined to deliver messages about white gender relations as he was about relations between the races. As we will see, these two foci of his writing intersect in crucial and insidious ways.

In *The Foolish Virgin,* published in 1915, the heroine, Mary Adams, is an old-fashioned young woman who believes God made women for "something more wonderful" than the world of work.[46] Mary's ideal is to find her Knight and be a wife and mother. As she looks down on the crowds of Manhattan, she believes that "[s]omewhere among its myriads of tramping feet, walked the one man created for her. She no more doubted this than she doubted God himself. It was His law. He had ordained it so" (*FV* 14). Although not fond of "dish-washing and pot-polishing and scrubbing," Mary undertakes her tasks cheerfully, for such was the price women paid for their ideal home (*FV* 20). For Mary, men and women were complementary, not equal. In men is "the strength which lifts and tugs and fights the elements." In woman are "the finer qualities of the Spirit turned toward the source of all spirit in God" (*FV* 29).

Then, at the New York Public Library, Mary meets Jim Anthony, with whom she falls in love at first sight. Even though he uses vulgar expressions like "Gee," "shucks," and "Kiddo," her "surrender was too sudden to realize that she was being driven by a power that obscured reason and crushed her will" (*FV* 62). In their first kiss, "[h]er whole being, body and soul, responded to his" (*FV* 84). She was sure it was love, for she had heard "the voice of God" (*FV* 85). In Mary's beliefs, "marriage is a holy sacrament" that binds forever (*FV* 102), and Mary insists that Jim is "the one man God made for me of all men on earth" (*FV* 142). They get married, with Jim ominously chuckling at the phrase "Until death do us part!" (*FV* 154).

They head South for their honeymoon, and the closer they get to the North Carolina mountains, the more coarse and menacing Jim becomes. Jim takes her to an ugly shack, the home of Nance Owens, whom he reveals to be his mother. Here Mary also learns that Jim is a drunkard and a robber and that he had murdered a neighbor of hers during a burglary. When Mary tries to leave, the "beast" inside Jim is unleashed, and he chokes her until she passes out (*FV* 253).

Dixon gives Jim a history that explains his criminality and is a direct descendant of his Social Gospel sermons. Jim's "drunken brute of a daddy" was a bigamist (*FV* 247). When Nance threw her husband out, he kidnapped Jim to spite her. Jim's father was a vicious man. He stuck pins in his son and once "pushed a live cigar agin his little neck" until it burned the flesh and left a scar (*FV* 248). Jim's dad then took him to New York, and Jim's first memory is of "hidin' under a stoop from a brute who beat me every night" (*FV* 79). Jim ran away and slept on the streets like a "stray dog" (*FV* 306). To add insult to injury, as a young adult Jim sees an invention of his stolen by two lawyers who become millionaires from it. And all around him are examples of sin. Wall Street has taught him that money is "the god that knows no right or wrong." The only "god in this world now," Jim admits, is the "Almighty Dollar!" "A burglar kills but one to get his pile, and then only because he must, in self-defence. A big gambling capitalist corners wheat, raises the price of bread and starves a hundred thousand children to death to make his," he adds. "Steal a hundred dollars, you go to the penitentiary," he tells Nance, but "Steal a million and go to the Senate!" (*FV* 252–53).

Mary is rescued when Nance Owen (unaware Jim is her son) tries to kill Jim and take the money he had stolen. A doctor whisks Mary, who collapses of "brain fever," off to recover (*FV* 302). Alas, Mary discovers she is pregnant, and she is terrified that she will give birth to a criminal. The wise doctor calms her down by pointing out that "the part the male plays in the reproduction of the race is small," for his job is merely to announce the "arrival of the queen," the mother.[47] Mary is the sole influence on the child, for "Almighty God can speak His message only through you" (*FV* 313). She has a "divine opportunity," for "nine-tenths of the spiritual traits out of which character is formed are the work of the mother," the doctor tells her (*FV* 315). As Mother, Woman is the ruler of the world and "the redemption of humanity" (*FV* 317). Mary's mistake was privileging physical attraction. The sanctity of marriage is based on more than "the violence of the passion of love" (*FV* 339); "marriage binds for life" because husband and wife are united in the child. "It was *your* business to *know* [Jim's true character]," the doctor tells Mary, "before you made him the father of your child" (*FV* 344).

Meanwhile, Jim, deeply regretful, has decided to win Mary back. He is "born again" as a Christian (*FV* 323) and develops a work ethic. In the beauty of the Carolina mountains this "transplanted child of the slums" grows into a "sturdy manhood" (*FV* 326). He atones for his crimes and decides to make Mary and the baby a home. He studies under an Asheville craftsman and makes every nail, hinge, board, table, and cabinet himself. Making furniture is a peculiarly western North Carolina form of redemption (*FV* 333). Yet it works. Mary takes him back and the family is reunited.

The Fall of a Nation, published in 1916, was a plea for the United States to build a strong defense as well as a commentary on current events. Though Dixon billed it as a sequel to *Birth of a Nation*, this novel is not about race or Reconstruction. Yet it is clear that Dixon felt his message in *Fall of a Nation* was urgent and needed. When planning the movie version, which he directed and produced, Dixon wrote Woodrow Wilson, no doubt hoping to obtain the president's imprimatur on the "sequel" as he had done with *Birth*. Wilson tried to discourage Dixon, claiming that the nation was "already soberly and earnestly aware of its possible perils and duties." The president deplored the idea of "excitement stirred up in so grave a matter."[48] Dixon forged ahead, securing the esteemed composer Victor Herbert to write the first original score for a motion picture. The film was only moderately successful, but Dixon's various efforts on the story's behalf show how important he considered it.

The fantastical plot of *Fall of a Nation* centers on Virginia Holland, a suffragist whose cause is funded by a Wall Street billionaire, Charles Waldron. Little does Holland realize that the reason Waldron supports woman suffrage is that he wants the United States to remain militarily weak; "hysterical women[,] utterly unfitted for [the] responsibilities"[49] of the ballot, are pacifists who will vote against military appropriations, allowing Waldron and his evil compatriots to take over the country. Dixon's hero, Congressman John Vassar, adamantly favors the build-up of the armed forces and proposes a bill to strengthen the navy as the novel opens. Vassar is, unlike most of Dixon's protagonists, not from the South but an immigrant from Poland. Vassar's father fled imperial repression in Eastern Europe and escaped with his five-year-old son, John, to the Promised Land.

Ostensible opposites attract, and Vassar falls for Holland, who, he is surprised to learn, is not an "ugly, disappointed, soured" woman (*FN* 62). Yet her charm makes woman suffrage that much more appalling, for "the man who desires a woman will sell principle, country, right, God, for his desire" (*FN* 75). "The government of a democracy was a difficult task under present conditions," Vassar maintains. "What would it become when the decision on which the mightiest issues hung could be decided by the smile of a woman's lips or the dimple in her cheek?" (*FN* 75–76). The congressman warns Holland of the "sinister significance" of her beauty in the political arena: "You take my judgment by storm because you're charming. You stop the process of reasoning by merely lifting your eyes to mine. Such a power cannot be used to further the ends of justice or perfect the organization of society. The power you wield defies all law" (*FN* 79). Holland is unconvinced by his arguments and refuses his courtship unless he admits her to be his equal. Vassar cannot lie, even to win the woman he loves.

Women get the vote and promptly kill Vassar's military appropriations bill. Soon America is overrun by foreign imperial troops who answer to a "federation of crowned heads of Northern and Central Europe" (*FN* 202). Waldron becomes the Governor-General of the Provinces of North America. The occupiers close schools, churches, and saloons; they suspend the bill of rights; they ban all newspapers; anyone caught with a weapon is executed. Holland realizes the error of her ways; she had been too "proud to surrender"—surrender is the word Dixon always used for women in love[50]—her "will and mind, my body and soul to any man" (*FN* 259). She pledges her love to Vassar and resolves to do her part in helping redeem America. "I have betrayed my country by folly beyond God's forgiveness," she cries, "I shall do my part now to retrieve that error" (*FN* 308).

To atone for her "folly," Holland organizes a million American women into a secret group called the Daughters of Jael, named after the Old Testament heroine. In Judges, Jael lures the commanding general of the army oppressing the Israelites into her tent, feeds him milk, and then, while he sleeps, hammers a tent spike through his head, killing him. Dixon's Daughters of Jael train to wield machetes with eight-inch blades. They are tasked to win over key enemy soldiers in the imperial army. Those who will not defect are to be plied with alcohol or killed when the coup begins. Although some of the Daughters would have to sacrifice their "honor" and seduce the enemy, "risking what we hold more precious than life," American women, who had brought this takeover on themselves, would be redeemed in this sacrifice (*FN* 339). America's heroic men, who have been training and arming themselves in the West, were to swoop in after the Daughters and conquer the last enemy soldiers. After a bloody battle, America is once again a democracy. Congress quickly builds up the military.

In 1919, Dixon published *The Way of a Man: A Story of the New Woman*. In this book, the enemy is solely feminism, not socialism or foreign empires. The "New Woman" of the tale, Ellen West, believes that the "woman movement," to succeed, "must destroy the family . . . . and replace it with the free individual." In lieu of "legal and sacerdotal marriage" would be "a free alliance,"[51] since marriage is economic slavery and "the death of personality" to women (*WM* 86). Ellen falls in love with Ralph Manning, a southern gentleman who believes in the traditional family. She cannot bring herself to "surrender," yet it is true love, for "[s]he felt the [same] strange elation which swept her heart in her first emotional experiences in the religion of her childhood." She stops to ponder how the "impulse of love and the religious instinct" are so similar (*WM* 59). To Ralph, she is a goddess, and "home is the temple in which" he hopes "to build the high altar of this religion" (*WM* 91–92).

Ellen seduces Ralph, and he becomes trapped in a no-strings relationship with her even though he desperately wants "a home and babies" (*WM* 231). And Ellen finds that without a wedding ring, women see Ralph as fair game, which makes her insanely jealous. Just as Ralph is about to leave her, Ellen's niece, Rose O'Neil, comes into the picture. Looking eerily like a young Ellen, Rose has one goal in life: to marry and have a huge family. Rose's "whole personality radiated faith, worship, tenderness, and the spirit of self-effacement," the opposite of Ellen's (*WM* 230). Ralph falls in love with the niece but is too honorable to pursue her. At the last moment, Ellen renounces her creed and agrees with "a woman's complete merging in the life of her mate" (*WM* 265). But it is too late. Ralph no longer loves her. In an act of sacrifice, Ellen arranges for Ralph to marry her niece.

The morals and themes in Dixon's novels are half Social Gospel theology and half his unique gender ideology.[52] Every one of Dixon's white villains is a drinker. The city's greed and heartlessness make brutes of men. City governments are so corrupt that ordinary men lose hope in fairness and justice. Despite the depths of evil into which white men sink, they are capable of redemption.[53] Marriage is holy, as is woman's surrender to a deserving man. Once a man and woman conceive a child, they are forever bound together by God. Woman is the queen of the universe, the most important person in the family, yet her role is as mother and homemaker. Women who step out of their place, such as the pacifist suffragists or the feminist who eschews marriage, will have to suffer and atone for their folly. Women are strong of will and body, but they too often fall prey to their lust. Romantic love is holy. Falling in love is like converting to Christianity.

Scholars have noted that Dixon idolizes white women; Joel Williamson astutely observes that Dixon viewed them as "goddesses."[54] Yet it is just as true that he idolizes—even *fetishizes*—white romantic love. Dixon's race novels repeat these themes. His first-ever fictional hero, Charles Gaston of *The Leopard's Spots*, embodies both of these notions. To Charles, women are "divine"[55]; "If I ever saw the face of God it was in my mother's face," he confesses. Yet for Charles, love is equally divine. "He had never spoken a word of shallow love-making to a woman in his life," the narrator says of him.

"To him love was too holy a mystery. It would have been the blasphemy of the Holy Ghost—a sin that would not be forgiven in this world or the world to come" (*LS* 235). When courting Sallie Worth, Charles reveals that "One chamber of my soul has always been sacred. It was the throne room of Love, reserved for the One Woman waiting for me somewhere whom I should find" (*LS* 274). After professing his passion to Sallie, he returns to his room to pray, for "Love the great Revealer had led him into the presence of God" (*LS* 277). Dixon often uses religious language to describe romantic love. His hero in *The Black Hood*, to cite an example, views love as "the mysterious force that could make anew the impulses of the soul. It had gotten him. He had been born again."[56] Or consider Nan Primrose in *The Root of Evil*. Nan rejects Jim Stuart, the man she loves, to marry a millionaire she has no affection for. Jim agonizes about the wedding, calling it an "act of blasphemy" because it was "stripped of the sanctity of love."[57] His faith in love was so bound up with his faith in God that Nan's betrayal forces him to fight "to hold the last shred of his faith in anything human or divine!"[58]

Where Dixon's racism and his gender ideology overlap in the keenest way is in his depiction of black gender relations as irredeemably disordered. It is useful to return once more to Dixon's ministry in New York and the height of his commitment to the Social Gospel. Dixon attacked Tammany Hall, he harangued against the exploitation of immigrant labor, he bemoaned the lure of the saloon, and he condemned churches for neglecting the poor. But it is clear that Dixon's Social Gospel, his Progressivism, was for whites only. Dixon never seemed to *see* black New Yorkers, an elision all the more striking when we recall that the Twenty-Third Street Baptist Church was situated on the very edge of New York's Tenderloin District, an area full of African American clubs, dance halls, and residences.[59] The few mentions of African Americans in Dixon's published Social Gospel sermons came when he discussed the "Southern Question."[60] Jacob Riis's expose of New York's "other half" included a chapter on blacks in New York, but to Pastor Dixon, they were invisible or beneath notice.[61] Until he turned South. Dixon had a great deal to say about southern blacks.

The most obvious problem Dixon claimed to see in black gender relations is apparent in his depiction of the black male as the bestial rapist of white women. Although he condemned the second and subsequent Klans for their lawlessness and for their persecution of Catholics, Jews, and even innocent blacks, he continued to see the first Klan as righteously heroic, never abandoning his belief that black men lusted after white women and that lynching was a justified response.[62] The most famous such scene in Dixon's fiction climaxes with Marion Lenoir and her mother jumping to their deaths from *The Clansman*'s Lover's Leap because they had been "ruined" by black men. *The Leopard's Spots* has not one but two such rapes, both of which happen to fair-haired daughters of Tom Camp, a one-legged Confederate veteran and Dixon's counterpart and answer to the other long-suffering Tom, Uncle Tom. Dixon's last novel, *The Flaming Sword*, has a graphic and indeed pornographic black-on-white rape scene in it, followed by a horrific depiction of the rapist's lynching.

But there are other scenes and tropes in Dixon's race novels that are equally disturbing. In Dixon's fiction, black women are all workers. They cook, clean, and care for the children in white households. Despite the fact that their labor is grueling, monotonous, and performed to relieve white women of the hardest domestic labor, Dixon has no sympathy for them. Black maids and cooks, when they are not serving Dixon's white families, are presented as comic buffoons. Dixon deplored women working for wages when those women were white. Black women do not count, for Dixon, *as women*. Black men fare no better. Recall that Nelse, of *The Leopard's Spots*, is identified as "a black hero of the old regime" and is the loyal slave of Old South mythology (*LS* x). How much more significant, then, is the fact that the black character Dixon created to be most sympathetic was regularly beaten by his wife and thus emasculated. Eve has pulled his hair out, hit him over the head with a biscuit board, made him lame by hitting his leg with a fire shovel, and whacked him with a flatiron. This same novel purports to show that black women have no maternal instinct. One freedwoman, in the midst of a "drunken orgie [*sic*] with dissolute companions," "knocked" her unwanted son "in the head and burned the body" (*LS* 93). Dixon's counterpart to Harriet Beecher Stowe's Topsy, Dick, was beaten and abandoned as a boy. Rather than being reformed, as Topsy is, Dick becomes more savage; it is he who rapes Tom Camp's second fair-haired child (*LS* chapter 5).

Dixon links these disordered gender relations to the supposed deterioration of African American religion in the postwar period, which he dates to the beginning of the black separation from white-controlled churches.

"In the old slavery days," his white preacher tells the freedmen, "you were taught the religion of Christ. It didn't mean crime, and lust, and lying, and drinking.... Your religion has come to be a stench" (*LS* 308). In slavery times, the white preachers spoke to "many men of character, carpenters, bricklayers, wheelwrights, farmers, faithful home servants that loved their masters and were faithful unto death." After emancipation, there were only "thieves and jailbirds and trifling women" in black churches (*LS* 308).

Dixon brings all of these notions together in Julius: a black character who appears in both *The Traitor* (his third Reconstruction novel) and *The Black Hood*. After emancipation, Julius takes the name of Julius A. Postle and preaches social and political equality to his audience. Julius lives with the two-hundred-pound Laura, who before the war was Henry's wife. Henry, the only black loyal to his former master in the novel, had been beaten up by Julius, which convinced Laura to dump him for the preacher. The only way for Henry to win her back is to beat Julius worse than Julius had beaten him.[63]

Julius and Laura routinely fight. Laura suspects Julius of cheating on her with the Methodist sisters he converts at his meetings. Julius determines to cast the devil out of his woman, even if by force. In one lengthy scene that Dixon intended as comic relief, Julius starts by whipping Laura with a hickory switch. Not to be outdone, Laura hurls an iron at Julius, but misses. Julius "whipped her around the room, threw her down, grasped her by the hair and banged her head against the floor" (*BH* 99). Henry happens upon this scene and comes to Laura's rescue. Yet Laura defends the man who beats her and tries to strangle her rescuer. A later chapter, sarcastically entitled "The Course of True Love," is also presented as comic relief. While the white characters in the novel are equating true love with salvation and holiness, the black characters continue to pervert gender relations. Henry lies, telling Laura that he has killed Julius, who earlier had skipped town. Before the Apostle died, Henry says, he sputtered "Ye kin have ole Laura. She ain't no count nohow—" (*BH* 286). At that moment, however, Julius appears in the doorway, a hatchet in one hand and a headless chicken in the other. Henry flees and none of these characters appear in the novel again. There is no resolution. Just change the names of everyone but Julius A. Postle and we have the same scenario in *The Traitor*.

A novel that bridges Dixon's interests in race and romantic love is *The Sins of the Father*, published in 1912, his singular effort to deal in depth with miscegenation between white men and black women. His hero, Major Norton, Confederate veteran, Klansman, newspaper editor, and rabid segregationist, has an affair with a seductive and conniving octoroon named Cleo, who has finagled her way into working as nurse for Norton's son. In Dixon's universe Norton is not to blame; as a friend tells him, "with that young animal [Cleo] playing at your feet in physical touch with your soul and body in the intimacies of your home, you never had a chance."[64] Even Norton's mother-in-law holds him innocent; she, too, believes that the proximity of black and white, coupled with the absolute power masters historically held over black women, made such affairs inevitable (SF 136). Norton begs his wife's forgiveness and stresses that "there's a difference as deep as the gulf between heaven and hell, in the divine love that binds my body and soul and life to you" and his momentary surrender to the Beast within (SF 155).

Years later, Norton is led to believe that his daughter with Cleo, Helen, has fallen in love with his white son, Tom, and that the two want to marry. Unwilling to reveal to Tom that Helen is his half-sister, the Major first tries to dissuade Tom from marrying a "negress." "Marriage is not merely a question of personal whim, impulse or passion," he tells Tom. "It's the one divine law on which human society rests" (SF 403). Yet Tom is willing to suffer degradation until his father reveals all. The Major shoots Tom and then himself. Miraculously, Tom lives, and he discovers that Helen was not his half-sister or a "negress," after all. Tom takes on his father's cause—the colonization of freedpeople in Africa—and refuses to let blacks "cross the threshold or enter [the] gates" of his ancestral home (SF 462).

Although Cleo already represents a dire threat to white marriage in the novel, Dixon still throws in scenes that ridicule black romantic love. There are three blacks in the Norton household workforce: Cleo, Andy, and Minerva. Minerva, the cook and housekeeper, is the counterpoint to the seductive and beautiful Cleo; her skin color is dark black (for Dixon, "coal-black" and "shining"), and she weighs two hundred and fifty pounds (SF 279).[65] Andy, a former slave of the family, is the lazy, cowardly, thieving, yet congenial butler. Andy decides he wants to marry Cleo, but Minerva has an eye for him. He confides in Tom Norton that he has a crush on Cleo and tries to enlist Tom's help. Tom at first is confused and assumes Andy wants to court Minerva. Andy is horrified at the idea: "I can't stan' er fat 'oman! . . . Man, ef we wuz walkin' along tergedder, en she wuz ter slip an' fall she'd sqush de life outen me!" Besides, he adds, "I nebber could stan' dese here coal-black niggers. Miss Minerva's so black she kin spit ink!" (SF 270). When Tom points out Andy is black, too, Andy demurs, describing himself as "tantalizin' brown" (SF 270). Cleo is almost white, "an' dat's what make me want her so," Andy confesses (SF 272). Andy has even been bleaching his skin and straightening his hair to become more attractive. Tom advises Andy to tell the truth and ask Minerva's help in his pursuit of Cleo.

Yet Minerva has plans, too; she "had decided that [Andy] was the best man in sight for a husband, and made up her mind to claim her own" (SF 278). As Andy tries to find the words to tell her the truth, Minerva misinterprets his intentions. "Well, des 'spose m'am dat a po' man wuz ter fall in love wid er beautiful lady, fur above him, wid eyes dat shine lak de stars," he begins (SF 282). Minerva giggles, thinking that he is talking of her. Before he can explain, she exclaims: "I sho do admire de indelicate way dat yer tells me of yo' love!" (SF 283). Sputtering and confounded, Andy cannot bring himself to correct her.

Soon, bolstered by mint juleps, Andy resolves to confront Minerva again and confess his love for Cleo. "I'se tangled up wid annuder 'oman!" he blurts out (SF 357). Minerva, in a rage, curses "[d]at yaller Jezebel" for trying to steal her man. Andy takes another tack, calling himself a "bad nigger" who is not worthy to be Minerva's husband (SF 358). But Minerva reminds him that she always knew that she was a cut above him; she loves him regardless. Desperate, Andy tells Minerva that he is a wife beater. "I beat her scandalous," he says of his first wife, "I pay no tenshun to her hollerin!—huh!—de louder she holler, 'pears lak de harder I beat her!" (SF 360). Though Andy claims he hit his ex-wife with an axe handle and a fire shovel, Minerva is delighted. Her first husband lacked the courage to beat her, and she could never respect him as a result. "I'se yo woman an' you'se my man!" she exclaims to Andy (SF 361).

These scenes mocking black love derive their racist potency not simply from their intrinsic bigotry but also from their juxtaposition in the novels with white romance. Many of these purportedly comic chapters come between moments of high drama and tension for the white characters. Thus, in *Sins of the Father*, Minerva and Andy's interactions are placed amid the pathos of the elder Norton's dilemma over his son's love for Helen. In *The Black Hood*, the confrontation between Julius A. Postle and Henry over Laura takes place in the middle of the novel's most angst-ridden scenes between the hero and heroine. Claudia Hawkins, the inamorata, falsely believes that the man she desires, John Craig, killed her father. Yet she cannot prove it. To exact vengeance for her father's murder, she asks John to confess that he had been a Clansman, an admission that would violate the oath of secrecy he made to the Klan and would result in *his* death at the hands of other Clansmen. This dilemma causes John great anguish, for Claudia has made it a test of his love for her that there will be no secrets between them. As John debates whether to choose love over loyalty, the plot is interrupted by the dysfunctional antics of Julius, Henry, and Laura. By shifting from the high drama (and melodrama) of white romantic love to the low comedy (as Dixon presents it) of black attempts at romance, Dixon highlights the racial difference he has constructed. The vulgarity of love manifested as violence is set in sharp contrast to the emotionally poignant and spiritually uplifting meeting of two souls, and, as Dixon intended, his novel's blacks appear even less humane as a result.

In Dixon's fictional and ideologically charged universe, there is no such thing as pure love between African Americans. Blacks have no capacity for the refined sensibility and spiritual elevation that motivate white lovers. Even the blacks Dixon identifies as "good" can express pure love only for their master and his family. Black women's only maternal instinct is for their white charges. After flatly claiming that blacks should not vote or govern, Dixon fondly recalled "memories of the dear old nurse in whose arms the weary head of my childhood so often found rest." He invoked this memory to prove he had only the "kindliest and tenderest feelings for the negro race," but that statement is patently false (*LP* 253). The violence that characterized black gender relations in Dixon's works served his white supremacist and separatist agenda well.

Dixon was not departing from his earlier roots in the Social Gospel movement when he endorsed lynching and racism. His Social Gospel was meant to help whites only. However low a white man had sunk—whether he be a drunken wife beater or an adulterous murderer—he could be redeemed, especially if a pious woman loved him. Throughout his life, Dixon preached—in fiction, on stage and screen, and from the podium—against rampant greed, political corruption, drink, and the exploitation of labor. He was clearly capable of substantive thinking. Recall how he understood that women in the garment trades were caught in a vicious cycle of hopelessness. But when it came to African Americans, Dixon's thinking was always superficial. And his God, evidently, was powerless to redeem them. In Dixon's universe, blacks could only have nightmare relationships where whips and beatings were more common than kisses and courtship. In Dixon's world, whites alone were capable of the finer and holier aspects of human emotion and intimacy. Just as there is more continuity than we have recognized between Dixon's earlier and later careers, Dixon's work also shows how race and gender ideologies can become entangled in both obvious and subtle ways.

NOTES

1. Dixon turned many of these novels into plays and a few into films. *Fall of a Nation*, for example, was turned into a motion picture in 1916. Victor Herbert, who was already known for composing operas and operettas, wrote the musical score for the film, the first ever originally composed for a movie. Herbert's score was "for full orchestra of seventy pieces," and he conducted on the film's opening night (*New York Times*, May 28, 1916, X7, and May 3, 1916, p. 11). Such publicity meant that these works had an impact far beyond the readership of each novel. Dixon's other plays include *The Clansman, The One Woman, The Traitor, Sins of the Father, The Leopard's Spots, Red Dawn, Man of the People,* and *Robert E. Lee,* and his films include *The One Woman* and *The Mark of the Beast*.

2. "Rev. Thos. Dixon Resigns," *New York Times*, March 11, 1895, p. 8.

3. Michael H. Hunt, "Ideology," *Journal of American History* 77 (June 1990): 108–15.

4. "Race relations" is actually imprecise here, as Dixon did not disdain Native Americans or the Chinese and expressly condemned anti-Semitism. When Dixon thought in terms of the "race problem," he thought exclusively in terms of blacks, whites, and (for him the worst horror) mulattoes.

5. In addition to his novels, see his statements in "Atlanta Views on Riots," *New York Times*, September 24, 1906, p. 2, and "Rockefeller a Hero of Romance," *New York Times*, August 10, 1907, p. BR486.

6. Thomas Dixon Jr., *The Failure of Protestantism in New York and Its Causes* (New York: Strauss and Rehn Publishing Co., 1896), 125.

7. Dedication page, Thomas Dixon Jr., *Living Problems in Religion and Social Science* (New York: Charles T. Dillingham, 1889).

8. Dixon, *Failure of Protestantism*, 125.

9. He was pastor of Twenty-Third Street Baptist until 1895, and he resigned from the People's Church in 1899. The biography of Dixon available for the basic facts of his life is Raymond Allen Cook, *Fire from the Flint: The Amazing Careers of Thomas Dixon* (Winston-Salem: Blair, 1968). A more critical view is offered in Joel Williamson, *The Crucible of Race: Black-White Relations in the American South since Emancipation* (New York: Oxford Univ. Press, 1984). For Progressivism and the Social Gospel, see C. Vann Woodward, *Origins of the New South, 1877–1913* (Baton Rouge: Louisiana State Univ. Press, 1971); Dewey Grantham, *Southern Progressivism: The Reconciliation of Progress and Tradition* (Knoxville: Univ. of Tennessee Press, 1983); William Link, *The Paradox of Southern Progressivism, 1880–1930* (Chapel Hill: Univ. of North Carolina Press, 1992); Donald Gorrell, *The Age of Social Responsibility: The Social Gospel in the Progressive Era, 1900–1920* (Macon, Ga.: Mercer Univ. Press, 1988); and Ralph Luker, *The Social Gospel in Black and White: American Racial Reform, 1885–1912* (Chapel Hill: Univ. of North Carolina Press, 1991).

10. See "Other Discourses," *Boston Evening Transcript*, October 8, 1888, p. 7, and "Sects and the Schools," *New York Times*, September 24, 1889, p. 1.

11. "The Rev. Thomas Dixon, Jr., Talks of the Power of the Editor," *New York Times*, June 9, 1890, p. 5.

12. "City and Suburban News," *New York Times*, September 18, 1890, p. 2.

13. For the earliest mention of Dixon's attacks on Tammany, see "The Tammany Incubus," *New York Times*, October 24, 1890, p. 5.

14. For example, Dixon was one of the prominent clergymen involved in the People's Municipal League, which sought to return honesty to the city's politics. "Work or Hire a Substitute," *New York Times*, August 13, 1890, p. 5.

15. "The Rev. Thomas Dixon, Jr., Talks of the Power of the Editor," *New York Times*, June 9, 1890, p. 5.

16. "Religious Notices," *New York Times*, October 11, 1890, p. 6.

17. "Religious Notices," *New York Times*, February 22, 1891, p. 7.

18. "Religious Notices," *New York Times*, March 14, 1891, p. 6.

19. "Religious Notices," *New York Times*, April 25, 1891, p. 6.

20. "Religious Notices," *New York Times*, December 5, 1891, p. 7.

21. "Religious Notices," *New York Times*, December 13, 1890, p. 6.

22. These sermon topics were advertised in the *New York Times* in January and February of 1891.

23. "Rev. Thos. Dixon Resigns," *New York Times*, March 11, 1895, p. 8.

24. Dixon, *Living Problems*, 150, and Dixon, *Failure of Protestantism*, 13.

25. Dixon, *Living Problems*, 179 (hereafter cited in text as *LP*).

26. Dixon, *Failure of Protestantism*, 13 (hereafter cited in text as *FP*). Dixon, like others in this era, used "woman," not "women," as his collective noun for white women as a group. This usage evoked the idea of women as singular and eternally the same.

27. Dixon admitted his early flirtation to a *Times* reporter. See "Rockefeller a Hero of Romance," *New York Times*, August 10, 1907, BR486.

28. Thomas Dixon Jr., *The Foolish Virgin* (New York: D. Appleton and Company, 1915), 6.

29. Dixon, *Failure of Protestantism*, 18; Dixon, "Is Christianity on the Decline?" *New Broadway Magazine* 20 (May 1908): 149–53. Although Dixon never joined his famous brother A. C. in the fundamentalist movement, fundamentalists were nonetheless reacting to perceived feminization, too. See Betty DeBerg, *Ungodly Women: Gender and the First Wave of American Fundamentalism* (Minneapolis: Fortress Press, 1990), and Margaret Bendroth, *Fundamentalism and Gender, 1875 to the Present* (New Haven: Yale Univ. Press, 1993). Billy Sunday was concerned by the absence of men as well. See Roger Bruns, *Preacher: Billy Sunday and Big-Time American Evangelism* (New York: Norton, 1992).

30. For gender and the Social Gospel, see Gail Bederman, "'The Women Have Had Charge of the Church Work Long Enough': The Men and Religion Forward Movement of 1911–12 and the Masculinization of Middle-Class Protestantism," *American Quarterly* 41 (September 1989): 432–65; Clifford Putney, *Muscular Christianity: Manhood and Sports in Protestant America, 1880–1920* (Cambridge: Harvard Univ. Press, 2001); and Susan Curtis, "The Son of Man and God the Father: The Social Gospel and Victorian Masculinity," in *Meanings for Manhood: Constructions of Masculinity in Victorian America*, ed. Mark C. Carnes and Clyde Griffen (Chicago: Univ. of Chicago Press, 1990). For the "crisis" in turn-of-the-century masculinity, see Gail Bederman, *Manliness and Civilization: A Cultural History of Gender and Race in the United States, 1880–1917* (Chicago: Univ. of Chicago Press, 1995); Anthony Rotundo, *American Manhood: Transformations in Masculinity from the Revolution to the Modern Era* (New York: Basic Books, 1993); Peter Filene, *Him/Her/Self: Gender Identities in Modern America*, 3rd ed. (Baltimore: Johns Hopkins Univ. Press, 1998); and John F. Kasson, *Houdini, Tarzan, and the Perfect Man: The White Male Body and the Challenge of Modernity in America* (New York: Hill and Wang, 2001). For a challenge to the traditional view of this era as one in which masculinity was in crisis, see Clyde Griffen, "Reconstructing Masculinity from the Evangelical Revival to the Waning of Progressivism: A Speculative Synthesis," in Carnes and Griffen, eds., *Meanings for Manhood*.

31. Roosevelt, "The Strenuous Life," address to The Hamilton Club, Chicago, Illinois, April 10, 1899, in *Theodore Roosevelt: Letters and Speeches*, ed. Louis Auchincloss (New York: Library of America, 2004), 755–56.

32. Quoted in Putney, *Muscular Christianity*, 42.

33. "Preacher Dixon Defiant," June 6, 1892, p., 9; "Preacher Dixon Rampant," June 27, 1892, p. 8; and "Dr. Potter and Mr. Dixon," December 13, 1892, p. 8, all in the *New York Times*.

34. Rotundo, *American Manhood*, 224.

35. "Mrs. Gougar Mr. Dixon's Equal," *New York Times*, July 13, 1896, p. 8.

36. "Dixon's Church the People's," *New York Times*, March 18, 1895, p. 2.

37. See the display ad in the *New York Times*, November 28, 1896, p. 7.

38. Dixon's magazine ran an ad for the Liberal Congress in each issue. See *Dixon's Sermons: A Monthly Magazine* (F. L. Bussey: New York, 1898).

39. Thomas Dixon Jr., *The One Woman: A Story of Modern Utopia* (New York: Grosset and Dunlap, 1903), 5 (hereafter cited in text as *OW*).

40. The most famous strike by shirtwaist makers took place in 1909, but union organizing and strikes had been going on for years before the massive strike of 1909.

41. See also Ruth's thought that "The sense of motherhood, the feeling of kinship to all women, brings to me again the certainty that I am right, that one great love unto death can alone give the soul peace and strength, and give to man and the world happiness" (*OW*, 262–63).

42. "Books That Sell Well," *New York Times*, December 12, 1903, BR19.

43. As some reviewers noted at the time, Dixon occasionally throws in a romance that is not relevant to his plot, as he does in his fictional "biography" of Lincoln, *The Southerner: A Romance of the Real Lincoln* (New York: Grosset and Dunlap, 1913).

44. Dixon's letter to the editor appears on February 25, 1905, in *New York Times Book Review*, 118.

45. Quoted in Cook, *Fire from the Flint*, 199.

46. Dixon, *Foolish Virgin*, 6 (hereafter cited in text as *FV*).

47. Mary cannot leave Jim, as marriage is forever to her. Nor is suicide an option to her "pious mind" (272). Dixon, *Foolish Virgin*, 312–13.

48. Arthur S. Link et al., eds., *The Papers of Woodrow Wilson*, vol. 34 (Princeton: Princeton Univ. Press, 1980), 426–27.

49. Thomas Dixon Jr., *The Fall of a Nation: A Sequel to The Birth of a Nation* (Chicago: M. A. Donohue and Company, 1916), 19 (hereafter cited in text as *FN*).

50. See the heroine's use of "surrender" in both *The Traitor: A Story of the Fall of the Invisible Empire* (New York: Doubleday, Page, 1907), 203, and *The Black Hood* (New York: D. Appleton and Company, 1924), 278.

51. Thomas Dixon Jr., *The Way of a Man: A Story of the New Woman* (New York: D. Appleton and Company, 1919), 5–6 (hereafter cited in text as *WM*).

52. Dixon's plots became predictable, as did his heroes and heroines. In 1925, for example, he reworked the ideas of *The Foolish Virgin* in a novel he published as *The Love Complex* (New York: Boni and Liveright, 1925). *The Love Complex* adds a fiancé to the mix, but it is still a critique of "love at first sight" unmitigated by reason and concern for the greater good of society. In *Love Complex,* the villain's personal history is partly to blame for his criminality. He was straight before his service in World War I, which was "a scientific orgy of murder." While Prohibition was enacted in America, Wallis's commanders at the front were getting their men drunk to "deaden brains and steel muscles" before battle. "To murder is to murder whether I'm in uniform or civilian clothes," he observes (171). Dixon also republished *The One Woman* under a new title, changing only, as far as I can tell, the characters' names. See *Companions* (New York: Otis Publishing Corporation, 1931).

53. This was part of Dixon's Social Gospel, too. In one sermon, Dixon said: "True Justice is love in action. Our courts will not be courts of justice until they shall be administered in love for the reclaiming of those whom they try" ("Low Denounced by Dixon," *New York Times,* September 13, 1897, p. 10).

54. Williamson, *Crucible of Race*, 152.

55. Thomas Dixon Jr., *The Leopard's Spots: A Romance of the White Man's Burden—1865–1900* (New York: Doubleday, Page, 1902), 245 (hereafter cited in text as *LS*).

56. Dixon, *Black Hood*, 90.

57. Thomas Dixon Jr., *The Root of Evil* (New York: Grosset and Dunlap, 1911), 86.

58. Ibid., 96.

59. Linda Elsroad, "Tenderloin," in *The Encyclopedia of New York City*, ed. Kenneth T. Jackson (New Haven: Yale Univ. Press, 1995), 1161.

60. Dixon, *Living Problems*, 253. Only once did Dixon approve of black male suffrage, and it was in a very limited context. He had a practice of speaking briefly on current events before preaching, and on September 21, 1890, he spoke on the Force Bill. In this speech, extensively reported on in the *Times*, he stated that "the Negro" was "making progress in education, accumulating wealth, and establishing himself on the solid basis of real manhood. When he is so established, and not until then, will he be able to exercise the functions of a true citizen" ("The Force Bill Condemned," *New York Times*, September 22, 1890, p. 8).

61. A decade later, after publication of *The Leopard's Spots* and *The Clansman*, Dixon paid more attention to northern blacks, especially those he saw as agitators. In one interview, Dixon blamed northern blacks for race riots in the South. Black immigrants to northern cities, he alleged, wrote home to describe mingling with whites, which provoked, he claimed, the southern blacks to commit "some atrocious crime on a white woman," which in turn led to race rioting ("Atlanta Views on Riots," *New York Times*, September 24, 1906, p. 2). Dixon predicted race riots in northern cities and condemned all miscegenation in them, which he believed was epidemic. See "Rockerfeller a Hero of Romance," *New York Times*, August 10, 1907, p. BR486.

62. "Klan Is Denounced by 'The Clansman,'" *New York Times*, January 23, 1923, p. 23. In this article Dixon explicitly opposes persecution and harassment of Jews and Catholics. When in Boston and New York pastorates, Dixon did preach anti-Catholic sermons, but in 1923 he disavowed his earlier anti-Catholicism, claiming that "the history of the United States and the loyalty and service of its Catholic citizens" had changed his mind. Dixon's novels *The Traitor* and *Black Hood* are fictional denunciations of the second Klan. Yet Dixon's last novel, *The Flaming Sword*, ends in a race war.

63. Dixon, *Black Hood*, 43 (hereafter cited in text as *BH*).

64. Thomas Dixon Jr., *The Sins of the Father: A Romance of the South* (New York: Grosset and Dunlap, 1912), 123 (hereafter cited in text as *SF*).

65. The two are perfect examples of the "Mammy" and "Jezebel" stereotypes whites constructed about black women. See Deborah Gray White, *Ar'n't I a Woman? Female Slaves in the Plantation South* (New York: Norton, 1989).

Portrait of Thomas Dixon by A. J. Conant. *Courtesy the Portrait Collection, Wake Forest University Art Collections, Winston-Salem, North Carolina.*

Thomas Dixon Jr. and Harriet Bussey (shown here in 1903) married in 1888, when Dixon was twenty-four years old. *Courtesy of Wake Forest University.*

Dixon in 1879, the year he enrolled at Wake Forest College at the age of fifteen. *Courtesy of Wake Forest University.*

Dixon at the age of seventy-two.
Courtesy of Wake Forest University.

Thomas Dixon's Great Lecture
THIS COUNTRY OF OURS

THOMAS DIXON, distinguished author and orator, has just made a Continental Tour speaking as a special representative of the National Recovery Administration, translating into terms of ringing conviction and inspiration the fundamental meaning of the NRA program. For the past four months he has held thousands spellbound by his matchless eloquence reaching new heights of power in his long career as an orator.

He closed his Tour in Boston, Massachusetts with a speech before the combined Rotary Clubs of the district that created a profound sensation and placed him at the head of the list of a thousand chosen speakers for the Administration. Everywhere he has pleaded for faith in our future based on the glorious story of America's past. Everywhere the response has been electric.

Books by Thomas Dixon

The Leopard's Spots; The Clansman (The Birth of a Nation); The Traitor; Comrades; The Root of Evil; The Life Worth Living; The Sins of the Father; The Southerner; The Victim; The Foolish Virgin; The Fall of a Nation; The Way of a Man; A Man of the People (A Play); The Man in Gray; The Black Hood; The Love Complex; The Sun Virgin; Companions; The Harding Tragedy (With H. M. Daugherty).

Dixon lectured around the country in support of the National Industrial Recovery Act during the Depression. *Courtesy of Wake Forest University.*

Thomas Dixon Sr. and his three sons, 1888. *Courtesy of Wake Forest University.*

Dixon in 1904. *Courtesy of Wake Forest University.*

"Ours Is a Century of Light": Dixon's Strange Consistency

DAVID STRICKLIN

When most people think of the Social Gospel, they think of an activist, "this-worldly" approach to applying Christian principles to social problems, often with a generous application of "liberal" political and theological views. Many people, in fact, draw a fairly straight line from the work of such Social Gospel leaders as Walter Rauschenbusch to the social justice and civil rights activism of Martin Luther King Jr. and his colleagues and compatriots. Few observers among the generally educated public, people for whom Thomas Dixon Jr. is known for one thing and one thing only— his authorship of the notorious book *The Clansman* and the resulting film *The Birth of a Nation*—would think to include him among the numbers of thinkers, writers, and activists who promulgated the religious ideology, as Cynthia Lynn Lyerly might say, known as the Social Gospel.

Indeed, someone who read the following five statements might be tempted to think of the person being quoted as quite a progressive: One, "[T]he sphere of religion is the sphere of the human conscience; . . . religion has to do with this world and not with the next."[1] Two, "Knowledge is social. All who know the secrets of an art or a science are of a brotherhood. . . . The impartation of knowledge . . . is a sacrament of the great universal church."[2] Three, "[H]umanity is intrinsically divine. Sin is inhuman essentially. It is the violation of the human. . . . If you do not believe sin is a fact, . . . open your eyes and walk down the streets of our great city [New York]. See written upon the faces of men and women the record of shame and crime and selfishness and greed."[3] Four, "[H]eaven is a redeemed municipality; a holy social organization. . . . Politics . . . is religion in action."[4] Five, and reflecting some of the optimism of the Social Gospel, "The sun of the Twentieth century is tinging [sic] the horizon. The new sun is rising on a world of brighter faith. I veritably believe that it will be an impossibility for an atheist or an infidel to live in the Twentieth century. Those words are destined to be lost from the language of the world."[5]

If that reader then found out that the five statements came from the notorious Thomas Dixon Jr., the likely first reaction might be confusion. How could the arch-southerner, whose region was synonymous with resistance to liberal change of any sort, be capable of even one of the sentiments just mentioned, let alone all of them and many others like them? Only a few years earlier he had preached and written in a somewhat more orthodox manner, holding onto the idea of a literal hell, for instance, embracing standard understandings of what churches were to be and do.[6] Before his northern sojourn and during his brief service as a minister in North Carolina, he was hardly a typical Southern Baptist pastor. He was not, however, shockingly out of step with his religious and regional compatriots. But now at the end of the nineteenth century, there is Dixon, calling for attention to the claims of the poor and to the need for economic reforms and a more activist church response to those claims and that need. It is Dixon in process, surely, but Dixon nonetheless, and parting company with the overwhelming majority of his fellow Southern Baptists, both pastors and laypeople, whose theological pronouncements scarcely ever departed from expressions of concern for the security of their everlasting souls and those of the objects of their fervent and heartfelt evangelistic efforts. Most Southern Baptist conversation, proclamation, and action concerning conditions in the earthly realm dealt with sin, the impediment to salvation that it represented, and the surest method of removing that impediment—the only one that they believed counted—the salvation experience available through Christ's sacrifice. Most Southern Baptist understandings of the world focused on the belief that it was the way God intended it to be, with all its racial, gender, and economic hierarchies. To such Southern Baptists, there simply was no question of injustice in the post–Civil War South they were in charge of because a merciful Providence had put them in charge of it.

Social Gospel advocates in the North particularly challenged the notion that the status quo was divinely ordained, sometimes employing Marxian criticisms and promoting socialist or quasi-socialist solutions to the grinding social and economic problems of the day, especially those of the nation's great industrial cities of the Northeast and upper Midwest. Though, as Robert Handy points out, the term "social gospel" was not widely used until after 1900, what was called "social Christianity" developed in the late nineteenth century.[7] The Social Gospel movement anticipated and helped inspire in several respects the initiatives and reforms of the Progressive Era of the first two decades of the twentieth century. Its purveyors often called for government action and unionization to combat social ills, especially the exploitation of urban, most especially immigrant, workers by the powerful, newly arisen corporations. These workers often belonged to religious communities, but the churches and other institutions that served those communities often were almost as marginalized as their ethnic-minority congregants, whose temporal needs were seen to under the auspices of frequently corrupt political machines. Otherwise, those religious bodies did what they had been doing for centuries. They told their members that the sufferings of the present life occupied but the twinkling of an eye compared to eternal bliss in heaven. In other words, suffer now, or not; it matters very little. Get through this life and die in good standing with the church, then the real life will begin. Often, these workers, like poor people throughout the country, simply had no one to look after their interests.

It was no accident that outcries against mistreatment of urban workers arose among labor organizers and some liberal pastors and laypeople at roughly the same time as the leaders of what became the Populist revolt began crying out for better conditions for rural workers in the South and Midwest. The principal difference in the two groups, though, was that Populists and their forerunners advocated changes that would benefit themselves, while Social Gospel advocates tended to be fairly well-to-do and well-educated persons who called for better conditions for those less advantaged than themselves. The Populist movement faded from view almost overnight after the 1896 presidential campaign and the heart-breaking loss of "fusion" (Democratic and Populist) candidate William Jennings Bryan, whom Dixon opposed,[8] to Republican William McKinley. Bryan's loss was not the only thing that caused the decline of Populism. One factor was the inability of the largely rural People's Party to make common cause with labor unions and other mostly urban entities such as the liberal churches associated with the Social Gospel. These natural allies never joined forces to challenge the grip that big business and industry and their partners in state and federal government in the 1890s had on the workers whose labors did so much to create the dizzying corporate profits of the day. This failure was especially ironic because many Populists combined socialist principles with the Christian gospel just as some of the more prominent Social Gospel figures did. An unfortunate coincidence of that failure was that racism played a role in the development and decline of both Populism and the Social Gospel.

Enter Thomas Dixon Jr. His views on race relations in the early twentieth century are well known. What is less well known is that he formulated those views after having first embraced certain Social Gospel principles. It might be tempting to assume that his racist views of the early 1900s, embodied in *The Clansman* and other novels, represented a departure from his Social Gospel thinking of the late 1890s. But, actually, his racist and sexist views were entirely consistent with his pronouncements in favor of a social-action approach to the gospel. To know how this was possible, it is necessary to take a look at the times in which Dixon was working, the ways other Social Gospel advocates thought and wrote, and the intellectual and rhetorical correspondence among the views of Social Gospel figures on reforming and re-forming society according to Christian principles, some approaches to which sometimes seem fairly heavy-handed. First, though, it might be helpful to try to sort out the content, origins, and development of Dixon's Social Gospel pronouncements.

Dixon's Social Gospel credentials depend largely on sermons and essays he produced during his work as a minister in New York City during the late 1890s, celebrated at the time by various observers, including reporters and editorialists for the *New York Times*, and collected and published almost immediately after their composition. Many of Dixon's sermons were published in 1898 and 1899 in *The Free Lance, a Monthly Magazine*, by the People's Church in New York and then reissued in hardback. *The Free Lance* published materials on behalf of what was called the Liberal Congress of Religion, made up of "independent liberal churches," mainly in the Northeast and upper Midwest, including Dixon's New York church at the time. The magazine's masthead listed officers of the church, including women deacons, or "deaconesses." Although these attributes were quite foreign to most southern church people, let alone Southern Baptists, Dixon's people, the roots of his acceptance of such practices and his thought in this period generally lay in his southern upbringing and education.

Much has been made of Dixon's intellectual versatility. Samuel S. Hill refers to Dixon as both "Theist and Deist, progressive and reactionary, child of a vanished age and enthusiast for the future."[9] To an extent, such variability and volatility could be traceable to the nature of intellectual and emotional ferment in the nation at the time and among educated southerners. At a time when people were debating the merits of industrialization in the South, the prospects for an empire for the United States, and the further concomitant reintegration of the South into the national mainstream, on one level it might have been natural for Dixon to feel swayed by the various viewpoints on the great national and regional issues of the day, possibly even to seem to drift among them. But Dixon had serious reasons for believing as he did, and several of those reasons had connections to his southern origins.

For one thing, in his biography of Dixon, Raymond Cook names two favorite professors of Dixon's at Wake Forest. One was William Royall, and the other was William L. Poteat, a member of a legendary family of Southern Baptist progressives. The Poteats led a number of initiatives in North and South Carolina in the last decades of the nineteenth century and first several of the twentieth that sought to inspire Baptists to translate faithfulness to the gospel into concern for the suffering and degradation of so many of their fellow southerners, people who were victims of problems, the Poteats sometimes reminded Southern Baptists, they had helped create.[10] Readings in Darwin, Huxley, and Spencer at Wake Forest "tore apart" Dixon's childhood conceptions of biblical literalism, Cook says, and contributed to his realization in college that he was an agnostic. When Dixon reported this news to William Royall, rather than scolding Dixon or expressing the kind of alarm one might expect a faculty member at a Victorian Era church-related institution to exhibit, Royall assured Dixon that he was just going through a "phase," according to Cook. He did not imply that Dixon's status as a Christian was of no consequence, but the fact that Royall gave Dixon permission, in a sense, to try out agnosticism probably had an effect on Dixon's willingness to challenge the received wisdom of the age, at least with regard to theology and its relations with social issues.[11]

Dixon's experiences after graduation from Wake Forest continued the process of liberating him to an extent from the intellectual and theological norms of his time and place. His postgraduate studies at Johns Hopkins University connected him to the latest European methods and content in historical and political theory. Although the university had many traditional ties to the South, it was at that moment engaged in something of a reinvention of graduate studies, especially in history, based on the new German model. The climate at Johns Hopkins embraced the German notion that historical scholars could achieve a fairly pure level of "objectivity," an intellectual cloak under which prejudiced elitists could pass off biased interpretations of the past as factual. Hopkins also gave Dixon an important friendship with Woodrow Wilson, no liberal in the Social Gospel sense, but another intellectually active southerner and one who was not long afterward drawn into the Progressive movement. When Dixon's wandering spirit got the better of his scholarly aspirations, he headed for New York early in 1884 to try his hand at acting, met with precious little success, but took advantage of the opportunities the metropolis afforded to hear such speakers as Robert Ingersoll, a fellow agnostic, and Henry Ward Beecher, who swayed him despite Beecher's legendary anti-southern views. Raymond Cook says Dixon pronounced Beecher "the greatest preacher in the world."[12]

His acting career a failure, Dixon returned to North Carolina, went to law school, and won election to the state legislature before attaining voting age. He exhibited his loyalty to the defenders of the Old South and the limits of his nascent liberalism by introducing the first bill in a state legislature to grant pensions to Confederate veterans, according to Cook, but the young legislator also supported the idea of industrial education. Many southerners saw industrialization in particular and modernization in general as a capitulation to the New South ideal of moving the region closer to the U.S. mainstream by diversifying the southern economy—moving it away from its agrarian/idyllic past—and to the urban and northern advocates of this ideal. The main thing he gained from his short career in politics was a deep sense of disillusionment. He perfected an articulate contempt for political corruption and despaired of finding political solutions to problems as long as politics was dominated by the self-serving party hacks so often the archetypal "public servants" of the day. Possibly inspired by his disillusionment with politics, he re-found his faith and became an ordained Southern Baptist minister in 1886. In pastorates in Raleigh and Boston, Dixon sought to rejoin the fight against political corruption not through direct involvement in politics but through his preaching. His crossing the boundaries of the Baptist South to go to Boston offered him a strange experience: accosting a Boston hotel manager for refusing to grant lodging to an African American nurse who had accompanied his family from North Carolina to Massachusetts. According to Cook, Dixon castigated the man "in the name of William Lloyd Garrison and Wendell Phillips," two of the great abolitionists who had helped destroy the Old South beloved in Dixon's memory, and refused to stay in the hotel.[13]

If only for that story, one would have plenty of evidence to make a case for the dramatic presence of irony in the life and thinking of Thomas Dixon Jr. But there is more here than irony. In the time between his arrival at Wake Forest and return to New York to take up his brief pastorates, Dixon moved away from the rigid traditionalism of his upbringing, became exposed to the latest intellectual and theological currents, acquired role models who reinforced his desire to press the edges of the accepted and the acceptable, met with some frustration in his attempts to offer temporal—that is, political—solutions to the problems of the day, and found himself using his considerable gifts as a public speaker and actor in the ministry, another form of speaking out on behalf of what he saw as good and challenging what he saw as evil. If not for what he went on to do later—only a few years later, as it turns out, but a lifetime in the compressed chronology of Dixon's vocational wanderings—one might think that the only surprising turn of events would have been if he had *not* found his way into the Social Gospel movement.

Though he is more concerned in these writings with the traditional measures of churchly success (such things as church growth and budget receipts, for example) than were many better-known Social Gospel figures of the day, he makes it plain that a church that only has eyes for the afterlife is a church wasting its time and effort. He says, "It is useless to prate about the inspiration of the Bible, or this or that doctrine, if, in the vital struggle, in the hand-in-hand conflict with sin and hell, there is failure and retreat and defeat," and he defines the vital task as using "the disposition and power [of Christ] to save the lost and weak and helpless." Further, he pulls no punches on behalf of his coreligionists. He cites the work of Jacob Riis in exposing the wretched living conditions of urban workers as a rebuke of the downtown New York churches within whose shadows the poor suffer, especially the Protestant churches, which he derides as a new "bourgeois aristocracy."[14] The otherworldly stance—which had worked for so long to dull churches' ability to hear the outcry of the poor, something Marx exploited for rhetorical purposes with great effect—simply left out much, perhaps most, of what Dixon believed Jesus lived on earth to inspire. Dixon did not deny the power or the need for the saving work of Christ on behalf of the soul of the individual believer, but he thought that the saving work of Jesus on behalf of society had just as much power and addressed needs even more desperate, needs that only grew as U.S. society became more urban, more industrialized, and more focused on the acquisition and display of wealth.

Dixon and the Social Gospel arose together during a time of increasing calls for the United States to join the world roster of empires. Partly because of this, more than a few Social Gospel advocates held views that seem to modern ears nothing more than racist. In his 1885 book *Our Country*, for instance, minister and missionary Josiah Strong promoted notions of economic uplift for the downtrodden, a central tenet of the Social Gospel, along with a signal commitment to the weighty joys of the "white man's burden." One of the earliest supporters of applying "Anglo-Saxon" political, cultural, and economic values to the groaning needs of the benighted masses in other parts of the world through open calls for U.S. imperialism, Strong inspired many people, including Dixon,[15] to link the robust, manly vigor of "Young America" to the idea of bringing light to those poor wretches living in non-American darkness. This was probably the principal reason Dixon went against his home region in supporting Republican William McKinley in the presidential election of 1896. That the poor wretches in question mostly consisted of people with dark skin made Strong's and Dixon's logic only more compelling to them. One could say the same thing about Dixon's admiring references to social Darwinist Herbert Spencer and U.S. historian John Fiske, one of the most graphic of American imperialists and someone who was somewhat famous for celebrating the European voyages of discovery and conquest of the New World as some of the great moments in all of human history.[16]

Dixon's remarkable series of sermons during his pastorate at the People's Church in the spring of 1898 fairly drip with eagerness to see that great day of U.S. hegemony arrive, a day that would replace the darkness with the light of American and Christian virtue. In "The Anglo-Saxon Alliance," for example, Dixon combines his racial politics, faith in the beneficent nature of prospective U.S. dominion, and conviction that white, western Christians will not only civilize the world but also hasten the disappearance of the darker races. To this end, he says, "The Anglo-Saxon race has the peculiar power of absorbing into a consistent unity all races that flow into its life." He adds that "from the last [possibly intending to say "the first"] drop of blood that ever came from my heart, to the last drop in my finger-tips, I am all over an Anglo-Saxon."[17] Though it is not clear how he connected these concepts with intermarriage, something few white southerners of his day welcomed, Dixon employed the idea of the "unity" of humanity in some strange ways, saying, "The world tends toward unity. That unity is the dream of all souls that love humanity."[18] His interpretation of unity, however, was that of a world melting pot, with Americans doing the melting. Though he says, "I count myself free from the prejudices [sic] of races and nationalities," his recognition of the debt "Anglo-Saxons" owe to other races extends principally to consumer goods such as the ivory brought forth by "the naked African." He acknowledges that the United States is not a nation only for "native Americans," though he means, of course, the same thing by that ironic expression that nativists have always meant by it, for ultimately the purpose of this unity and open-mindedness is the realization of the new life of "Young America" by its true "king," the "citizen soldier."[19] Conquest will bring about world unity, both the conquest of the gospel and that of the mighty United States. One had only to acknowledge the power and logic of the modern age to face these facts, for, as Dixon said in 1896, "Ours is a century of light, knowledge, investigation, analysis, facts. Woe to that creed or cult that dares to flinch beneath the searchlight of the dawning century."[20]

That the great figures in the Social Gospel movement kept largely quiet on the subject of race has puzzled readers and observers for decades. They often think that the advanced views of these pastors and theologians on economic matters, especially their concern for the plight of industrial workers, should be paralleled by progressive views on race relations. That present-day readers may be troubled by the absence of progressive views on race relations in Walter Rauschenbusch's work, for instance, says as much about those readers as it does about the pastor of Hell's Kitchen or about Washington Gladden or any number of other Social Gospel figures. Robert Handy says that Social Gospel advocates "tended to accept the views of race held by progressives generally." These varied somewhat but included those of Josiah Strong, who Handy says was "closer to being obsessed with the idea of Anglo-Saxon superiority than most other advocates of the social gospel, though there was some reflection of his sentiments in what they had to say." He goes on to say that Gladden "was troubled by the plight" of African Americans. He just "did not focus on it."[21] In Dixon's case, his continued use of negative stereotypes about African Americans in sermons and writings that also embrace the Social Gospel indicates a late nineteenth-century sensibility quite different from that of the twenty-first century, when seemingly no one who embraces the progressive views of the Social Gospel would also embrace racism.

Dixon certainly offers clues that might throw the hounds off his scent. Writing only thirty-three years after the end of the Civil War, he offers the tried-and-true gambit of the Lost Cause, that the Civil War was not fought over slavery.[22] But he also attacks the idea of biblical sanction for slavery,[23] refers admiringly at times to Abraham Lincoln, and even quotes the "Battle Hymn of the Republic"! Still, one has a difficult time avoiding at least asking a couple of questions: Are his comments about slavery and Lincoln and the rest just things he said to gain favor with his New York City audiences, or did he really believe these statements he made? Is he more candid in his sermon "A Friendly Warning to the Negro," in which he praises Booker T. Washington and other moderate African American leaders who held that the proper place for their people was at the bottom of the economic and social ladder of U.S. society? Dixon naturally links his treatment of the subject to his Anglo-Saxonism. Even his criticism of "Pitchfork Ben" Tillman, the South Carolina racist (and erstwhile Populist) firebrand, whom he calls "a freak" and "an abnormality" who "no more represents the Southern white race than the wildcat represents the animal life in the South," cannot take away his comment that "The blackest day for the negro was the day he became a voter in the South." Dixon was utterly consistent on this point, no matter how many other references he made to the needs of the less fortunate in U.S. society or the ill effects of the corruption of powerful forces. He railed against the "enfranchisement of hordes of ignorant slaves," for example, expressing his view of how, "under the leadership of adventurers and villains" in Reconstruction North Carolina, "They wrecked the state government [and] stole everything they could get their hands on."[24]

There are additional problems in trying to square Dixon's various views. He accepts social Darwinism, yet he holds that the love of Christ dispels social distinctions.[25] Again, perhaps the clue lies in his faith in the benevolent effects of white-Christian-American domination of the world. Listen to his praise for Theodore Roosevelt in "Roosevelt, the Heroic Leader" and "Roosevelt's Personality"[26] and to his various paeans to American exceptionalism, his celebration of "God's special providence in the creation and sustenance of the United States."[27] The most merciful God, he feels, surely would not entrust a special destiny to a nation incapable of bringing improvement to the lives of the downtrodden. When benighted lands receive the light of American leadership, their renovated societies will offer the poor the same possibilities for advancement that the Gilded Age offered their counterparts in the United States. He acknowledges and laments the existence of wage slavery in the U.S. industrial economy, but when the subject turns to imperial prospects, the United States looks better and better to Dixon by comparison with other nations. One had to accept a certain amount of Horatio Alger's faith in luck and pluck, along with large doses of Spencer's faith in the survival of the fittest, to believe that a genuinely poor person could advance to a position of social and political equality with the holders of the great wealth of the day, but Dixon believed it was better to hold a lowly position in a land under U.S. guidance than an exalted one in a land of darkness.

Other views get blended in Dixon's thought. Like most traditional ministers, he opposes the use of alcohol, but in "Bishop Potter and the Saloon" he goes beyond the usual objections to drink as a threat to one's spiritual status. He links a reform agenda with the idea of social control and works in an approving quotation from Knights of Labor leader Terence Powderly against the debilitating effects of liquor on workers.[28] He also denigrates gambling and other forms of "debauchery of young manhood and young womanhood," not just because young people should refrain from carrying on, but because "[to the saloons] young workingmen and young working women go in search of pleasure and recreation and begin their downward career." The cost of drinking is not just the disappointment of Jesus or the chagrin of one's mother. It is the loss of any hope of working one's way up the economic ladder of the industrial United States.[29]

In these and many other ways, Dixon's career points to the problem of what biblical students call "prooftexting" in trying to explain the views of a complicated, driven, restless intellectual, a religious and cultural ideologue. The expression "prooftexting" refers to the use, mainly, of Bible verses taken out of context for the purpose of proving an often shaky point. For instance, one might quote Jesus, sometimes known as the "Prince of Peace," as favoring war when he said, "I come not to bring peace, but a sword" (Matt. 10:34). In context, Jesus is actually referring to the costs his followers will incur by going against society's usual ways of doing things, presumably including its addiction to war, which his overall teachings suggest fairly strongly he abhors. Prooftexting from Dixon's writings can create confusion, indeed. One could take various quotes from his writings, use these "texts," and, depending on one's perspective, "prove" all kinds of things about his views, or one could take passages out of context to confound depictions of him as a Social Gospel figure or a racist or a socialist or even a Christian. It seems that all of these things, all the ways readers approach Dixon, should be tempered by reference to the overall shape of his life and thought and to the times in which he did his work. In some ways, Dixon's notions seem remarkably advanced for his time, ideas that certainly resonate with the Social Gospel. In addition, other more-or-less progressive thinkers and activists of the day also had racial blind spots or overt racist sentiments. Woodrow Wilson was only the most prominent of these; the phenomenon was certainly not limited to Dixon. The problem is to try to reconcile Dixon's seeming progressivism with his fondness for Old South ways and values. Or is it?

In the first place, Dixon's ecumenical instincts and ideas, including his views of church life in the South in comparison with that in the North, need comment. That his sermons and essays were endorsed and marketed by an organization that amounted to an early council of churches and that he called church "federation" the solution to the problems that marked urban churches as failures[30] are enough to set him apart from most southern church leaders of his day or, for that matter, of the contemporary era. Southern church leaders dragged their feet on "federating" and otherwise linking their congregations and judicatories with others. Even the connectional churches, such as the Methodists and Presbyterians, showed a long reluctance to cede any authority to councils of churches. With very few exceptions, Southern Baptist congregations, associations, state conventions, and the national structure known as the Southern Baptist Convention steadfastly refused to join councils of churches. For Southern Baptists, this refusal sprang partly from historical and theological reasoning, including the power of a view called Landmarkism, an exclusivist viewpoint that developed among Southern Baptists in the nineteenth century and centered on a radical notion of the primacy of the local congregation and the identification of Southern Baptist congregations, and them only, with the one true church. In large part, however, the reluctance of most Southern Baptists to accept the affiliation of their congregations or judicatories with councils of churches stemmed from the fact that church councils tended to promote liberal causes with which most Southern Baptists wanted nothing to do. For the most part, councils did and do exactly that, and most Southern Baptists did and still do avoid them judiciously.[31] In the minds of many Southern Baptists, therefore, the terms "ecumenical," "social gospel," and "liberal" became almost interchangeable and came to mean "anti-Christian" or at least "anti-evangelical." Part of the suspicion toward church councils, somewhat akin to the attitudes of many conservatives toward the one-world threat they perceive in the United Nations, stemmed from the associations of councils with Social Gospel reform agendas. Among many southerners, particularly, the thought of going against the dominant culture repulsed them completely. That culture had given them much of their identity, rooted in the Old South, the fight for slavery and states' rights, and the post–Civil War struggle against northern attempts to reconstruct their racial views, and that culture was bolstered dramatically and graphically by the churches of the South. Ceding any authority to church bodies beyond local or regional control was unthinkable for most southerners, and this was especially true of Southern Baptists. Dixon's New York ecumenism marks him as someone who checked a large part of his Southern Baptist identity at the door of the metropolis.

His place in the cultural and intellectual landscape, however, points to a strong continuity between that crucial transition zone known as the New South and the twentieth-century United States. To a great extent, the New South made the modern United States, and it did so because of people such as Dixon. In the first decade of the century, one sees Theodore Roosevelt beginning to do battle with Ben Tillman, inviting Booker T. Washington to the White House, but backing away from racial reform agendas in much the same way his cousin-president did in the 1930s and 1940s. Between their presidencies, one sees Woodrow Wilson's reversal of anything even resembling racial tolerance and his famous admiration for the Dixon-Griffith morality play whereby, Wilson purportedly said, history was "written with lightning." Consider also Wilson's authorship of a U.S. history text endorsing the views of the notorious "Dunning School," an interpretation of Reconstruction that centered on the ways the South supposedly was made to suffer under corrupt, wasteful, and inept northern- and black-dominated state governments intent on humiliating white southerners and imposing hateful changes on the noble region. Volume five of Wilson's *A History of the American People*, subtitled *Reunion and Rationalization*, employs uncritically the scholarship of William A. Dunning and his Columbia University colleague John W. Burgess, the two of whom taught generations of graduate students that African Americans were simple, childlike creatures who were incapable of self-government, let alone abstract thought. Dunning and Burgess depicted Reconstruction as a monstrous fraud and said the South was saved when the federal troops went home and the white elites who were meant to run the region were allowed to resume their control of it and their domination of their black neighbors. Wilson called Reconstruction "the rule of negroes and adventurers,"[32] a sentiment, shared by Dixon, that found its way into *The Clansman*. If Dixon needed any reassurance of the validity of his grotesque appraisal of the Reconstruction era, it was widely available through some of the leading scholars of his day.

In his classic history of Reconstruction, Eric Foner said that such views "did much to freeze the mind of the white South in unalterable opposition to outside pressures for social change and to any thought of breaching Democratic ascendancy, eliminating segregation, or restoring suffrage to disenfranchised blacks."[33] With such a political background clearly in mind, Wilson and the two Roosevelts made the modern U.S. presidency and set the tone for much racial intolerance of the twentieth century, and they did so in large part out of deference to the prejudices of the "New South," which based its claims to newness on a promise of accommodation to the need for economic modernization while holding on to its perceived need to keep down its African American masses. They achieved their goals, in large part, by the way, because of the failure of Populism to take control of the liberal end of the U.S. political spectrum and challenge the Democrats to stand up for the rights and needs of working people, both black and white, when southern Democrats scared white Populists into joining them and repudiating their alliances with African American Populists. This left the Solid South Democratic, and segregated, until the 1960s and made even northern liberal Democrats who aspired to national prominence reluctant to offend southern racist sensibilities. There, at the creation of the formal Jim Crow system in the 1890s, the failure to link concerns for poor whites with any sense of justice for African Americans, and the setting in motion of decades of further suffering is Dixon, questioning some of the verities of the Old South but embracing others, calling for modernization while endorsing the most callous disregard for the rights and aspirations of black citizens. There is the New South. There, for most of the twentieth century, is the United States.

There also is the further irony of Dixon's uneasy relationship with the burgeoning fundamentalist movement of his day. One of its key southern leaders was none other than his own brother A. C. Dixon. By the mid-1890s, Thomas had gotten agnosticism out of his system, and he and Clarence did public battle with Robert Ingersoll, both on fairly conservative grounds, but the brothers parted company on theological and ecclesiological matters. Again, it would be natural to assume that someone with Dixon's racial views and sense of American triumphalism might embrace the exclusivist position of fundamentalists. After all, so many people with such views in the twentieth and early twenty-first centuries embraced beliefs such as biblical literalism, fervent evangelism aimed at regeneration of lost souls through the experience of being "born again," premillennialism, and anti-Darwinism. Further, they refused to keep fellowship with those who held different views and blended these tenets with a resistance to social and cultural changes such as racial integration and hawkish interpretations of the special purposes of U.S. foreign and military policy. During his Social Gospel period, Dixon held the last two views—militarism and racism—without holding the first five. Rather than excluding people from the ranks of one's church or denomination because of disagreements over how to interpret scriptural texts, a fundamentalist hallmark, Dixon says that the "church triumphant" should set aside obsessions with doctrinal disputation lest it "damn a world to save a syllogism." He goes on to say that it "must preach a sociological as contradistinguished from a merely individual gospel."[34] His aforementioned ecumenism further separates him from the fundamentalists of his day. He even goes so far as to speak kindly of Catholics, something unheard of among southern fundamentalists until the abortion issue created a common cause between them that surprised both groups in the 1970s and 1980s. In his book *The Failure of Protestantism in New York and Its Causes*, though he still refers to himself as a Baptist in its pages, Dixon is remarkably free of the anti-Catholic bias typical of so many Protestants (especially Baptists) of the day, let alone fundamentalists, adding, "From Catholicism to-day we should learn the concrete application of truth in everyday life." The purpose of this insight, he says, is to align church practice with a sensitivity to the needs of the masses, again, something that precious few fundamentalists cared to engage in because they were so eager to do battle with Darwin's teachings, which intrigue Dixon, and to prepare for the fast-coming end-time, which strikes him as a way of dodging greater responsibilities of churches to address earthly concerns.[35]

Like other cultural leaders of his day with active imaginations and fervent longings for a future shaped by a selective view of the past, Dixon held seemingly contradictory ideas in balance. He did not do this effortlessly or perfectly, but also he did not do it alone. Students of progressive tendencies in U.S. and southern history can learn much from considering the often strange mixtures of impulses and ideas that swirled in Dixon's mind. His life helps remind people of the dangers of trying to apply current notions of political and cultural consistency to historical personages, and his work shows the dangers of taking selected passages out of context to try to digest the thinking of a complicated individual. His life also shows the need to keep in mind how personal needs and proclivities can affect the ways a public figure's thought develops. Dixon's intense ambition drove him to excel as a student at Wake Forest, led him into a variety of short careers before the arrival of his fortieth birthday, and whetted his appetite for public recognition and for the continuing sound of applause. He genuinely desired to influence people, often in ways that would have prompted them to improve the living conditions of the less fortunate, hardly a selfish impulse on his part. But his desire for fame led him at times to forsake elements of his own past for less pure reasons, as when he left the Baptist fold in New York because he thought removing his denominational identity would increase the crowds of people who came not so much to worship, perhaps, as to hear him speak.[36]

Also, his life and work show the need to be reminded that the Social Gospel era did not mark the first time personal behavior, rather than right belief alone, was linked to Christian faithfulness. In fact, it makes some sense to connect the Social Gospel ideal to that of the Puritan commonwealth. Broadening somewhat, one could see how both the Roman Catholic sacramental system and the Puritan commonwealth ideal performed some regulation of personal and social behavior in order to help assure good standing with the governing church and, thus, the prospect of a "good death" and resultant entry to heaven for Catholics and some reassurance of predestination for election for Puritans. Thus, for much of the Catholic Middle Ages and for the colonial phase of "American" history, concerns for the afterlife were connected with some attention to behavior during this life. With the decline of Calvinism and the rise of theologies based more on notions of free will, especially during and after the Second Great Awakening in the first years of the nineteenth century, heirs of Puritanism, riding the burgeoning wave of evangelicalism, sought and advocated social reform. This was true especially in urban areas, where the drunkenness of wayward husbands inspired the involvement of the temperance-minded women who helped so much to drive the revivals. The passion for reform focused on behavioral failings that marred daily life, indeed, but that also threatened the salvation standing of wrongdoers. Stamping out drunkenness, licentiousness, and Sabbath breaking reflected a concern for the afterlife, not "just" the concerns of the day. The subject matter of the theological debates of the nineteenth century, especially the various millennial theories, also contributed to a linkage of "this-worldly" behavior and future prospects for believers. By the end of the century, activist Christianity, reformism, Populist combinations of socialist theory and Christian revivalism, and in some respects the simple awakening of the conscience of the better-off in the face of the suffering and exploitation of the working masses came in and out of the thinking and action of any number of Social Gospel adherents. In one way or another, from time to different time, Thomas Dixon Jr. came in and out of each of those perspectives. That they grew alongside, and possibly even grew out of, the reprehensible racial views for which he is internationally famous represents no signal departure or inconsistency within his thinking and action. To him, his was a century of light, an American century, a Christian century, a century of the disappearance of darkness, in all its forms.

NOTES

I would like to thank Cynthia Lynn Lyerly for the many insights into Dixon that she shared with me during the year and a half we worked on the presentations for our joint session at the Wake Forest conference, where the default response to almost any question on Dixon's life became "Ask Lynn Lyerly." I would also like to thank Michele Gillespie, Randal Hall, and Bill Leonard for inviting me to participate in the conference and for their many acts of kindness and guidance; and I would like to thank the great Sam Hill for his perceptive comments on our session.

1. "Alger, and Why He Should Resign," in Thomas Dixon Jr., *Dixon's Sermons, Delivered in the Grand Opera House, New York, 1898–1899* (New York: F. L. Bussey, n.d.), 64.

2. "The Bulwarks of the Nation," ibid., 82.

3. "What Is Sin?" ibid., 92, 94.

4. "The Larger Church," ibid., 98, 103.

5. "Dixon on Ingersoll," ibid., 128.

6. Thomas Dixon Jr., *Living Problems in Religion and Social Science* (New York: Charles T. Dillingham, 1889), 74–75. See also Dixon's caustic remarks about Catholicism, which he later moderated, ibid., 31, 189–91.

7. Robert T. Handy, ed., *The Social Gospel in America, 1870–1920* (New York: Oxford Univ. Press, 1966), 5.

8. Raymond Cook, *Fire from the Flint: The Amazing Careers of Thomas Dixon* (Winston-Salem, N.C.: Blair, 1968), 91.

9. Samuel S. Hill, "My Response to Lyerly and Stricklin Papers," Thomas Dixon Jr. and the Making of Modern America conference, Wake Forest University, April 12, 2003.

10. See Randal L. Hall, *William Louis Poteat: A Leader of the Progressive-Era South* (Lexington: Univ. Press of Kentucky, 2000).

11. Cook, *Fire from the Flint*, 37–38, 48.

12. Ibid., 49, 50–51, 52–54.

13. Ibid., 57, 59–60, 61, 65, 66–67, 68–69.

14. Thomas Dixon Jr., *The Failure of Protestantism in New York and Its Causes*, 2nd ed. (New York: Strauss and Rehn, 1896), 24, 26, 35.

15. See Dixon, *Failure of Protestantism*, e.g.,116; Josiah Strong, *Our Country: Its Possible Future and Its Present Crisis* (New York: Baker and Taylor, 1885), 191, 194, 211, 213.

16. "Dixon on Ingersoll," 124, 125; Cook, *Fire from the Flint*, 91, 93. See also John Fiske's book *The Discovery of America* (New York: Houghton and Mifflin, 1892).

17. "The Anglo-Saxon Alliance," in *Dixon's Sermons*, 11. See also "The New Fourth of July," ibid.

18. "Destiny of America," ibid., 76.

19. Ibid., 78, 80.

20. Dixon, *Failure of Protestantism*, 12. It was very strange to be reading Dixon's sermons on his hopes for war against Spain and a coming American empire during the months leading up to the Wake Forest conference, which took place during the U.S. invasion of Iraq in the spring of 2003. His arguments in favor of and attacks on the opponents of imperial adventures retrace many of the points made as the country moved toward war in Iraq. His excoriation of the French for failing to side with the United States against Spain and praise of Britain for supporting the United States sound particularly familiar. See "Anglo-Saxon Alliance," 9–10, for instance.

21. Handy, *Social Gospel in America*, 29.

22. "New Fourth of July," in *Dixon's Sermons*, 39.

23. See, for example, "The Larger Church," in *Dixon's Sermons*, 102.

24. "A Friendly Warning to the Negro," in *Dixon's Sermons*, 112, 114, 117, 118; Dixon, *Living Problems*, 251.

25. "Dixon on Ingersoll," 124, 125, and "Ingersoll's Mistakes," in *Dixon's Sermons*, 143.

26. "Roosevelt, the Heroic Leader," in *Dixon's Sermons*, 58–63; "Roosevelt's Personality," ibid., 88–91.

27. "Ingersoll's Mistakes," in *Dixon's Sermons*, e.g., 145.

28. "Bishop Potter and the Saloon," in *Dixon's Sermons*, 150.

29. Ibid., 151.

30. Dixon, *Failure of Protestantism*, 134, 145–48.

31. The principal exception to Southern Baptists' avoidance of affiliation with councils of churches developed in North Carolina, where a handful of congregations historically affiliated with the Southern Baptist Convention joined the North Carolina Council of Churches in the 1960s and 1970s. Most of them were predominantly white and "dually aligned" with the American Baptist Churches, which for white congregations in the South usually means they are fairly liberal.

32. Woodrow Wilson, *A History of the American People*, vol. 5, *Reunion and Rationalization* (New York: Harper and Brothers, 1901), 76, 113. See also a fairly famous narrative history written by another Columbia University professor, David Saville Muzzey, *An American History* (Boston: Ginn, 1911), 389, wherein is posed the question, "Why did the North put upon the South the unbearable burden of negro rule supported by the bayonet?"

33. Eric Foner, *Reconstruction: America's Unfinished Revolution, 1863–1877* (New York: Harper and Row, 1988), 610.

34. Dixon, *Failure of Protestantism*, 123–24, 125; Cook, *Fire from the Flint*, 83–85.

35. Cook, *Fire from the Flint*, 87, 89.

36. Ibid., 89.

Thomas Dixon and the Literary Production of Whiteness
SCOTT ROMINE

Long ignored as an embarrassing, if not aberrant, purveyor of white supremacy who wrote bad novels, Thomas Dixon has gathered recent critical attention as a central, even normative, voice in the racial discourse of the early twentieth century. Historians and critics such as Sandra Gunning, Grace Elizabeth Hale, Cathy Boeckmann, Joel Williamson, Walter Benn Michaels, and Mason Stokes have focused attention on Dixon as a foundational figure in the modern project of, as Hale puts it, "making whiteness." Where Williamson writes that "Dixon probably did more to shape the lives of modern Americans than have some presidents,"[1] it is Michaels who perhaps affords Dixon the greatest impact on American history and culture. Fully elaborated by the 1920s, according to Michaels, Dixon's brand of nativism helped to reconfigure American culture into a set of beliefs and practices dependent on, but irreducible to, race. In this crucible, Michaels argues, "Americanness" itself is transformed into a "project," something that could be "lost or recovered, defended or betrayed."[2] Such assertions risk putting the literary cart before the cultural horse, of positing Dixon as a cause and not an effect. But even if Dixon partially symptomizes broader cultural trends, it seems clear that his idiosyncratic articulation of white supremacy intervened crucially in the production of modern American identity.

This essay addresses a claim Williamson makes of Dixon's *The Leopard's Spots* (1902): "it is probably significant that the one work nearest to a codification of Radical [racist] dogma came not at all in a scholarly form, but in a novel."[3] It is precisely that significance that I wish to explore, mostly by destabilizing the relationship between novels and dogma. How, that is, does Dixon's narrative form intervene in or enable a white supremacist project? With caveats for the potential redundancy here—*The Leopard's Spots* is, after all, a novel—I want to address this question in two distinct, although interrelated, ways: first, with respect to narrative itself as a mode of organizing experience, and, second, with respect to the kind of novel Dixon wrote. Briefly, I will argue that, far from being a passive vehicle into which Dixon inserted his racial ideologies, narrative and white identity exist in a mutually constitutive relationship. In *The Words of Selves*, Denise Riley argues that "any act of identification necessarily entails a scenario,"[4] and in building on this crucial insight, I want to examine how Dixon does not so much *represent* whiteness as a stable, fixed essence, but *tells* it as a story of traumatic origins, heroic defense, and grandiose recovery. This argument will reorient a dominant pattern in recent criticism of Dixon's work that seeks to expose or deconstruct his contradictory, illogical, and fragile construction of whiteness. Cathy Boeckmann typifies this trend in arguing that Dixon's racial contradictions are "inconsistent with the genre of prose romance and . . . ironically undermine the efficacy of written characterization to contain and transmit racial messages."[5] While granting the importance of Boeckmann's argument (and with the generically related work of Judith Jackson Fossett and Kim Magowan[6]) that Dixon anxiously and incompletely disentangles white manhood from its feminized, black counterpart, I want to turn such arguments on their head and argue that "the genre of prose romance" (among other genres) *produces* white identity—not as a "racial message" to be transmitted, but as a racial fantasy to be played out. In other words, I am interested in how white identity works, not how it fails—in how Dixon's fluid and dynamic production of whiteness mobilized readers to privilege white identity over competing forms of identification. Part of Dixon's efficacy in this project lies in how he embeds whiteness in a wide array of genres, each with its own distinctive set of formal and affective structures. That the premises of these genres are often quite different (if not mutually exclusive) points not only to the conceptual incoherence of Dixon's narrative, but also to its dramatic power. To recognize that whiteness is both the traumatized object of melodrama and the heroic agent of epic adventure—that *The Leopard's Spots* is both historical narrative and utopian fantasy—is to recognize that whiteness does not make sense. It is also to begin to understand the malignant genius of Thomas Dixon. As Fredric Jameson observes, that which "comes before the purely contemplative mind as logical scandal or double-bind, the unthinkable and the conceptually paradoxical, that which cannot be unknotted by the operation of pure thought . . . must therefore generate a whole more properly narrative apparatus—the text itself—to square its circles, and to dispel, through narrative, its intolerable closure."[7] Dixon offers whiteness not as essence, but as action; not as purity, but as purification; not as fact, but as affect; not as noun, but as imperative verb—more precisely, he stages and restages a compelling drama between the latter, dynamic terms and the former, static ones.

In *Towards the Abolition of Whiteness*, David Roediger suggests that "whiteness is now a particularly brittle and fragile form of social identity,"[8] to which we should add that brittle, fragile social identities are often the most compelling and intensely fetishized. Certainly this is true in Dixon's work, which compulsively stages scenes of abjection, trauma, and violation as the origin of white identity. An extremely condensed version of Dixon's traumatic scenario occurs late in *The Leopard's Spots* when a Negro trooper meets a white couple on a sidewalk: "He ran into the girl, jostling her roughly, and the young white man knocked him down instantly and beat him to death."[9] What is striking here is not the violence, but the economy: a single sentence condenses an essential sequence of Dixon's narrative world. We might go so far as to label this Dixon's *primal scene:* black masculinity violates white womanhood; white manhood revenges itself upon the black body. (Reiterated ad nauseam, this scenario is also one, as we shall see, that Dixon seeks finally to transcend.) It is crucial that the actors in the scenario cannot be reversed. White men respond to violation with active heroism, black men with passive abjection. In a similarly condensed and equally evocative passage, blacks are disenfranchised by merely *warning* them not to vote. "Those who come," the Klan leader informs his subalterns, "will be allowed to vote without molestation. . . . Any man, black or white, who can be scared out of his ballot is not fit to have one. Back of every ballot is the red blood of the man that votes. . . . This is simply a test of manhood" (160). Needless to say, the freedman fails this test, his vote is sparse, and "Civilisation," as the chapter title tells us, "Was Saved" (153).

What I wish to foreground here is the imperative, contingent, sequential structure of the racial identities produced in these passages. If the white man of the first passage had not responded with violence, he would have forfeited his white identity; had the freedman voted en masse, he would have ceased being "Negro." The latter claim is, of course, complicated by the assumption (eventually proven correct) that the "red blood" behind a ballot cannot be "black blood," and hence that the Negro will naturally fail this "test of manhood." The ostensibly egalitarian scenario that "any man, black *or* white" has available this test is here posed as a *predictable* scenario—a foregone conclusion of racial difference. A similar logic informs the other scenario as well, since Dixon's premise is that any *true* white man will respond as this one does, by "instantly" defending white womanhood. Whiteness, then, is both the subject of the action and, paradoxically, predicated on the action. Here, as throughout the novel, Dixon vacillates between a pragmatic, performative understanding of race and an essentialist, predictive one that racially codes certain behaviors. What should be noted, however, is the moment of hesitation contained in both scenarios that, as we shall see, is extended into broader scenarios—specifically, the potential failure of white manhood to secure its survival and the parallel (and more threatening) possibility of Negro ascent. Whiteness resists representation simply as "essence" precisely because the necessity of "acting white" (and the possibility of not doing so) introduces a contingent dimension to racial identity or, to put the matter another way, makes it possible for race to become an identity. Indeed, to consider Dixon's understanding of whiteness in strictly essentialist terms—that is, as a set of stable racial characteristics that causes certain behaviors and precludes others—is to ignore that simply being white is not an especially accurate predictor of anything: white characters are as likely to threaten civilization as to save it. The paradox is that Dixon codes civilization itself as "white," in stark contrast to African barbarism that "has held one fourth of this globe for 3000 years [but] never taken one step in progress" (437). To say, however, that Dixon's depiction of whiteness fails because it lacks conceptual integrity is to miss the point that his multiple and often contradictory understandings of whiteness work to generate its *dramatic* integrity, by which I mean to collapse the narrative and affective dimensions of what it means to be white. Put simply, that whiteness is a moving target helps to make Dixon's narrative of whiteness a moving story.[10]

In arguing that white identity is *called into being* at the moment the white girl is "jostled"—cumulatively, when white womanhood is threatened—I should clarify first how Dixon explicitly racializes the scenario—how, in other words, the identity at stake is based on the abstraction of race rather than alternative abstractions of class, honor, or regional affiliation. (Indeed, one can read Dixon as grafting race onto an earlier southern shame culture based on precisely those alternatives.) Dixon's intervention is simply to nominate whiteness as the stake of the game, the name of the script. In one of the novel's several passages in which fragmented whiteness gives way to a homogeneous racial identity, "Every discordant element" is suspended in the ecstatic politics of the moment:

> Henceforth there could be but one issue, Are you a White Man or a Negro?
> They declared that there was but one question to be settled:—
> *"Shall the future American be an Anglo-Saxon or a Mulatto?"* (159)

It is not as a gentleman or as a southerner, but as a white man, that action is demanded; indeed, the former modes of identification, especially those based on social class, act as threats to the future American because they prevent white unity. In some ways, Dixon represents poor whites as the purest whites, since they are both untroubled by vestiges of paternalism and more directly threatened by black ascent. The lower-class Tom Camp claims to have "always hated a nigger since I was knee high" (28), and it is he whose two daughters are, in separate incidents, sexually assaulted by black men.[11] The first of these assaults, according to the novel's ideological hero, the Reverend John Durham, "will be the trumpet of the God of our fathers that will call the sleeping manhood of the Anglo-Saxon race to life again" (127). White manhood is thus posited as dormant prior to the "Negro Uprising" (100), just as it acquires a contingent dimension afterward—that is to say, not all men socially recognized as white will fulfill the imperatives of white manhood. The question "Are you a White Man or a Negro?" inquires not of skin color or social recognition, but of intentions; its grammar produces a predicate (what a white man must do; here, vote Democratic) upon which its subject (being a white man) depends. The "issue" thus parallels the "one question": A "White Man" is one who acts to ensure that the future American will be an Anglo-Saxon, a daunting task since, as one character puts it, "there is enough negro blood here to make mulatto the whole Republic" (242). The biological fragility of whiteness—its susceptibility to contamination by one drop of Negro blood[12]—helps to make white identity similarly tenuous. At the same time, it helps to make white identity possible, since only through the identification of themselves as White Men can the erstwhile white men "awaken" to fulfill, as Charles Gaston later puts it, "God's call to our race to do His work in history" (437). White supremacy thus becomes, curiously enough, the cardinal test of a White Man.[13]

Given Dixon's close association of whiteness and nationhood, race treason becomes literally possible and stands not as an obstacle to, but a condition of, white manhood, a test to be overcome if white manhood is to be achieved. We see this, for example, in Dixon's use of doubled characters: Simon Legree stands as the constitutive underside of the Reverend Durham; Allan McLeod, of Charles Gaston. The latter pairing is especially rich from a structural point of view, as Gaston nearly succumbs to the "Voice of the Tempter" (as the chapter is titled) when McLeod offers him a leading role in the evolving scalawag Republicanism that is also, as Gaston eventually recognizes, a form of Negro rule. If Gaston is to become the epic hero of the white nation, he must first undergo an education—a process of *bildung*—as he purifies himself from temptation and his race from contamination.[14] Since white manhood, as Dixon ultimately conceives it, is not a default condition, it can exist as a desirable object—the holy grail of Gaston's quest. In Dixon's writings, white people can never, as it were, be white enough.[15] Nor can they rest secure in their whiteness; the traumatized subjects of Legree's regime are threatened not merely with a loss of power, but a loss of identity, since Legree's politics lead directly toward a mulatto America. It is therefore essential to understand that whiteness is subject to, as Michaels says, recovery, defense, and betrayal precisely because it is embedded in contingent scenarios whose outcomes are in doubt.

To understand the resonance of this racial configuration, we shall need to consider how Dixon's narrative addresses and engages its reader—how, finally, it offers itself as primer in how to be white. *The Leopard's Spots* is a novel rich in what the narrative theorist Peter Brooks (borrowing from Freud) calls forepleasure:

> Forepleasure is indeed a curious concept, suggesting a whole rhetoric of advance toward and retreat from the goal or the end, a formal zone of play (I take it that forepleasure somehow implicates foreplay) that is both harnessed to the end and yet autonomous, capable of deviations and recursive movements. When we begin to unpack the components of forepleasure, we may find a whole erotics of form, which is perhaps what we most need if we are to make formalism serve an understanding of the human functions of literature. Forepleasure would include the notion of both delay and advance in the textual dynamic, the creation of the "dilatory space" which Roland Barthes, in *S/Z*, claimed to be the essence of the textual middle. We seek to advance through this space toward the discharge of the end, yet all the while we are perversely delaying, returning backward in order to put off the promised end and perhaps to assure its greater significance.[16]

The concept of forepleasure helps to elucidate not only the relationship between the novel's dilatory plot (its delays, deferrals, preliminary victories, defeats, humiliations, false starts, and so on) and its intensely pleasurable climax, but also the relationship between form, pleasure, and identification. Pleasure is important in Dixon because it conditions the reader to be white. In Freud's classic essay "A Child Is Being Beaten," the titular scenario produces the simultaneity of mutually exclusive scenarios ("the father beats the child," "the father beats [another] child," "I am being beaten by the father").[17] In Dixon, conversely, a race is being beaten, but it is being beaten sequentially: first, it is the white race, and then it is the black race. There is, moreover, no confusion in the field of the subject; as Dixon's implied reader, *we* are being beaten, and then *we* are beating. Although I want to return to the novel's affective dimension at the conclusion of this essay, suffice it to say for the present that there is a narrative trajectory at the level of affect, an organizing sequence of pleasures just as, when viewing a modern action film, we identify with the hero's preliminary degradation at the hands of the villain so that we can participate in the revengeful pleasures to come. Whiteness thus acquires an affective dimension as a way of feeling, an emotional protocol demanding certain patterns and sequences of empathy and revulsion, pleasure and pain. It is in this sequence of responses that the meaning of whiteness will ultimately reside.

Two features of Dixon's primal scene would have profound consequences in Dixon's novel and its cultural field. First, the sequence blurs in interesting ways the boundaries between erotic and political terrains. Where black men are concerned, this blurring is quite clear: political aggression merely encodes sexual aggression. One of Dixon's crucial sequences, familiar to any student of southern racial politics, works to situate "political equality" as a preliminary gesture toward "social equality" and miscegenation, if not outright rape. When Tim Shelby, for example, obtains a political position as school commissioner, he tries to force a white woman to kiss him in order to get a job as a teacher. Similarly, George Harris, the black protégé of the Radical Republican Everett Lowell, exposes the "preposterous" logic of Lowell's insistence that "Social rights are one thing, political rights another" (392) when he asks for Helen Lowell's hand in marriage. Conversely, white manhood expresses itself in the nation-state. Black men vote to rape, white men vote in order to save civilization, which is to say, to keep black men from raping. The erotic dimension of white politics is simultaneously preserved and concealed. Second, Dixon's sequence could be grafted onto a historical narrative; American history itself could be shown as a variation on Dixon's primal scene. As I hope to show later in this essay, Dixon effects a transfer of white identity from ritual to romance, from the repetitive demands of minstrel shows, lynchings, and dramas of consent to a grand (white) narrative of American history.

In *The Plague of Fantasies*, Slavoj Žižek writes that "the 'sublime object of ideology' is a spectral object that has no positive ontological consistency, but merely fills in the gap of a certain constitutive impossibility." Of the anti-Semitic figure of the Jew, for Žižek the quintessential example of this sublime object, he writes, "it is not the Jew who prevents Society from existing (from realizing itself as a full organic solidarity, etc.); rather, it is social antagonism which is primordial, and the figure of the Jew comes second as a fetish which materialized this hindrance."[18] That Dixon's Negro can substitute for Žižek's Jew is only too clear; we need only observe that all of Dixon's truly dangerous villains are white men who enable the trauma of Dixon's primal scene. Rather than rehearse the intricate patterns of American racial scapegoating upon which Dixon draws and to which he contributes, I want to consider what Žižek adds to the equation: specifically, the *narrative* character of the antagonisms involved. For Žižek, an effective ideology must resolve "some fundamental antagonism by rearranging its terms into a temporal succession,"[19] thereby permitting the experience of what Žižek calls *jouissance*, that orgasmic sensation of psychological wholeness whose lack can be retroactively displaced to a scapegoat who has "stolen" it. Whatever the intrinsic merits of Žižek's scheme, it sheds important lights on the collective plot at the heart of Dixon's novel: the white state achieves organic solidarity (and orgasmic gratification) by "eliminat[ing] the Negro from our life" (434).

The white state appears as the culmination of two dominant narrative movements: one toward a consolidation of white identity that intensifies group identification, the other toward a purification of white identity that maximizes its "whiteness." More precisely, consolidation occurs as a repetitive narrative movement throughout the text, not always with satisfactory results. As Sandra Gunning observes of one lynching, the "regenerative violence" practiced by the white mob "not only threatens to taint white morality and humanity, but also resembles the very bodily distortions threatened by black rape as the white avengers merge with the beast they originally set out to destroy."[20] The consolidation of white identity here is excessive; although "the rich and the poor, the learned and the ignorant, the banker and the blacksmith, the great and the small . . . were all one now" (368), the crowd, as the lynching proceeds, "seemed to melt into a great crawling swaying creature, half reptile half beast, half dragon half man, with a thousand legs, and a thousand eyes, and ten thousand gleaming teeth, and with no ear to hear and no heart to pity!" (380). As Gaston realizes, this degrading cycle of "Godless revenge" threatens to devolve into a war between *two* "thousand-legged beast[s]," one black, one white (382). That this cycle is not narrative enough—that, specifically, it lacks a happy ending—necessitates the purification of white identity—that is, its absolute separation from "the Negro." Yet, as Dixon offers the white state as the means of transcending the eroticized cycle of black sexual predation and white punishment, his final solution (connotation intended) remains anything but stable and fixed.

In examining Dixon's fantasy of a purified, consolidated white identity, we might begin by interrogating the radical circularity of the white state that is both called into being by black rape and devoted more or less exclusively to its eradication. As Charles Gaston says, it is "on account of the enfranchisement of the Negro" that "the people of the South had to go into politics" (280). Moments after this claim, however, Gaston defines politics in a very different way. "Government is the organized virtue of the community," he says, "politics is religion in action" (281). Against the reactionary, contingent politics of his earlier claim, Gaston here describes politics as a positive expression of virtue, an immanent form of transcendent value. The apparent contradiction can be reconciled if we recognize that Gaston's earlier claim is incorrect as a textual matter: the enfranchisement of the Negro makes southerners go not into politics, but into the Klan. (And as we have seen, it is the Klan's threat to kill black voters that drives the Negro, for the moment at least, out of politics.) But Dixon insists here, as he does more explicitly in *The Traitor*, that the Klan be disbanded precisely because of its natural tendencies toward chaotic, unauthorized violence—its gravitation toward a condition of ontological blackness. By "violat[ing] for the moment the statutory law" (161), the Klan can *save* civilization, but it can never *be* civilization itself. In fact, it is the Klan's disbanding—which is to say its self-censorship, its self-discipline—that ensures its purity as an object of piety.[21]

In the final analysis, civilization can only *be* the white state, which stands in a prophylactic, not punitive, relation to black rape, and hence can apparently evade or transcend the degrading cycle of sexual violation and revenge. But as the "post-sexual" state emerges, we should note a few of its curious characteristics that emerge, climactically, in Gaston's "Speech that Made History." For one thing, as Mason Stokes has shown,[22] the scene itself is highly eroticized: Gaston "played with the heart-strings of his hearers in this close personal history as a great master touches the strings of the harp. His voice was now low and quivering with the music of passion, and then soft and caressing" (439); "These patient, kindly people, slow to anger, now terrible in wrath, were trembling with the pent-up passion and fury of years!" (443). Presented as a mechanism of censorship and discipline, the white state ironically emerges out of a virtual political orgy. Moreover, the specifically political dimension of the white state is nonexistent. In fact, Gaston is in total "accord with the modern Republican utterances at almost every issue" (197), while he disagrees vehemently with a Democratic party dominated by "old moss-backs" (193). Still, as he tells the scalawag Allan McLeod, "The name Republican will stink in the South for a century, not because they beat us in war, but because two years after the war, in profound peace, they inaugurated a second war on the unarmed people of the

South, butchering the starving, the wounded, the women and children.... Their attempt to establish with a bayonet an African barbarism on the ruins of Southern society was a conspiracy against human progress" (194). This is identity politics plain and simple, yellow-dog Democracy in its original incarnation as a reactionary practice of white identity. Told as a story originating in trauma, in reaction to a "conspiracy against human progress," the progressive, identitarian narrative of the white state, coupled with its resistance to potentially divisive matters of policy, can produce only what Žižek calls the zero-institution, "the empty signifier with no determinate meaning ... a specific institution which has no positive, determinate function [except] the purely negative one of signaling the presence and actuality of social institution as such, in opposition to its absence, to pre-social chaos."[23]

And yet for all Gaston tells the story of the white state as transitional and progressive—as a narrative of the Law emerging out of chaos, of protected white female virtue following a precarious, threatened white female virtue—he must do so by compulsively rehearsing the trauma *necessitating* the white state. Gaston offers his resolution "to eliminate the Negro from our life" as a solution to the scenario in which "His insolence threatens our womanhood," as the condition of permanently censoring the illicit expression of black sexuality. But in order to do so, Gaston reveals that the white state can never be precisely that—a state, a condition—since its ecstatic climax depends upon recirculating the trauma that it wishes to prevent. In other words, while Gaston tries to tell the story of how "they" were raping "our" women and now we can make them stop, the story he tells reveals that "their" raping "our" women is the very condition of white identity, its obscene supplement, its constitutive fantasy. Only by *telling* the white state as a narrative of progress can Gaston square the circle of his primal scene, or rather transform its unpalatable circularity into a linear sequence that can be swallowed.

In making this claim, I do not mean to suggest that white identity does not "work," but that it depends upon the contradictory fantasies of being constantly traumatized and having transcended that trauma: the question is not one of logic, but of sustaining emotional intensity. Whiteness cannot, as it were, live happily ever after, despite Dixon's assurance that it does. The contradictory logic of *The Leopard's Spots* thus compels its reader toward an awareness that his whiteness is besieged, while simultaneously directing him toward a promised land of racialized pleasure. For this reason, it is crucial that Dixon's narrative terminates where it does, in a moment of pure ecstasy and gratification. For Gaston, the reduction of the world to his frame of fantasy is doubled in politics and love, since in addition to Gaston being acclaimed as the Lord's "messenger anointed to lead His people" (444), his new bride rejects his offer of a public life by affirming, "You are my world" (464). Identified by the Reverend Durham as the "heroine who inspired Charles Gaston with power to mould a million wills to his" (463), Sally is the ideal helpmeet of the new white Adam. Her "wealth and beauty" will "mate with the genius and chivalry of the South" as exemplified by Gaston, thereby producing, her father hopes, "children's children . . . as the sands of the sea!" (463). By this point, Gaston's is, quite literally, the only will left. *The Leopard's Spots* thus concludes with Gaston's (politicized) erotic union with white womanhood and his (eroticized) political union with white men, and in both cases the ecstatic moment of merger comes as an absolute transcendence of recalcitrant reality. If the splitting of white identity is the primary narrative obstacle to be surmounted, the aggregation of the "souls of white folk" (to borrow Michaels's evocative phrase) produces gratification that borders on the explicitly utopian. Though Gaston's speech "fixed the history of the state for a thousand years" (434), not one of those years can be represented, since there is no logic of dénouement that might return the narrative to the world of the everyday. This is why simply being white is, as a formal matter, impossible for Dixon, whose eschatological impulse consistently situates white identity in a narrative progression toward the millennialist fantasy of the thousand-year state that is, simultaneously, a return to a white Eden.

In turning to the question of genre, I want to address more specifically how Dixon's use of historical romance and melodrama work rather brilliantly to generate and consolidate white identity. Briefly, I want to argue that *The Leopard's Spots* grafts the psychosocial dynamics of a lynching onto a grand narrative of American history and destiny. If lynching is, in Trudier Harris's evocative phrase, a ritual of "exorcising blackness,"[24] Dixon offers a kind of exorcism of ritual—a transcendence of ritual's repetitive demands as a condition of expressing white identity. The transition from a repetitive, ritualistic mode of racial discipline to a romance of the white man's burden begins in a series of racial representations that imply a ritual to be superseded. For purposes of classification, we might identify three ritualistic modes of white supremacy, each producing its own racial type: rituals of consent, which produce the figure of faithful retainer; rituals of racial hierarchy, which produce the figure of the comic "darky"; and rituals of exorcism, which produce the figure of the black rapist.[25] Drawing from a dense cultural archive, Dixon produces racial stereotypes only to discard them as his narrative drives toward its fantasy of the white state.

Dixon's first significant black figure is Nelse, the faithful retainer of Charlie's father who accompanies him to the battlefield and bears the dead soldier's sword back to his son. Drawn directly from Thomas Nelson Page's Sam in "Marse Chan,"[26] Nelse loyally evades the "millyons" of Yankee soldier who seek, ineffectually, to emancipate him (11). But while he ritualistically confers manhood on Charlie, he is not much of a man himself, as we see in his comically abortive courtship of his wife. When informed that his slave marriage has no legal standing, he thinks to cow his wife by pretending to consider "odder gals" as matrimonial candidates, only to have his wife quickly establish her supremacy, forcing him to "sleep in the barn for three weeks, court her an hour every day, and bring her five cents worth of red stick candy and a bouquet of flowers as a peace offering at every visit" (62). I need hardly add that the female dominance in this relationship inverts Dixon's normative gender roles, nor that Dixon ultimately has no place for Nelse, as the recipient of paternalistic regard, in his white state. Of narrative necessity, as several critics have observed, he must therefore be killed off, as he is in a chapter entitled "The Old and the New Negro," which efficiently transfers the burden of black representation from Nelse to Charlie's boyhood companion Dick. When Charlie breaks down in tears over the death of his "best friend," Dick responds simply, "I wouldn' cry 'bout er ole nigger" (164).

If Nelse begins as the faithful retainer and ends as the comical darky, Dick enacts a more symbolically dense transition: he begins as the star of a minstrel show and ends as the star of a lynching. As Gunning has noted, Dick is modeled directly on Stowe's Topsy.[27] Like Topsy, Dick comes complete with exaggerated dialect, unkempt appearance, and commitment to his white companion. But Gaston is no little Eva, and where Topsy's "mighty wicked"[28] nature comically masks a Christian waiting to happen, Dick's comic mask conceals true wickedness lurking beneath. After disappearing for a period of years, he appears again as the rapist of Tom Camp's youngest daughter and, subsequently, as the victim of a lynching against which Charlie ineffectually protests. It is necessary both that Charlie protests and that he fails. On the one hand, Dick's lynching is necessary as catharsis; on another, as we have seen, it produces the white mob that fails to differentiate itself from the black "beast" that it punishes. Charlie's protest that the lynching is not sanctioned by law is necessary so that he can go on to produce a superior, law-abiding mob, the "two thousand men [gone] mad" at the conclusion of his climactic speech. Again deployed against Negro "insolence [that] threatens our womanhood," this mob of "citizen kings" bears no taint of blackness, nor does its final solution threaten an endless cycle of degrading violence. As a bulwark against the taint of the black body and the potential contamination of the white (female) body, Dixon offers the purity of the white (male) body politic.

To the psychosocial dimension of this drama that we have already addressed, we can now address how history itself—the years 1865–1900, referenced in the novel's subtitle—is used to ground and validate white identity. One way in which it does is by defining black identity as the product of historical forces. Alongside the essentialist discourse that portrays the Negro as intrinsically barbarous, Dixon tells a contradictory story in which Legree's Regime results in "the complete alienation of the white and black races as compared with the old familiar trust of domestic life" (200)—a story, in other words, that explains the ascendancy of the black rapist over the faithful retainer in historical, not essentialist, terms. More importantly, the exorcism of the ascendant rapist obtains historical coordinates. Through the various symmetries that align Dick's lynching and Gaston's speech, Dixon has Gaston make history by remaking history—that is, by telling Reconstruction and its aftermath as a story of black rape, an iteration of Dixon's primal scene. And here we should note that Dixon is merely extending to a world-historical scale the narrative production of black rape that pressured lynching itself toward pure formalism—that is, an expressive, performative ritual that required only a symbolic "rapist." (We see this pressure especially in the contemporaneous discourse of lynching, which is always about black rape, whereas actual lynchings more often punished other "crimes.") In transposing his racial psychodrama (to which we must afford primacy) to history, Dixon produced a meaning for Reconstruction just as Lost Cause mythology produced a meaning for the Civil War and New South mythology produced a meaning for the Old South. Nationalism generally, as Tom Nairn and many others have observed, tells progressive narratives through regressive means by constructing usable pasts, by "looking inwards, drawing more deeply upon . . . indigenous resources, resurrecting past folk-heroes and myths . . . and so on."[29] But Dixon's "resources" are not limited to the South, nor does he use mythology proper as a vehicle for expressing white supremacy. Here we can usefully juxtapose Dixon with Charles Carroll, whose *The Tempter of Eve* reconstructed the Genesis story so that the tempter is actually a "*negress,* who served Eve in the capacity of maid servant."[30] Where Carroll grounds his white supremacy in a theologically idiosyncratic reading of the Eden myth,[31] Dixon draws from a more ostensibly empirical archive—American history itself. As he did for works throughout his career, Dixon claimed for *The Leopard's Spots* an almost literal factuality. In the "Historical Note" that precedes the novel, Dixon writes that "all the incidents used in Book I . . . were selected from authentic records, or came within my personal knowledge," before going on to claim that the "only serious liberty" he has taken "with history is to tone down the facts to make them credible in fiction." While we may be tempted to dismiss such claims as incredible, it is worth remarking that many contemporary reviews of the novel explicitly affirmed its purported historical authenticity.[32] More importantly, only five years after its publication, Dixon's basic narrative of Reconstruction as a "struggle through which the southern whites, subjugated by adversaries of their own race, thwarted the scheme which threatened permanent subjection to another race"[33] prefaced the northern historian William Archibald Dunning's landmark study of the subject. While simple influence is far too neat an explanation to account for these similarities, neither are they entirely coincidental.

But if Dixon deploys history as "evidence" that white supremacy is the cardinal test of an American and the central theme of American history, its latent content made manifest in the aftermath of Reconstruction, we should reiterate here the novel's trajectory toward pure fantasy. Despite

Dixon's fetishistic attitude toward evidence, *The Leopard's Spots* is accurately labeled as romance and not as history or even historical novel as that genre is usually understood. Indeed, to consider *The Leopard's Spots* in light of the historical novel as practiced by Walter Scott and theorized by Georg Lukács is to help identify its curious amalgamation of fact and fantasy. Peter Schmidt, who identifies numerous parallels between Scott's *Ivanhoe* and *The Clansman*, suggests that Dixon anxiously adapts Scott's dialectical and culturally synthetic narrative of a nation in crisis.[34] But where *The Clansman*'s narrative of sectional reconciliation necessitates at least a simulated dialectic, *The Leopard's Spots* conspicuously lacks this understanding of historical crisis. For Lukács, Scott's great genius was the creation of a "mediocre," "middle-of-the-road hero" able to bring together the extreme social forces "whose struggle fills the novel, whose clash expresses artistically a great crisis in society." "Through the plot," Lukács writes, "at whose centre stands this hero, a neutral ground is sought and found upon which the extreme, opposing social forces can be brought into a human relationship with one another."[35] (As an American example, Lukács offers Cooper's Natty Bumppo, who mediates between Indian and English cultures.) But despite Dixon's stated admiration for Scott,[36] it is precisely this synthetic, mediating function that is impossible in a novel about the clash of two "hostile armies . . . the Black against the White" (84). Given Dixon's insistence on collapsing all antagonisms into this racialized contest, he cannot imagine an alternative politics, and hence political opponents must be discarded as pathetically misguided (Susan Walker), utterly depraved (Legree and his regime), or cravenly opportunistic (Allan McLeod). Progress can only be understood as purification, never as negotiation. This limitation produces, in Lukács's terms, a regression from Scott and Cooper's "real and genuine" historical novels (that is, novels that register history's properly dialectic character) to a "modern attempt to galvanize the old epic artificially into new life"—epic here understood as a literary mode organized around heroes that are, in Hegel's terms, "total individuals who magnificently concentrate with themselves what is otherwise dispersed in the national characters" and who "acquire the right to be placed at the summit and see the principal events in connection with their individual persons."[37] By centering his narrative around such a hero, Dixon returns to what Lukács calls the "normative childlikeness of the epic,"[38] a world in which history is divested of its historicity and subjugated totally to the psychological terrain of trauma and wish fulfillment.[39]

Given the inherent fragility of such a world, we must inquire as to how Dixon maintains it. In turning to the novel's rhetorical dimension, I want to situate *The Leopard's Spots* within the context of melodrama and sentimental power. As they are usually understood, these terms refer to a distinctively feminine tradition in nineteenth-century American literature epitomized by Harriet Beecher Stowe's *Uncle Tom's Cabin*, the novel, of course, to which Dixon was directly responding in *The Leopard's Spots*. But as Glenn Hendler shows in *Public Sentiments*,[40] the "logic of sympathy" underlying the sentimental tradition was not merely a privatizing, feminine affair opposed to the masculine rationality of the public sphere, but instead was a pervasive and widely disseminated strategy of public discourse, identification, and transformative politics.

In considering Dixon's rhetorical genius, we cannot avoid the presence of Stowe.[41] Dixon's revision of *Uncle Tom's Cabin* attempts to subvert the moral hegemony extended by Stowe's novel, understood by Dixon as a grotesque commitment to the Negro as the "sentimental pet of the nation" (261), a role dependent upon the (white) reader's empathetic identification with black suffering. The banishment of the Negro from this role requires, of course, that nationhood be revised as a collective identity organized around the fetish of whiteness, and "[w]hen the Anglo-Saxon race was united into one homogeneous mass . . . the Negro ceased that moment to be a ward of the nation" (409). In slight contrast to Stowe's internal essays and direct address, Dixon has characters (especially the Reverend Durham) repeat key ideas that he wishes to communicate. The use of melodramatic characterization—and we should observe with Schmidt that melodrama "as a genre constantly pushes toward the separation of opposites"[42]—demands, in both cases, extreme patterns of empathy and revulsion. There is no character in American literature more vile than Stowe's Simon Legree, unless it is Dixon's Simon Legree. The pathos of Uncle Tom's suffering is transferred, as Boeckmann suggests, to the character of Tom Camp and more generally, as Jane M. Gaines observes, to the South "cast as a woman."[43] More broadly, Dixon's rhetoric follows Stowe in producing a subject position that is at once demanding and effortless. On the one hand, there are few concrete demands made on the citizen kings hailed in *The Leopard's Spots*. Dixon's contemporaneous reader *already* has access to the white nation produced at the conclusion of the novel, and there is no particular political relation to it required. On one level, this may strike us as a logical scandal: in a novel where the reader is informed that "The name Republican will stink in the South for a century," we are provided with a heroic celebration of the Spanish-American War prosecuted by a Republican administration and starring the future Republican president Theodore Roosevelt, whom Dixon much admired. But at the level of policy, as we have seen, there are zero imperatives in the zero-institution of the white state. Conversely, Dixon is extraordinarily demanding in scripting emotional responses. To return again to Stowe, we might consider her injunction to her reader: "But what can any individual do? Of that every individual can judge. There is one thing that every individual can do,—they can see to it that *they feel right*. An atmosphere of sympathetic influence encircles every human being; and the man or woman who feels strongly, healthily and justly, on the great interests of humanity, is a constant benefactor to the human race. See, then, to your sympathies in this matter!"[44] In counterpoint to the potential quietism of Stowe's demand (merely) to "feel right," to "see, then, to your sympathies," we can offer Dixon's own assessment in *The Leopard's Spots*: "A little Yankee woman wrote a crude book. The single act of that woman's will caused the war, killed a million men, desolated and ruined the South, and changed the history of the world" (262).

If Dixon's concrete, transformative politics of sympathy must remain at least partially implicit, he is quite clear to situate his reader, even at the conclusion of the novel, in a narrative of racial threat. Earlier, he has mapped the declension of a totalized white identity, since after the Klan "saves civilization" early in the novel, Major Dameron predicts that the "redeemed" state can be maintained "so as long as the white people are a unit" (169). This unity is precisely what Allan McLeod and other scalawag race-traitors are able to dissolve in generating the racial threat that Gaston must heroically counter. Similarly, Dixon situates his reader in relation to an alternative future path available to the Negro. As the Reverend Durham observes, "If you train the Negroes to be scientific farmers they will become a race of aristocrats, and when five generations removed from the memory of slavery, a war of races will be inevitable, unless the Anglo-Saxon grant this trained and wealthy African equal social rights. The Anglo-Saxon can not do this without suicide" (335). In a similar vein, Gaston later recognizes that race war will result when "culture and wealth would give the African the courage of conscious strength" (382). Still, Gaston is planning at the very end of the novel "large appropriations for the industrial training of negroes along the lines of the new movement of their more sober leaders" (459),[45] before another lecture from Durham calls him to his senses. What I wish to call attention to here is the absence of inevitable resolution; in contradiction to Dixon's insistence elsewhere that the Negro cannot advance, here the potential for black ascent is an essential correlate to the imperatives of white nationalism. We might almost say the white state needs, on some level, a dangerous antagonist lest its heroic energy dissipate in a series of foregone conclusions. To return to an issue raised earlier, it is not that the possibility of black ascent undermines a racial message, but that it intensifies a scenario in which identity is at stake. Gaston's backsliding is inexplicable except as an attempt on Dixon's part to renew his reader's sense of racial threat.

From an ideological perspective diametrically opposed to Richard Wright's *White Man, Listen!*, *The Leopard's Spots* commands its reader to listen as a white man.[46] In attempting to awaken the "sleeping manhood of the Anglo-Saxon race," Dixon protects against future slumber by interpellating the white subject at the crux of the decision, "shall the future American be white or mulatto?"—by linking Marx's question, "what is to be done?," to a question of identity—"who am I?" Whiteness, as Dixon ultimately conceives it, cannot survive its status as an empowered, unthreatened identity, at which point the highly visible whiteness that activates the Invisible Empire threatens to recede into a whiteness that is merely invisible.[47] Still, it is important, as the emergence of whiteness studies has taught us, not to confuse the invisibility of white identity with its nonexistence, but rather to recognize such invisibility as the tacit, ostensibly normative condition of a group identity whose prerogatives have been assured.

For Dixon, conversely, the narrative production of whiteness demands that it *do something* lest it devolve into a mere fact. Hence his reiteration of the melodrama of besieged whiteness even after whiteness has survived its siege, his recirculation of trauma even after whiteness is no longer traumatized. Dixon's highly charged, almost exotic portrayal of white manhood was received in what might be characterized as a period of white American boredom, a pervasive anxiety over the regularization and standardization of American life around the turn of the century. We see this, as Richard Brodhead shows in his probing analysis of Charles Chesnutt's *The Conjure Woman* (1899), in the desire for exotic, alternative places and ethnicities that drove the genre of local color. Offering "the plot of cultural tourism" as the paradigmatic structure of local color, Brodhead notes that the white consumers of Uncle Julius's conjure tales "inhabit an organized way of life whose very decencies and 'superiorities' ... afflict them with a sense of experiential deprivation," while, for his part, Uncle Julius "wins an enhanced social place for himself by making African-American expressive forms and 'soul' available to others' imaginative participation and consumption."[48] The specter of experiential deprivation has haunted whiteness from its inception; as George Rawick says, the racist meets the symbolic Negro as "a reformed sinner meets a comrade of his previous debaucheries.... In order to insure that he will not slip back into the old ways or act out half-suppressed fantasies, he must see a tremendous difference between his reformed self and those whom he formerly resembled."[49] From minstrelsy to hip-hop, white fascination with blackness often turns precisely on the censorship, self-discipline, and deferred gratification denied the racial other. A year after Dixon published *The Leopard's Spots*, W.E.B. Du Bois describes a biracial American culture in terms that rehearse, if not this precise opposition, an organically related one. Looking forward to "some day on American soil [when] two world-races may give each to each those characteristics both so sadly lack," Du Bois catalogues Negro offerings—the "soul of the Sorrow Songs," for example—to a white "desert of dollars and smartness."[50] Against this vision of a biracial and mutually complementary America, Dixon offers a white America untroubled with experiential deprivation. His grandiose, heroic version of white identity simultaneously censors the illicit pleasures coded "black" and remains intensely pleasurable. In calling, as Gaston does, the "Citizen kings" of the white nation "to the consciousness of [their] kingship" (442), Dixon, like Huey Long after him, offers a promotion, a way of passively living in history on a world-historical scale. And we should reiterate here the immense scale of Dixon's novels: all of American history turns on the pivot of a small Piedmont town, thousands of years hang on a single moment. The imperatives of whiteness have, at every turn, implications that are grandiose and apocalyptic; civilization itself is at stake.

At the same time, we need not assume a perfect alignment between (to use the language of reader-response theory) Dixon's ideal reader and his real readers to assert the novel's efficacy in forwarding its ideological agenda. To be sure, many contemporary reviews offered blanket endorsements of Dixon's ideology.[51] But even among reviews sharply critical of the novel, one finds suggestions that Dixon has altered the terrain of American racial discourse. A hostile review in the *New York Times,* for example, concedes to the novel "a certain dramatic power" and, more significantly, that "the negro is not as Mrs. Stowe imagined him, an Anglo-Saxon bound in black." In going on to claim that "not a little sentimental gush characterized the early efforts for [the Negro's] improvement,"[52] has not the reviewer restated Dixon's characterization of the Negro as the "sentimental pet of the nation"? Similarly, a hostile review in *The Independent* denounces an author who, "with the bloodthirsty imagination of an outraged man . . . contrasts all the cruelties and villainies practiced by the whites in the South with the long suffering virtues and weaknesses of his own oppressed people." The author is Charles Chesnutt, the novel *The Marrow of Tradition,* and while the reviewer goes on to fault Dixon in similar (albeit more muted) language, has not *The Leopard's Spots* effectively radicalized Chesnutt by shifting the location of the "sensible middle," the position from which the reviewer can lament the tribal "war cry" of the extremists?[53] In calling for an "unashamedly 'dogmatic' and 'terrorist'" approach to public speech, Žižek writes, "If racist attitudes were to be rendered acceptable for the mainstream ideologico-political discourse, this would radically shift the balance of the entire ideological hegemony."[54] It is precisely against such a shift, I argue, that Kelly Miller pens his eloquent "open letter," his attempt to fix Dixon beyond the pale of acceptable discourse.[55]

Even among more sympathetic readers of Dixon, we still need not assume total capitulation to the novel's affective logic. Somewhat speculatively, we might consider the experience of Walter Hines Page, whose liberal, paternalistic doctrines are directly attacked in *The Leopard's Spots,* but who, if the story is to be believed, was so engrossed by the novel that he read it in a single sitting before firing off to Dixon a telegram "bursting with enthusiasm and congratulations."[56] Was Page engrossed as a publisher consuming a potential bestseller, or as a white man as Dixon constructs that category? Clearly, this is the kind of question for which the historical record leaves no answers, but I want to at least suggest that Page and many readers like him may be explained in terms of Žižek's assertion that "an ideological identification [interpellation] exerts a true hold on us precisely when we maintain an awareness that we are not fully identical to it, that there is a rich human person beneath it: 'not all is ideology, beneath the ideological mask, I am also a human person' is *the very form of ideology,* of its 'practical efficiency.'"[57] What I am suggesting, finally, is that Dixon enables white supremacist ideology by expanding its limits, by opening a space for a less virulent white supremacy—genteel racism, as Williamson calls it—whose effects may ultimately have been more pernicious. A striking irony of a novel without irony is that even as a *guilty* pleasure it may have done its work.

Writing of Thomas Dixon, Kim Magowan claims that "[n]othing is more central to white supremacy than the notion of identity being fixed and stable."[58] Let me reiterate why I feel such claims are wrongly premised. Conceived as an inert conceptual system to be passively imprinted on readers, Dixon's novels surely fail, but to say this is to imply that they *did* fail and to ignore in crucial ways what novels *do*.

As I have shown, Dixon's pernicious genius was to offer a compelling scenario of white identity—compelling not in spite of, but because of, the unfixed, unstable identities he produces. Dixon's white manhood, like the white nation in which it is finally articulated, is not a given, but an achievement, not a timeless essence, but a tenuous contingency. Dixon's intervention in American history was not to make whiteness coherent, but to make it desirable. Through his deployment of narrative structure and literary genre, Thomas Dixon helped to generate the affective structures of whiteness as identification and identity, making his story one of modern America's darkest chapters.

NOTES

1. Joel Williamson, *The Crucible of Race: Black-White Relations in the American South since Emancipation* (New York: Oxford Univ. Press, 1984), 140; Grace Elizabeth Hale, *Making Whiteness: The Culture of Segregation in the South, 1890–1940* (New York: Pantheon Books, 1998).

2. Walter Benn Michaels, *Our America: Nativism, Modernism, and Pluralism* (Durham: Duke Univ. Press, 1995), 185.

3. Williamson, *Crucible of Race,* 140.

4. Denise Riley, *The Words of Selves: Identification, Solidarity, Irony* (Stanford: Stanford Univ. Press, 2000), 13.

5. Cathy Boeckmann, *A Question of Character: Scientific Racism and the Genres of American Fiction, 1892–1912* (Tuscaloosa: Univ. of Alabama Press, 2000), 65.

6. Judith Jackson Fossett claims that "Dixon constructs an almost seamless Manichean racial, gender, and regional economy for the postbellum period"; still, she argues, "Despite Dixon's narratorial attempts to the contrary, the strict binaries are not entirely sustainable." See Judith Jackson Fossett, "(K)night Riders in (K)night Gowns: The Ku Klux Klan, Race, and Constructions of Masculinity," in *Race Consciousness: African-American Studies for the New Century*, ed. Judith Jackson Fossett and Jeffrey A. Tucker (New York: New York Univ. Press, 1997), 37. Noting a similar confusion of racial and gender identities, Kim Magowan writes that "when the white man cannot separate race and gender difference in his own body, the identity of the Ku Klux Klan as the unit that separates alleged difference dissolves." See Kim Magowan, "Coming between the 'Black Beast' and the White Virgin: The Pressures of Liminality in Thomas Dixon," *Studies in American Fiction* 27 (spring 1999): 83.

7. Fredric Jameson, *The Political Unconscious: Narrative as a Socially Symbolic Act* (Ithaca: Cornell Univ. Press, 1981), 82–83.

8. David R. Roediger, *Towards the Abolition of Whiteness: Essays on Race, Politics, and Working Class History* (New York: Verso, 1994), 12.

9. Thomas Dixon Jr., *The Leopard's Spots: A Romance of the White Man's Burden, 1865–1900* (New York: Doubleday, Page, 1902), 410. Hereafter cited parenthetically.

10. In a splendidly argued critique of white studies and its impact on historical scholarship, Eric Arnesen complains specifically of the "moving target" of whiteness offered by contemporary scholarship in white studies. To his critique of the "conceptual slippage between crucial terms—whiteness and white supremacy," I can only offer here that Dixon attempts to effect precisely this slippage, just as he attempts to subordinate alternative forms of identification to a specifically white identity—a totalizing move characterized by Arnesen (correctly, in my opinion) as being problematically reproduced in white studies itself. More broadly, Arnesen helps to define the problematic threshold between historiography and cultural studies, especially where the latter depends on literary texts. While this essay attempts to explain Dixon's production of whiteness as a matter of formal logic directed toward a hypothetical reader, it must remain largely speculative in determining the impact of that logic on a concrete historical formation. See Eric Arnesen, "Whiteness and the Historians' Imagination," *International Labor and Working-Class History* 60 (fall 2001): 3–32, especially 6–9, 15, 21–23.

11. It is equally true, as Sandra Gunning argues, that Tom Camp *least* fulfills the imperatives of white manhood, since he is effectively unmanned (as an amputee, he cannot protect his daughters) and animalized (he spearheads the lynch mob's descent into savagery). See Sandra Gunning, *Race, Rape, and Lynching: The Red Record of American Literature, 1890–1912* (New York: Oxford Univ. Press, 1996), 39–40. Ultimately, it is Camp's strategic location on the various thresholds of white identity—between female/male; victim/defender; civilized/savage; white/black—that makes him a compelling figure in Dixon's unfolding drama.

12. Throughout the novel, Dixon reiterates the fantasy of biological contamination through blood, most graphically perhaps when Lowell forbids George Harris from marrying his daughter (see discussion below). In that scene, Lowell affirms to Harris that he knows "the important fact that a man or woman of negro ancestry, though a century removed, will suddenly breed back to a pure negro child, thick lipped, kinky headed, flat nosed, black skinned" (394).

13. The circularity of this formulation allows us to revisit the question of racial essentialism. Is it not that identification precedes in Dixon (and in group identification generally, although usually less pathologically) the content upon which identification is ostensibly based? In Dixon, we see this in that only white men who identify themselves as such possess those racial characteristics that justify white supremacy. Reading essentialist definitions of race as an effect, not a cause, of identification helps explain the imperviousness of white racism (to take our immediate example) to logic: new racial characteristics can always be produced (as an object of psychological investment) once the identification is secured. What is essential, as I discuss below, is that these characteristics can be deployed to differentiate "us" from "them."

14. From the perspective of genre, *The Leopard's Spots* can be read as a *bildungsroman* grafted onto an epic—a kind of *A Portrait of the Epic Hero as a Young White Man,* if you will. The extreme generic eclecticism of *The Leopard's Spots* (see discussion below) fulfills M. M. Bakhtin's description of the novel as the genre into which all other genres are incorporated while simultaneously banishing any hint of dialogism (Bakhtin's label for the novel's dynamic mediation of "various different points of view, conceptual horizons, systems for providing expressive accents, [and] various social 'languages'"). See M. M. Bakhtin, *The Dialogic Imagination,* ed. and trans. Michael Holquist and Caryl Emerson (Austin: Univ. of Texas Press, 1981), 282. For an examination of Charlie Gaston's "purification of speech as the young representative of the post-war generation [who must learn] to speak Durham's untainted dialect of white supremacy," see Scott Romine, "Things Falling Apart: The Postcolonial Condition of *Red Rock* and *The Leopard's Spots,*" in *Look Away! The U.S. South in New World Studies,* ed. Jon Smith and Deborah Cohn (Durham: Duke Univ. Press, 2004), 187.

15. Michaels offers a similar argument, claiming that Dixon's Clansmen "wear sheets because their bodies aren't as white as their souls, because no body can be as white as the soul embodied in the white sheet"; see Walter Benn Michaels, "The Souls of White Folk," in *Literature and the Body: Essays on Populations and Persons,* ed. Elaine Scarry (Baltimore: Johns Hopkins Univ. Press, 1988), 187. Fossett and Boeckmann also thoughtfully explore the problematics of externalizing white identity. My concern here is more teleological in nature— that is, understanding whiteness as a *process* of purification—of, in fact, becoming white.

16. Peter Brooks, "The Idea of a Psychoanalytic Literary Critic," *Critical Inquiry* 13 (1987): 339.

17. Sigmund Freud, "'A Child Is Being Beaten': A Contribution to the Study of the Origin of Sexual Perversions," in *The Standard Edition of the Complete Psychological Works of Sigmund Freud,* trans. and ed. James Strachey, vol. 17 (London: Hogarth Press and the Institute for Psycho-Analysis, 1955), 179–204.

18. Slavoj Žižek, *The Plague of Fantasies* (London: Verso, 1998), 76.

19. Ibid., 11.

20. Gunning, *Race, Rape, and Lynching*, 40.

21. Thomas Dixon Jr., *The Traitor: A Story of the Fall of the Invisible Empire* (New York: Doubleday, Page, 1907). Dixon's emphatic denunciation of the post-1870 Klan is replicated in his well-documented opposition to the modern Klan, founded in 1915 at Stone Mountain, Georgia, on a date chosen to coincide with the Atlanta premiere of *Birth of a Nation*. See Raymond Cook, *Fire from the Flint: The Amazing Careers of Thomas Dixon* (Winston-Salem, N.C.: Blair, 1968), 196–97.

22. Mason Stokes, *The Color of Sex: Whiteness, Heterosexuality, and the Fictions of White Supremacy* (Durham: Duke Univ. Press, 2001), 150–51.

23. Slavoj Žižek, "The Matrix: Or, The Two Sides of Perversion," paper presented at the Center for Art and Media, Karlsruhe, Germany, October 1999, http://container.zkm.de/net condition/matrix/zizek.html (accessed August 11, 2003). I should also note my general indebtedness here to Joan W. Scott, "Fantasy Echo: History and the Construction of Identity," *Critical Inquiry* 27 (winter 2001): 284–304, especially 284–92.

24. Trudier Harris, *Exorcising Blackness: Historical and Literary Lynching and Burning Rituals* (Bloomington: Indiana Univ. Press, 1984).

25. Although even a preliminary taxonomy of such rituals and types is far beyond the scope of this essay, I want to emphasize Dixon's narrative regression through a series of already established racial types. This regression obtains an affective trajectory—from affection to smiling contempt to revulsion—that corresponds to the descending order of humanity associated with the type in question.

26. Thomas Nelson Page, *In Ole Virginia: Or, Marse Chan and Other Stories* (1887; reprint, Chapel Hill: Univ. of North Carolina Press, 1969).

27. Gunning, *Race, Rape, and Lynching*, 36.

28. Harriet Beecher Stowe, *Uncle Tom's Cabin: Or, Life Among the Lowly* (1852), in Harriet Beecher Stowe, *Three Novels* (New York: Library of America, 1982), 286.

29. Tom Nairn, *The Break-Up of Britain* (London: New Left, 1977), 348.

30. Charles Carroll, *The Tempter of Eve; or, The Criminality of Man's Social, Political, and Religious Equality with the Negro* . . . (St. Louis: Adamic Pub. Co., 1902), 402.

31. For an excellent analysis of Carroll's work in context, see Stokes, *Color of Sex*, 95–107. Although Stokes shows how the bizarre logic of *The Tempter of Eve* draws from contemporaneous theology and scientific racism, the structural advantages of Dixon's pseudo-historicism seem clear.

32. Lilian Bell offers a typical example, affirming that "most of the stern facts marshaled by the author are quite unknown to even the so-called enlightened people." See Bell, Review of *The Leopard's Spots*, by Thomas Dixon Jr., *Saturday Evening Post*, April 12, 1902, p. 15.

33. William Archibald Dunning, *Reconstruction: Political and Economic, 1865–1877* (New York: Harper, 1907), xv.

34. Peter Schmidt, "Walter Scott, Postcolonial Theory, and New South Literature," *Mississippi Quarterly* 56 (2003): 552–53; Thomas Dixon Jr., *The Clansman* (New York: Doubleday, Page, 1905).

35. Georg Lukács, *The Historical Novel*, trans. Hannah and Stanley Mitchell (Boston: Beacon Press, 1962), 36, 37, 36, 36.

36. See Raymond Cook, *Thomas Dixon* (New York: Twayne Publishers, 1974), 55.

37. Lukács, *Historical Novel*, 36.

38. Georg Lukács, *The Theory of the Novel*, trans. Anna Bostock (Cambridge: MIT Press, 1990), 71.

39. A reviewer in *The Independent* offers the perspicacious insight that "when historical facts are dramatized, as they are in this novel, they cease to be mere records of the past. They are infused with the spirit of a living personality and become accusations." See Review of *The Leopard's Spots*, by Thomas Dixon Jr., *Independent* 54 (June 19, 1902): 1549.

40. Glenn Hendler, *Public Sentiments: Structures of Feeling in Nineteenth-Century American Literature* (Chapel Hill: Univ. of North Carolina Press, 2001), especially 212–19.

41. One of the notable, although hardly surprising, features of Dixon's critical revival is the total absence of aesthetic recuperation, despite similar efforts made on behalf of women writers who share many of Dixon's stylistic and formal features. Jane Tompkins's celebrated defense of Stowe, for example, especially in its elucidation of Stowe's complex engagement with contemporaneous cultural myths, can be transposed almost effortlessly to Dixon. That it has not—that critics still routinely characterize Dixon as beyond the aesthetic pale—points to the continued (and perhaps inevitable) connection between politics and aesthetics. Put bluntly, Dixon's hideous racism makes his works aesthetically unsalvageable. See Jane Tompkins, *Sensational Designs: The Cultural Work of American Fiction, 1790–1860* (New York: Oxford Univ. Press, 1985), 122–46.

42. Schmidt, "Walter Scott," 552.

43. Boeckmann, *Question of Character*, 76–77; Jane M. Gaines, "Thomas Dixon and Race Melodrama," in this volume.

44. Stowe, *Uncle Tom's Cabin*, 515.

45. The allusion here to Booker T. Washington's "false solution" to American race relations predicts Dixon's own denunciation of the Washingtonian program in his 1905 essay "Booker T. Washington and the Negro," *Saturday Evening Post*, August 19, 1905, pp. 1–2.

46. Richard Wright, *White Man, Listen!* (Garden City, N.Y.: Doubleday, 1957).

47. The relatively secure position of white Americans in 1915 relative to earlier in the century may account for the very different reactions to *The Clansman* and *The Birth of a Nation* observed by John Inscoe. More importantly, it may account for Dixon's displeasure at the change. See John Inscoe, "*The Clansman* on Stage and Screen: North Carolina Reacts," *North Carolina Historical Review* 64 (April 1987): 139–61. The difficulty of sustaining white identity in the absence of threat may account for Gaston's ill-defined "conquest of the globe" (435), an imperialist project that seems motivated largely by the need to give white men something heroic to do.

48. Richard Brodhead, introduction to Charles W. Chesnutt, *The Conjure Woman and Other Conjure Tales*, ed. Richard Brodhead (Durham: Duke Univ. Press, 1993), 2, 11–12, 12. For several reasons, Chesnutt is an interesting author to read alongside Dixon, among them Chesnutt's use of the label "Future American" to refer to a *mixed-race* or postracial American and the fact that both authors were edited by Walter Hines Page.

49. George P. Rawick, *From Sundown to Sunup: The Making of the Black Community* (Westport, Conn.: Greenwood Press, 1972), 132–33.

50. W.E.B. Du Bois, *The Souls of Black Folk*, in W.E.B. Du Bois, *Writings* (New York: Library of America, 1996), 370.

51. Writing in *The Bookman*, Mansfield Allan offers a typical example, claiming that "When the negro problem is settled in the only way that can be settled so long as Anglo-Saxonism retains its solidarity and its pride, then in truth North and South will be 'triumphantly reunited.'" See Mansfield Allan, Review of *The Leopard's Spots*, by Thomas Dixon Jr., *Bookman* 15 (July 1902): 474. For some reviewers, Dixon erred on the side of caution. A review in the *William and Mary Quarterly*, for example, faults Dixon for portraying Lincoln too sympathetically; see Review of *The Leopard's Spots*, by Thomas Dixon Jr., *William and Mary Quarterly* 10 (1902): 283.

52. Review of *The Leopard's Spots*, by Thomas Dixon Jr., *New York Times*, April 5, 1902, BR10.

53. Review of *The Leopard's Spots*, by Thomas Dixon Jr., *Independent* 54 (June 19, 1902): 1548.

54. Žižek, *Plague of Fantasies*, 26.

55. Kelly Miller, *As to The Leopard's Spots: An Open Letter to Thomas Dixon, Jr.* (Washington, D.C.: Howard University, 1905).

56. Cook, *Fire from the Flint*, 109–10.

57. Žižek, *Plague of Fantasies*, 21.

58. Magowan, "Coming Between," 83.

Thomas Dixon and Race Melodrama

JANE M. GAINES

Many times in my work on the relationship between the cinematic power of *The Birth of a Nation* (1915) and the monumental African American answer to it, Oscar Micheaux's *Within Our Gates* (1920), I have thought about Thomas Dixon.[1] I have never considered him as an author, however. This is not to say that I am dismissing him as a literary figure. Quite to the contrary, I applaud recent attempts by renowned literary analysts to read *The Clansman* and *The Leopard's Spots* as sources of *The Birth of a Nation* for what these popular novels tell us about the rise of American nationalism and nationhood.[2] My stance is a challenge to the paradigm of authorship in which the accepted critical practice renders the life of the author synonymous with the life of the text.[3] Instead, I am proposing that authors and readers or viewers meet in a shared paradigm that takes the cultural form of a very popular genre: melodrama. Melodrama is here a shared conceptual structure that governs lives, that is shaped through, by, and as the popular cultural production which has its lived as well as its literary and cinematic forms. Within this article I will be talking about and defining the more historically circumscribed race melodrama.

I turn here to Dixon's account of himself as an audience member at his first viewing of *The Birth of a Nation*, the film he helped to produce. This involves not only analyzing parts of his memoirs but also interpreting his own recollections as a document of cultural reception. Let me set the scene. On this occasion, the film was screened for a small group just before the March 3, 1915, premiere in New York. This screening featured Joseph Carl Breil directing his newly composed score.[4] The scene is all the stranger since the hall is virtually empty. The Liberty Theatre at Broadway and 53rd Street, as Dixon recalls it, was a cold and cavernous two thousand-seat auditorium filled with only seventy-five select few. Far away in the pit, says Dixon, Breil was rehearsing a "weary" orchestra over an "incomplete score," frustrated to the point where he was "tearing his hair in a hopeless sort of frenzy."

> I crept up stairs into a shadowy corner to watch alone. I was prepared for the worst. I was in no sense prepared for what I saw and heard. The last light dimmed, a weird sound came from the abyss below. The first note of the orchestra, a low cry of the anguished South being put to torture. It set my nerves tingling with its call. And then the faint bugle note of the Southern Bivouac of the Dead. In it no startling challenge to action. No trumpet signal to conflict. It came from the shrouded figures of the shadow world. And then I saw my story enacted before my eyes in beauty and reality. And always the throb through the darkness of that orchestra raising the emotional power of each scene to undreamed of heights.[5]

There are two evocative images of sound that I want to single out here: the "weird cry," also a "low cry," and the "throb through the darkness" of the orchestra—crying and throbbing.

Some might say that this written recollection is hardly empirical evidence of anything. Clearly it can also be argued that Dixon provides us with an excellent example of someone whose perceptions of the world were entirely self-interested. He lived as well as reproduced in his creative work the epitome of the nineteenth-century "melodramatic world view." Dixon, after all, apparently understood everything in terms of "anguished cries" and "emotional depths."[6] The world seemed to this Baptist minister always divided into two camps: the victimized and the villainous, the sympathetic tortured and the heartless torturer. A reading of this chapter, "My First Picture," from Dixon's memoirs, *Southern Horizons*, also shows that he cast the critics of *The Birth of a Nation* in these same dichotomous camps—and conflated all enemies, old and new. "And now the sinister forces that had provoked me to write the story were gathering to suppress it," he wrote, describing the influential figures lined up to oppose the opening of the film on the East Coast.[7]

At the point of the dramatization of dichotomization and the plumbing of the depths of emotion—here is where Thomas Dixon meets the cinema.

The melodramatic scheme of things was made manifest for him as never before in the new moving picture machine. Of the motion picture he wrote that it was a "new process of reasoning by which the will could be overwhelmed with conviction."[8] This would seem to be his formulation of the old struggle between reason and emotion where he awards the day to emotion. And in this regard, it is important to note that Dixon's own emotional response, and certainly his recollection, seem to be based entirely on acoustic imagery. In his memoirs, Dixon describes not what he *saw* that first night but what he *heard*. No scene is recollected. What he recalls is not the first image but the "first note" played by the orchestra. His first impression of the powerful new medium is a sound and not a pictorial image. Or, better, he is impressed by an image produced by an acoustic sign, not an iconic sign. Why does this matter to the history of cinema?

The serious study of the sound track has come relatively late in the production of the history of cinema. Thus, work on this earliest period of sound and musical production for dramatic works opened up only in the last decade, after the publication of music theorist and film historian Martin Marks's seminal work on the silent score. While it was so often said that the silent film never was exactly "silent" that the refrain became a kind of joke, that bit of humor served the serious purpose of reminding the field of the incredibly rich area that still needed to be opened up for further research.[9] Under the question of sound, which includes effects, narration, and miscellaneous music, the score is perhaps the most complicated. Here the score for *The Birth of a Nation* is a monumental paradigm-setter as it looks backward to the miscellany of piano accompaniment and forward to the mellifluous underscoring of the classical Hollywood narrative. One way of talking about this difference is to refer to the way that Breil's score is two kinds of score in one. First, as a composite score it was somewhat of a throwback to the earliest silent film accompaniment, often sewn together from "bits" of music from a published anthology of appropriate phraseology such as "Hurry" music or nautical motifs. As a composite score, *The Birth of a Nation* score included both high and low music, familiar tunes such as "Dixie" and classical strains such as Wagner's "Ride of the Valkyries." In retrospect, however, it is Breil's originally composed music supplementing the composite score that sets a new standard for the industry. As film historians have understood it, the power of such a classical score derives from the way in which it tells the same story that the pictorial images tell, only in musical terms. The potency of what is called "underscoring" is in its capacity to meld the disparate pieces of the production in such a way that the viewer feels a fluid whole experienced as overwhelming emotion—not as individual pictures and certainly not as individual tunes. The legend of Breil's explosive score is founded on the premise that it was an original orchestral piece in its own right at the same time that it bridged the "unoriginal" musics, contradictory though this may seem.

There have been many attempts to come to terms with the cataclysmic power of *The Birth of a Nation*, particularly in the first troubled years of its exhibition and distribution in the United States.[10] I have argued before that these accounts, however, do not begin to consider the contribution that the orchestral score would have made to the controversial reception of the film.[11] My previous study was aimed at scholars in film theory and music theory and had as its goal the restatement of the importance of the score as a decided dimension of melodrama as a genre. This entailed recalling the origins of the term *melodrama* in the French term *mélo-drame* (music-drama), which understands the music-like dimension of other moving-picture signs—gestures, words, and rhythmically cut pictures.[12] Thus I am starting from the assumption that we need to think more about the musical component to melodrama-as-performance as well as the function of this melos as it is heard and felt. But here I want to go further to ask how one undertakes research on the reception of popular sound in history. How is one to take accounts such as Dixon's? Surprisingly, Thomas Dixon was not the only audience member to register his reaction to the orchestral score as played in the first year of *The Birth of a Nation*'s exhibition history. Others, from film critic and poet Vachel Lindsay to the NAACP's Francis Hackett, recalled the rhythms of the Breil score vividly, as we will see.

But before we talk about the retrospective accounts of what was heard, we need to turn to the orchestral score itself, with a few provisos. For in the research on the reception of musics, we are faced with more than one interesting asymmetry. First, there is the asymmetry on one side of the written score and recorded performance, and the personal recollection of having heard that music performed in a certain way on the other side. Asymmetry is also there in the phenomenological problem presented by written notation, which is interpreted as it is musically performed as well as interpreted as it is heard at the moment of reception—an interpretation on top of an interpretation. All of the literature in the new cultural studies of music suggests that music works on each of us in predictable cultural ways, but that because it reaches the listener via a more direct route than other signifiers it is often perceived as "my music." As Claudia Gorbman has said, "music directly accesses the psyche." The film music that reaches us so directly also fills things out suggestively (that is, unspecifically) for the viewer. It contributes to the evocative immersion of the spectator. Again, Gorbman describes this process: "Music removes barriers to belief; it bonds spectator to spectacle, it envelops spectator and spectacle in a harmonious space. Like hypnosis, it silences the spectator's censor. It is suggestive; if it's working right, it makes us a little less critical and a little more prone to dream."[13] This is all by way of helping us to think of Thomas Dixon as imaginatively immersed within the film score in which he hears the "throb through the darkness" of the orchestra and the "low cry of an anguished South being put to torture." We might say that he *hears* his *vision*. But what is that vision?

Now, by way of contrast with Dixon's interpretation-recollection of what he heard, let us turn to the printed musical score and the orchestral performance of the Joseph Carl Breil composition.[14] As Neil Lerner and I discovered when we undertook an exhaustive close analysis of the Breil score, the very "first note of the orchestra" is played in the introductory section, a section titled the "Motif of Barbarism" on the published sheet music that appeared for sale within the first year of the film's release.[15] Also called the "Negro theme," we have found this theme to be distinctive and persistent in Breil's score for *The Birth of a Nation*. While the motif is really introduced in the first four measures, we have looked at the first seven measures in the composer's score. (See Figure 1.)

The "Motif of Barbarism" music accompanies the first moving images of the entire film, the tableau of a minister standing in prayer above African slaves who kneel before him. At this point in the film, three measures have been added to the four-measure motif, measures that could be read as signifying the civilizing influence of the minister as they work toward a melodic resolution. Several features of this music contribute to the signification of "the primitive." Most noticeable in its first appearance is the insistent tom-tom rhythm that is beating underneath a mildly syncopated melody, a syncopation effected by accenting the weak part of the first beat of

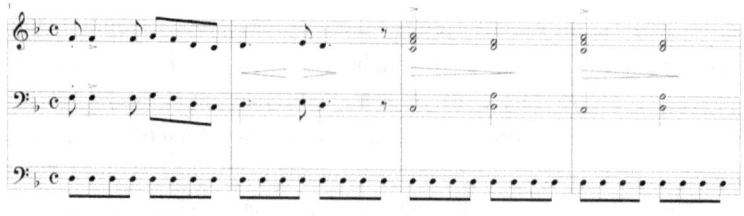
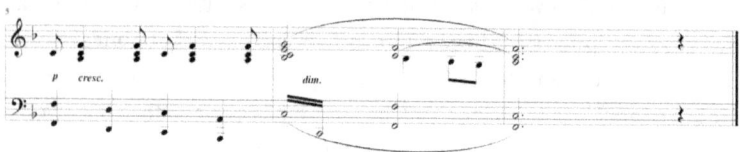

Figure 1. "Motif of Barbarism," first appeared (MOMA-LC, page 1) from *The Birth of a Nation*, by J. C. Breil.

the first measure. The origins of this kind of syncopation are important to recall since this draws our attention to the question of the cultural history of connotations. African musical traditions are rich in their use of cross-rhythms and polyrhythms, rhythms that produce syncopations, and it has been widely argued that African syncopation has had a profound influence on American popular music from the nineteenth century to the present. As we will see, in *The Birth of a Nation*, syncopation becomes attached to connotations of "primitive" sexual instincts that have the potential to become predatory and violent. Although at the outset the motif is attached to Africans in general, later it will become attached not to all black characters, but to those who are specifically positioned as sexually threatening (Gus, Silas Lynch, and Lydia Brown, Austin Stoneman's mulatta mistress).

The first occurrence of Breil's "Motif of Barbarism" sets up several contrasting oppositions, creating a musical signifier for "primitivism," a signifier that is defined against European art-music norms. Thus, syncopation is opposed to the melodic smoothness of European rhythms. In addition, musical textures are contrasted. Breil's "barbaric" melody is first given in octaves lacking the homophonic or polyphonic underpinnings so prized in European music since the rise of polyphony. (European art music privileges the trained coordination of multiple, simultaneous melodic lines.) In contrast, the "gapped" melody of the "Barbarism Motif" (in which there is a jump of a minor third between the fifth and sixth melodic notes) and a flat seventh scale degree establishes a pentatonic pitch collection, one frequently found in folk musics. Finally, the use of a D minor key, a sad and tragic key, is notable through the first four measures, through both the arrival on D and through its restatement in measure two, as well as through repeated modal cadences in measures three and four. Measures five through seven move to the parallel major key of F and a fuller homophonic texture.

In this introductory laying out of the "Barbarism Motif," the suspension in measure six helps add to the hymn-like character of this final part of the cue, the part associated with the image of the minister. The entire first statement of the Barbarism theme therefore uses musical binaries (such as minor/major) to set out the thematic binary—the black/white binary of the overall film.

The above analysis of the "Motif of Barbarism" in the introductory moments of the Breil score was undertaken in collaboration with an expert musicologist, and I have left it virtually intact here for a specific reason. Our earlier concern was less interested in Thomas Dixon's romantic memory and more concerned with performing a careful cultural reading of the motif. But in the context of this paper our careful description becomes useful as a check against personal recollections. We were struck most immediately with the "tom-tom" drums in the bass clef under the first four bars and noted that in the performed score the kettle drum beat was heard more than once accompanying the "Motif of Barbarism" melody. It seemed relevant to us that the memory of at least two other contemporary audience members focused on this same music, which emerged for them as a signifier of primitive passions. For instance, Vachel Lindsay objected to what he felt was a mismatch between music and scene where in his hometown of Rochester, Illinois, "hoochey koochey strains" were heard in the wrong places.[16] Similarly, Francis Hackett, the NAACP member, heard "hoochy-coochy" music. He particularly objected to its use in its relation to the scene in which, as he described it, Gus, the "lust-maddened Negro" pursues the "innocent white girl."[17]

Although Dixon is recalling the introductory strains of music over the arriving slaves and not what later became known as the "Gus chase" scene, the first two measures of "Motif of Barbarism" are fundamental to the underscoring in both, as I have said.[18] Thus we could pose the hypothesis that what others heard as "hootchy-kootchy" music was heard by Dixon as the "weird cry from the abyss below," the "low cry" and the "throb through the darkness" of the orchestra. But while his descriptive choices (weird, low, and throb) could be describing the polyrhythmic African syncopation, the gapped as opposed to the smooth melody, and the pentatonic pitch from folk music, how do we explain the "cry" that he heard? What in Breil's music signifies not only "cry," but "weird" and "low," connotations that lead Dixon to associate what he hears with the "anguished South being put to torture." Surely it must be the D minor key, that "sad and tragic key," that the author of *The Clansman* is hearing as the South in the historical throes of agony. There is here a perfect match between Dixon's sensibilities and those of the film, which, after all, epitomizes the tradition of nineteenth-century theatrical melodrama as it was being reinvigorated through this new form of light and shadow.

The case I want to make about Thomas Dixon's hearing, about his recollection of the orchestral score, is that this matching of sensibilities should be understood not as personal authorship but as the function of genre. Genre is a way around authorial influence, here corrected with an idea of shared rules and codes governing the narrative thread as well as the screen pictorialization. A genre approach has the advantage of allowing us to understand the relationship between Dixon and director D. W. Griffith, not as two authors but as two southerners sharing a melodramatic worldview. As reconceived in recent years by literary critics such as Peter Brooks, melodrama is increasingly understood as a structure that supports works of high literary culture as much as lower and more popular forms. Taken over by film theorists, melodrama is discovered as the underpinning for most of Hollywood cinema in its entire first century, its features particularly pronounced in the silent era. To say what some of these features are should help us to think about Thomas Dixon's relationship to the form that preceded him, that wrote him as much as or more than he wrote it.

Yet melodrama is also more than its features and is irreducible to its literary or cinematic form since its ideological sphere of influence may be the *lived* reality of an entire culture. Helping to specify this for us, Linda Williams has recently demonstrated the relationship between Harriet

Beecher Stowe's 1852 *Uncle Tom's Cabin*, *The Birth of a Nation*, and the televised O. J. Simpson trials of the 1990s. To state the premise of her book: "[S]ince the mid-nineteenth century, melodrama has been, for better or worse, the primary way in which mainstream American culture has dealt with the moral dilemma of having first enslaved and then withheld equal rights to generations of African Americans."[19] These "race" melodramas of black and white, exemplified by *The Birth of a Nation* as well as *Uncle Tom's Cabin*, function as a kind of national dialogue over the decades following the Civil War, where the sympathy toward the Uncle Tom of Stowe's novel is answered by the antipathy toward the mulatto in *The Birth of a Nation*, forged into what Williams here calls the anti-Tom. As she says, melodrama as a form was "yoked into a dialectic of racial pathos and antipathy."[20] Thus the "race melodrama" of my title refers to the form within which the warring took place, those cultural wars over having enslaved and been enslaved, forged in black and white terms by blackened and whitened groups.[21] The African American race melodramas on film from the same period as *The Birth of a Nation* are race melodramas of a different kind, as their rhetoric of uplift is meant to change the subject from slavery to success, but success always in racial terms against a history of overcoming and having overcome unspeakable adversity.[22]

Key features of melodrama lend themselves to this cultural discourse conceived in the broadest of terms and on the most elevated of scales. Of the many features we could identify, I want to mention three here: the tendency to privilege the point of view of the victim, the urge to hyperbolize, and the proclivity to dichotomize, to which I have already referred earlier. If there is one feature of nineteenth-century melodrama that most defines its political persuasion, it is the tendency to take the point of view of the victim, most dramatically seen in *Uncle Tom's Cabin*, where the lowly and beleaguered win the day as their values triumph. It has often been said that the difference in the melodramatic structure between *The Birth of a Nation* and *Uncle Tom's Cabin* is that the white woman has been switched with the black man as the sufferer and the object in need of saving. I would amend this somewhat, recognizing the way that in *The Birth of a Nation* the entire South is cast as a woman, but seeing also in Dixon's "low cry of the anguished South being put to torture" a downtrodden people emerge, a whole *people* whose point of view is privileged. One of the more interesting questions for melodrama theory arises here in the problem of the political valence of a melodrama like *The Birth of a Nation*. While melodrama itself has been understood as carrying over the legacy of a radical political vantage point from as far back as the French Revolution, we still need to understand the vulnerability of this structure to manipulation. *The Birth of a Nation* perhaps helps us to see that the reversal of fates in which the underdog triumphs over the forces of oppression does not translate automatically into a progressive political program. Suffice it to say that the proclivity to dichotomize where the victim stands helpless against the villain only really lends itself to the kind of inversion in which the wolf enters the stage in sheep's clothing.

Yet more interesting in our attempt to come to terms with the life of Thomas Dixon is the way melodramatic dichotomization and hyperbolization work together in the rhetoric that he spoke as well as the rhetoric that "spoke him."[23] For before Dixon, thus "speaking him," there was of course the tradition of the Southern Baptist ministry, the tradition of exhortation from the pulpit, of the rendering of life's challenges in the most exaggerated and apocalyptic of terms. Dixon in *Southern Horizons* refers to the "Crucifixion of the South" by Reconstruction politicians, slipping into a habitual rhetoric but also telling us the degree to which religiosity must have infused his thinking about every aspect of daily life.[24] Recall also that the three books upon which he was raised were the Bible, *Pilgrim's Progress*, and *Spurgeon's Sermons*. Aunt Barbara, the old slave, had read to him from that Bible.[25] In the Christian sermon as in the theatrical melodrama of pathos, overstatement is the name of the aesthetic. Everything felt must be hyperbolized; everything described must be vivid; and everything spoken must be thunderous. Thus the orchestral tones are especially appealing to Dixon because it is in their resonant terms that he attempted to reach the public, the masses, that he imagined he was serving first as minister and later as popular playwright and author. This passage, again from *Southern Horizons*, only reiterates the degree to which he saw the motion picture as a superior proselytizer as well as a miraculous equalizer: "I watched the effects of the picture on cultured spectators and realized for the first time the important fact that we had not only discovered a new universal language of man, but that an appeal to the human will through this tongue would be equally resistless to an audience of chauffeurs or a gathering of a thousand

College Professors."[26] The goal of the melodramatic rhetoric of the sermon would be to reach and conquer, to produce its effect swiftly and, above all, viscerally. And this is the visceral response that Dixon himself reports having felt on hearing that "low cry of the anguished South being put to torture." "It set my nerves tingling with its call," he says. Dixon tingles, but today we shudder.

In conclusion, let me say that we have something not a little remarkable here in the object of study. It is not only that our starting point of reception is not an untainted audience but a thoroughly interested producer. It is most unusual to study the reactions of authors to what might be considered "their own" material. But that is the point. As rehearsed and as scripted as Dixon is, in this instance we catch him off guard at the opening of *The Birth of a Nation*. In Thomas Dixon's exaggerated emotional response *to his own film*, we understand the definition of race melodrama that he attempted to set forth in earlier films and theatrical productions as well as literary works. This particular American race melodrama tells the story of who enslaved whom in the rawest of terms and in the end recruits its political converts to the same sides that they already occupied.

NOTES

1. Most of this has been work on the prolific African American filmmaker Oscar Micheaux, who, it is now agreed, over his 1918–1950 career as producer and director, was committed to answering the challenge of D. W. Griffith's *The Birth of a Nation*, particularly in the extant silent films such as *Within Our Gates*. See Jane M. Gaines, *Fire and Desire: Mixed Race Movies in the Silent Era* (Chicago: Univ. of Chicago Press, 2001), and Pearl Bowser, Jane M. Gaines, and Charles Musser, eds., *Oscar Micheaux and His Circle: African American Filmmaking and Race Cinema of the Silent Era* (Bloomington: Indiana Univ. Press, 2001).

2. See Linda Williams, *Playing the Race Card: Melodramas of Black and White from Uncle Tom to O. J. Simpson* (Princeton: Princeton Univ. Press, 2001); Walter Benn Michaels, *Our America: Nativism, Modernism, and Pluralism* (Durham: Duke Univ. Press, 1995).

3. See Jane M. Gaines, "Of Cabbages and Authors," in *A Feminist Reader in Early Cinema* ed. Jennifer Bean and Diane Negra (Durham: Duke Univ. Press, 2002).

4. Martin Marks, *Music and the Silent Film: Contexts and Case Studies, 1895–1924* (New York: Oxford Univ. Press, 1997), 135–41.

5. Thomas Dixon Jr., *Southern Horizons: The Autobiography of Thomas Dixon* (Alexandria, Va.: IWV Publishing, 1984), 296.

6. Ibid., 299. The degree to which Dixon was impressed by this score can be measured in the little-known history of the musical composition he commissioned for the next film he

wrote and produced, *The Fall of a Nation* (1916). All accounts point to his efforts to rival the achievement of Griffith's film, but little has been written about the score he commissioned from Victor Herbert for the now lost film. Anthony Slide, *American Racist: The Life and Films of Thomas Dixon* (Lexington: Univ. Press of Kentucky, 2004), argues that Herbert was the first major American composer to produce an entirely original composition for the screen. Slide should be consulted for the most recent and most thorough account of Dixon's career in the film industry.

7. Dixon, *Southern Horizons*, 296.

8. Ibid., 298.

9. See Richard Abel and Rick Altman, "Introduction," in *The Sounds of Early Cinema*, ed. Richard Abel and Rick Altman (Bloomington: Indiana Univ. Press, 2001); Rick Altman, "The Silence of the Silents," *Musical Quarterly* 80 (winter 1996): 648–718.

10. See Nickieann Fleener-Marzec, *D. W. Griffith's The Birth of a Nation: Controversy, Suppression, and the First Amendment as it Applies to Filmic Expression, 1915–1973* (New York: Arno Press, 1980).

11. Jane M. Gaines and Neil Lerner, "The Orchestration of Affect: The Motif of Barbarism in Breil's *The Birth of a Nation* Score," in Abel and Altman, eds., *Sounds of Early Cinema*.

12. Christine Gledhill, "The Melodramatic Field: An Investigation," in *Home Is Where the Heart Is*, ed. Christine Gledhill (London: British Film Institute, 1987), 19.

13. Claudia Gorbman, *Unheard Melodies: Narrative Film Music* (Bloomington: Indiana Univ. Press, 1987), 55.

14. The score discussed here is the piano conductor score found in the Library of Congress and corresponding roughly with the print of *The Birth of a Nation* in the Museum of Modern Art (MOMA-LC). It should be made clear here that during this period there would never be a perfect correspondence between the printed score and the music that accompanied the images. The conductor or musical director would be in the position to decide what music would be played through each cue, aware that tempo change and repetition were always options and that the goal was continuous music over every sequence in the film. The difficulty of trying to recreate some semblance of the Breil score as performed was brought home in this study as we watched the Kino International VHS version of the film and listened to the New Zealand symphony orchestra DVD version of the performed score. See Gaines and Lerner, "Orchestration of Affect."

15. It is in the piano score published in 1916 that the melody is titled "Motif of Barbarism." See *Selections of Joseph Carl Breil's Themes from the Incidental Music to "The Birth of a Nation"* (London: Chappell and Co., 1916).

16. Vachel Lindsay, *The Art of the Moving Picture* (New York: Macmillan, 1915), 191.

17. National Association for the Advancement of Colored People, Boston Branch, "Fighting a Vicious Film: Protest Against The Birth of a Nation" (1916), in *The Movies in Our Midst*, ed. Gerald Mast (Chicago: Univ. of Chicago Press, 1982), 128.

18. See Jane M. Gaines, "Birthing Nations," in *Cinema and Nation*, ed. Mette Hjort and Scott MacKenzie (London: Routledge, 2000), for a reading of Flora's death in relation to her

brother the Little Colonel's fear of menstruation, as well as an overview of other readings of this scene.

19. Williams, *Playing the Race Card*, 44.

20. Ibid., 100.

21. This more specific formulation of melodrama as a genre into "race melodrama" is relatively recent and has developed entirely out of the study of nineteenth-century American culture. In Williams, *Playing the Race Card*, it is the most well developed, especially in relation to film, but more recent work on literature (Susan Gillman, *Blood Talk: American Race Melodrama and the Culture of the Occult* [Chicago: Univ. of Chicago Press, 2003]) promises to elaborate, expand, and establish the productivity of the concept. It promises more even, I think, than the concept of domestic melodrama, which is both European and American. Gillman, for instance, reads the work of Mark Twain as well as African American literary figures such as Pauline E. Hopkins as race melodrama.

22. See Bowser, Gaines, and Musser, eds., *Oscar Micheaux and His Circle*.

23. The best discussion of melodramatic hyperbole can be found in Peter Brooks, *The Melodramatic Imagination* (1976; reprint, New Haven: Yale Univ. Press, 1995). Important to note here is that while *The Melodramatic Imagination* was first published in 1976, it had very little impact on literary theory, although, beginning in the 1980s, its importance to film theory has been huge. Brooks's primary examples, however, are not drawn from popular forms but from, among other things, the high art of novelist Henry James.

24. Dixon, *Southern Horizons*, 300.

25. Raymond Allen Cook, *Fire from the Flint: The Amazing Careers of Thomas Dixon* (Winston-Salem: Blair, 1968), 4, 9.

26. Dixon, *Southern Horizons*, 301.

The Cinematic Representation of Race in The Birth of a Nation: A Black Horror Film

CHARLENE REGESTER

The Birth of a Nation, considered a cinematic achievement for its time, was equally well known for receiving public plaudits and for evoking public protest. Although it has become an icon in American culture for the historical perspective it formulated, it was actually one of the most volatile cinematic representations of America's racial politics. In spite of its racial divisiveness, it has become the signifying historical moment that film historians can never forget, and the signifying moment that contemporary film scholars can never avoid referencing.

Numerous extensive examinations of this film have evolved from Thomas Dixon's discourse on the racialization of the South. But a glaring void in the study of the film is an analysis of *The Birth of a Nation*'s construction as a horror film. Deconstructing the film—this time as a horror film or a film that evolves out of the horror film genre—will fill this void.

This essay examines the way in which Griffith employed the paradigm of the horror film genre, overwritten on a racially and sexually charged text. Whites became caught up in identifying with the film's *heroes,* who led valiant and vigilant struggles to reclaim the (white) South. Whites were pitted against blacks, and southern whites were pitted both against the North and against the blacks. Griffith's strategy succeeded in forcing black spectators to project an "oppositional gaze,"[1] and this was transformed into mobilized action off the screen, resulting in the most vigorous battles waged in film history to prevent the exhibition of a motion picture. Griffith, while revealing his, as well as Thomas Dixon's, deep-seated psychological views, played upon the psychological constructions of race and sex in the white and black imagination. Whites were portrayed as *brave* and *heroic*, blacks as *dastardly* and *scary*. The mixed reception the film provoked led to the paths this essay pursues in examining and assessing the infamous *The Birth of a Nation* by investigating Griffith's employment of the horror film paradigm.

Negative responses to the film were particularly vigorous in urban areas. According to the *Chicago Defender,* when *The Birth of a Nation* opened in Philadelphia:

> It was billed at the Forest Avenue Theater. When the doors were opened thousands of people crowded at the theater to see if the race really meant to show its backbone and resent the disgraceful play. Five thousand members of the race, old and young went to the theater and demanded that the play be stopped. Policemen were called and a riot call was sent to the nearest station. There was a general melee. Policemen beat women of the race who took part in the fight, and never before in the history of this city was there such a riot.[2]

The spectators' negative response, a combination of anger and fear, translated into violence as some of the public expressed their opposition to the film. This two-pronged negativity of anger and fear is the impetus for expanding on the investigation of *The Birth of a Nation* as it conforms to the horror film paradigm.

Previous scholars have affirmed the use of horror film techniques in *The Birth of a Nation*. Thomas Wartenberg argues that the monster figure in *King Kong* (1933) parallels that of the black male reconstructed in *The Birth of a Nation*. James Snead, in comparing *The Birth of a Nation* and *King Kong,* suggests that Griffith's film achieves "a desired political end (the erasure of the black/savage from white/civilized society)," an ending replicated in *King Kong*. Gerald Butters makes the analogy between the monster figure in *The Birth of a Nation* and *Frankenstein,* arguing that "as Dr. Frankenstein makes his monster, not fully realizing what he is doing, Stoneman makes Lynch."[3]

Griffith closely linked fear, terror, horror, and monstrosity with blackness, so that black spectators could not extricate themselves from the on-screen horrors. Charles Derry asserts that "Some horror films deal with our fears more directly than others, but in general, horror films speak to our subconscious and—like our dreams—deal with issues that are often painful for us to consciously and directly address."⁴ Griffith, applying the techniques of the horror film genre to *The Birth of a Nation*, chose to present blackness as a threat to the safety of whiteness, embodied in the preservation of the white South—blackness that must be excised in order for the white South to exist and reclaim its position of power.

The Birth of a Nation was produced early in the development of horror films. The genre's official inception in American cinema reportedly began with Tod Browning's *Dracula* (1931),⁵ many years after Griffith's *The Birth of a Nation* (1915). But Browning, one of the progenitors of the horror film genre, had had an earlier association with Griffith, so perhaps Browning's influence on Griffith should be noted. According to David Skal, Browning was introduced to Griffith, a fellow Kentuckian, in 1913 and offered Griffith an acting role (as an undertaker) in a two-reel comedy, *Scenting a Terrible Crime* (1913).⁶ In that association, Griffith may have been influenced by Browning's predilection for the horror film genre, and it is even conceivable that Browning may have been influenced by Griffith and Dixon. Actually, Griffith may have been introduced to the horror film genre in cinematic works produced in Germany, Hungary, and France, countries where such techniques were already employed. Perhaps Griffith's applying the technique of the horror film genre was a subconscious act, as it paralleled his conscious decision to construct blackness as horrific. Conforming to the horror film genre, *The Birth of a Nation* (a) positioned white women as victims, (b) constructed a monster represented in the image of the black male rapist, and (c) created fear among both black and white spectators. An examination of these three components of *The Birth of a Nation* follows, demonstrating how the film conforms to the horror film genre and how it forces black spectators to resist identification with the film, while explaining the furor and outrage that erupted in the film's aftermath.

According to Karen Hollinger, it was not uncommon for classic monster films to position women as victims of the monster's aggression. In *The Birth of a Nation*, both Elsie and Flora assume the position of victimized females. While Elsie resists Silas Lynch's marriage proposals and implied sexual desires, Flora resists the sexual lustfulness of her alleged black rapist, Gus. Hollinger adds, "Just as the classic horror monster is commonly defined as male, so the primary object of his desire is almost exclusively female."⁷

Positioning the female as victim empowered the predominantly male audiences; identifying with a female figure in distress allows them to contemplate their own "passivity, humiliation, and penetration."[8]

Linda Williams asserts that the failure and frustration of the female victim's vision (denying herself the right to look at her attacker) is the most important mark of her sexual purity. For example, in *The Birth of a Nation*, when Elsie is pursued by her attacker, she vows to look at him but then in terror proceeds to cover her face and eyes as though to erase the all-too-real moment that she cannot deny. Williams argues that by activating the gaze of the monster, this act becomes synonymous with the female's victimization. In fact, by looking at the monster, she acknowledges her sameness to the monster in that both are similar in their freakishness.[9] This is important to the extent that if women become linked to the black monster, as is the case in *The Birth of a Nation*, the fear that they provoke (castration anxiety, as posed by women, and the castration anxiety as posed by blacks) and the threat that they provide to white manhood is rendered even more visible. Michael Rogin astutely observes that "White supremacists invented the black rapist to keep white women in their place."[10]

White females' positioning as victim is also played out in other ways in *The Birth of a Nation*. Barbara Creed posits that the horror film constructs the mother as abject—meaning spiritless, humiliated, downcast. Drawing upon the views of Julia Kristeva, Creed suggests that "the mother-child relation [is] one marked by conflict; the child struggles to break free but the mother is reluctant to release it."[11] Of direct relevance to *The Birth of a Nation*, Flora, prior to her attack, is warned by her brother to be careful, as a black assaulter might be in search of a victim. That Flora does not heed her brother's warning demonstrates how she becomes a victim and subtly implies that women should defer to the opinions of men. According to Russell Merritt, prior to Flora's attack, her relationship with her mother is unveiled:

> Flora, the budding adolescent, is trying to be helpful to her mother, who tends to patronize her. Her mother won't let Flora join in sewing Klan costumes but finally compromises by giving her the exciting if menial task of hiding completed Klan outfits inside sofa pillows. When mother winces at the taste of the stale drinking water, Flora jumps off a sofa arm volunteering to fetch a fresh supply from the spring in the woods. The resistance comes

not from brother Ben, who is nowhere in sight, but from her mother who mimes that the trip is not worth Flora's effort. But Flora grabs the water bucket with determination, proving she is a grown-up and can be useful.[12]

Flora's contentious relationship with her mother speaks to the mother-child dynamic associated with horror films, wherein the maternal figure is constructed as abject. Added to this, Creed suggests that "Images of blood [and other bodily secretions] are central to our culturally/socially constructed notions of the horrific. They signify a split between two orders: the maternal authority and the law of the father."[13] Thus, following Flora's leap to her death as she escapes her attacker, the black Gus, her body is cradled in her brother's arms as blood seeps from her mouth. Jane M. Gaines affirms, "Blood drips from her virginal mouth, wiped away by the Little Colonel who holds the limp and battered body, no longer of any use to anyone."[14] Creed argues that the horror film's obsession with blood, particularly the blood of women, represents not only women's menstruation but also males' castration.[15] If this is the case, then in *The Birth of a Nation*, the castration anxiety that white males experience gets displaced onto white women and is transformed in the not visibly seen, but implied, castration and lynching of the black Gus. According to Stephen Neale, castration is an underlying subtext to the horror film genre.[16]

That the female is victim is consistent with the horror film genre, as one critic observes, "[T]he killer is with few exceptions recognizably human and distinctly male... [H]is victims are mostly women, often sexually free and always young and beautiful ones."[17] Certainly, in *The Birth of a Nation* both Flora and Elsie conform to this criterion of representing youth and beauty as implied by the standards unique to this historical period. Moreover, that they are pursued and victimized further demonstrates how the film conforms to this genre. Manthia Diawara contends that in the Gus/Flora attack, "Being watched unawares here connotes not the lures of voyeurism and exhibitionism, but danger, and equates Gus, intertextually, with the unseen danger that stalks the innocent in many thrillers and horror movies."[18] The white female's victimization is then rendered visible in the fact that she is stalked by her attacker—an act that attests to her innocence as the victim of an attack.

Added to this, the reduction of the victim to the body further demonstrates how *The Birth of a Nation* conforms to the horror film genre. Carol Clover argues, "It may be through the female body that the body of the audience is sensationalized, but the sensation is an entirely male affair." In *The Birth of a Nation,* the fact that both females are raped, or at least that rape is implied, suggests how they are reduced to the body. Moreover, male sexuality then becomes the weapon, and in this instance black male sexuality also points to the victimization of women. "Cinefantastic horror . . . succeeds [in] violating that [feminine] body—which recoils, shudders, cries out collectively—in ways otherwise imaginable, for males, only in nightmare."[19]

The following brief synopses of the Gus/Flora attack and the Lynch/Elsie assault present scenes from *The Birth of a Nation* that support the inclusion of techniques unique to the horror film genre, concerning both the victimization of the white female and the demonizing of the black male as monster. The two characteristics become a blend, inseparable from each other.

It is of note that when Gus is introduced as the monstrous beast in pursuit of Flora (the symbol of white innocence and purity), the title cards characterize him as "Gus, the renegade, a product of the vicious doctrines spread by carpetbaggers." Griffith's reference to Gus as a renegade, defined as an individual who rejects lawful behavior, automatically codes him as out of control. Moreover, Gus is positioned on the other side of a fence, while Flora and Elsie are seated underneath the trees, engaged in an intimate conversation. Gus stares at the two women, his eyes fixated on the victim, his mouth slightly open. The fence becomes a metaphor for the South/North; black/white; and good/evil dichotomies that Griffith appropriates in the film. Gus walks past the women but then returns for another, longer-lasting look, indicative of a stalking of his victim. This monster-beast/white victim juxtaposition exacerbates a reaction of fear, as Cameron (the Little Colonel) warns Gus to stay away from these women.

After exchanging words with Cameron, Gus puts his hands in his pockets as though his hands represent a phallic symbol that has to be contained or controlled. Positioning his hands in his pockets implies that he is attempting to control the uncontrollable. Additionally, Gus's beastly persona is amplified by the fact that his jacket is unbuttoned, revealing the shirt underneath, suggesting that he is not a soldier who holds respect for his uniform. His unbuttoned shirt hints also at his hypersexuality embodied by both his blackness and his Otherness. At this point, Gus is clearly established as a problem—a monstrous beast.

Following a cutaway, the film returns to Flora's attack. When Flora, against her brother's warning, goes to a stream in the woods to fetch a bucket of water, she is distracted by a squirrel perched on a tree. While she attempts to coax the animal down from the tree, Gus, nearby, observes Flora. Now Gus, carrying his jacket on his arm to indicate that he is disrobing, moves toward her, in a hunched position. It seems as though he is being transformed—from human to beast—in a metamorphosis from normality to abnormality. Fear is obviously constructed in this implied transfiguring. Gus approaches Flora, telling her that he is now a captain in the military and wants to get married. He grabs her arm, but she resists his embrace, hits him, and flees. Terrified, Flora attempts to hide behind a tree, but Gus is relentless in pursuit of his victim; only the whites of his eyes are now visible (again the beast-image).

By this time, Cameron realizes that Flora is alone in the wilds. Cameron knows that Gus is in pursuit of Flora when he sees Gus's jacket on the ground, a filmic hint at a sexual attack. Next Flora is seen fleeing her attacker. Reaching a cliff, arms extended, Flora turns to her attacker, vowing, "Stay away or I'll jump." As Gus continues to approach his victim, the camera provides a shot from the bottom of the cliff upward to Flora; her death appears to be imminent.

On another level, but presented as being equally sinister, there is the affair between Lynch and Elsie. While Stoneman, Elsie's father and a white man of liberal views, participated in shaping Lynch's political career, Lynch (a mulatto) is seen to be "betraying" him, because Lynch expresses a desire for Stoneman's daughter. Compared to Gus, Lynch is sophisticated in his appearance and demeanor, and the fact that he is a politician allows him to be viewed as less offensive as an attacker than the beastly looking Gus. But the film conveys the message: blacks, despite their sophistication, cannot disconnect themselves from beastliness; being black renders them beastly attackers, desirous of white women.

Elsie refuses Lynch's marriage proposal. Pointing her finger at him, she shakes her arms emphatically and then heads for the door. Lynch rushes to lock the door, announcing that he will build an empire and she shall be his queen. Elsie, while fearful, seemingly does not take his proposition seriously until he kisses the hem of her dress—a not-so-subtle implication of sexuality. Again, Elsie heads for the door and flails her arms in the air. When she turns around to look at her attacker, he is crouched in a chair, in a beastly posture. Like Gus, Lynch now seems to make the transformation from human to beast. The camera cuts back and forth between Elsie's resistance and the riding of the Klan who are coming to save the white South. Lynch embraces Elsie, but she struggles to free herself from his embrace; then she faints in his arms.

According to Michael Rogin, the black rapist as a beast in *The Birth of a Nation* grew out of the racist views of Griffith and Dixon, who "imagined a monstrous America of the future, peopled by mulattoes. Stopping black men from penetrating white women gave birth to a redeemed nation."[20] Marie Helene Huet suggests that the monster's origin can be traced to early history, when it was believed of monsters that "Their strange appearance— a misleading likeness to another species, for example—belies the otherwise rigorous law that offspring should resemble their parents."[21] If the monster is linked to parental origin, the black monster in *The Birth of a Nation* can certainly claim lineage to a white paternity that seeks to admonish the very black that this paternity helped to create. (This is not so different from Rogin's assertion that Gus and Lynch are Thomas Jefferson's children.[22]) But more importantly, that the monster as Other is linked to the white self further explains the fear that the black monster likely posed.

That *The Birth of a Nation* conforms to the horror film genre is apparent in the fact that the "monster is overtly, even excessively masculine."[23] Showing the monster pursuing a female victim, as in *The Birth of a Nation*, where Gus pursues Flora and Lynch pursues Elsie, affirms that "It is commonplace for the monster to carry off a scantily clad woman."[24]

Consistent with the horror film genre, as evident in the parallels between *The Birth of a Nation* and *King Kong,* the black male in the former is constructed as a monster. Many scholars have linked the beast figure, King Kong, to black maleness. For example, Harvey Roy Greenberg notes that "Kong, then, is the epitome of the white man's day dream of the brute black, the heartless, mindless foreigner, feasting on violence and rapine." Such an assertion can also be made of the black attackers in *The Birth of a Nation*. Added to this, Greenberg claims that implicit in the racism appropriated by *King Kong* is that "the Negro should be portrayed as the degraded repository of the white man's forbidden impulses."[25] A similar case can be made for *The Birth of a Nation,* in which the black male attacker became the object and scapegoat for the failings, discontent, and unrest that existed in white society. The black male attacker was made responsible for the political divisions that existed between the North and the South. Gail Dines claims that "The notion of the Black man as a sexual monster has been linked to the economic vulnerability that white working-class men feel in the face of a capitalist economy over which they have little power."[26] The black then becomes synonymous with the monster or beast, an idea whose origins can be found in racist ideology.

Griffith consciously constructed Gus as a sexual predator. Donald Bogle asserts that Griffith's construction of the black male parallels the brutal black buck, whose animalism is perceived as being inherent to the black male. According to Bogle, Griffith depicted "the black bucks of the film [as] psychopaths, one always panting and salivating, the other forever stiffening his body as if the mere presence of a white woman in the same room could bring him to a sexual climax. Griffith played hard on the bestiality of his black villainous bucks with the intent of arousing hatred."[27] Griffith's monster figure is also associated with violence. As Stephen Neale contends, "Violence also marks the horror film, most evidently in films where a monster—werewolf, vampire, psychopath, or whatever—initiates a series of acts of murder and destruction which can only end when it is either destroyed or becomes normalized."[28]

The analogy of the black as monster extends to other films as well. One of these is *Bride of Frankenstein* (1935)—a film that also introduces the notion of lynching as punishment for the monster's violent acts and that parallels the presentation in *The Birth of a Nation.* According to Elizabeth Young, *Bride of Frankenstein* presents "the monster in a condition of continual flight from a murderous mob. Captured partway into the film, he is strung upon a tree as an angry cluster of men surround him. This visual moment is so shockingly reminiscent of the imagery of lynching that, as with the monster's 'blackness,' the film here radically rewrites boundaries between the 'fantasy' of horror film and the 'realism' of other cinematic genres." Young continues that there is "an uncomfortable circulation between horror films and acts of lynching as viewer 'spectacles.'"[29] *The Birth of a Nation*'s reconstruction of a lynching (symbolically if not literally) conveys the meaning that such acts were merely punishment for those who violated southern codes—in particular, for those blacks who violated racial and sexual codes by committing sex crimes against white women. Even if audiences sympathize with the monster figure in *Bride of Frankenstein*, they will be less sympathetic to the monster in *The Birth of a Nation* because of his race and his violation of the white female. Therefore, lynching is rendered an appropriate punishment for the monster figure in both films but more so for the monster in *The Birth of a Nation*.

Fear constitutes another means by which to distinguish horror films, and *The Birth of a Nation* certainly has its share of fear. Again, there is a blending of characteristics, so that "the white female as victim," as well as "the black male as monster," become natural parts of the fear factor. Just as fear is such an intangible—a feeling, an emotion, an expression—so also is the manner of evoking fear many-faceted.

The fear of what could potentially happen in real life, even though not fully orchestrated on screen, was an obvious means of creating fear not only for whites but for black spectators as well. Edward Guerrero affirms that "[to attest] to the film's broad and vile influence; on Thanksgiving night, 1915, some twenty-five thousand Klansmen marched down Peachtree Avenue in full menacing regalia to celebrate the film's opening in Atlanta. So, considering the racism, discrimination, and brutality at large in that historical moment, African Americans had every reason to fear that what was depicted on the screen could easily be acted out against them in reality."[30]

Fear was evoked by *The Birth of a Nation* in the public imagination both for what could potentially happen and what was constructed in the mainstream press. While many assume that blacks did not react negatively to *The Birth of a Nation* when it toured the South, this truly is not the case. North Carolina, the home of Thomas Dixon, offers a sample representation of the southern black reaction to *The Birth of a Nation*. Unfortunately, only a few reports documenting black reaction to the film are available, and relying on the mainstream press yields a questionable assessment of how the press may have participated in fueling the inflammatory sentiment that the film provoked. Below is a report from a black newspaper, the *Chicago Defender*, on how the film created a volatile atmosphere in the town of Salisbury, North Carolina:

> *The Birth of a Nation* was shown here several years ago and its showing was accompanied by threats of a racial outbreak when members of two races took exception to the applause given at certain occurrences which particularly pleased them. Whites from the ground floor of the theater threatened to "come up there and get you" when non-white patrons in the balcony vociferously applauded a part which pleased them. "Come on up," was the reply and a near riot precipitated. The matter was quieted without damage.[31]

The current investigation suggests that the mainstream newspapers that generally catered to predominantly white audiences actually fueled the horror experienced by blacks due to this film.

There is also a record (though scant) of Dixon's play *The Clansman*, on which Griffith's film *The Birth of a Nation* was based. According to John Inscoe, who chronicles the reception among North Carolinians of both Dixon's play and Griffith's film, the play was regarded as even more offensive than the film. Inscoe reports that the play may have aroused more opposition among North Carolinians than did the film. He asserts: "When *The Clansman*, a stage production . . . toured the state in 1905, the reaction to the lessons it taught was, for the most part, just what Dixon had wanted. His inflammatory racist message came through loud and clear to North Carolina audiences in 1905, with the majority of critics and reporters extolling the timeliness of Dixon's warning and accuracy of his depiction of the dangerous situation at hand. But ten years later he was to find North Carolinians reacting very differently to the filmed version of his play, and their reaction disappointed him greatly."[32] However, even though the film did not elicit quite the same audience responses as did the play, the film did create fear among blacks. The North Carolina mainstream press coverage created fear among them, and demonstrated how the press reports could continue the horror that had been reconstructed on screen in both its visual and verbal representations.

According to Inscoe, Thomas Dixon, in collaborating with Griffith on the production of *The Birth of a Nation*, "maintained in 1915, as he had in 1905, that his purpose was 'to create a feeling of abhorrence in white people, especially white women, against colored men,' and that he hoped the film would accomplish his plan, like that of Lincoln, 'to have all Negroes removed from the United States."³³ If these were Dixon's opinions and intentions, although the film may not have elicited the same provocative response that the play had achieved and ultimately failed to conform to Dixon's expectations, he did succeed in provoking fear among blacks by injecting such racially infused views into *The Birth of a Nation*. As the film was screened in some North Carolina cities, "the racial issues, so much the focus of the play and fully as evident on the screen, were for the most part either ignored, minimized, or substantially altered. Most reviewers felt compelled to comment on the Northern protest against Griffith's masterpiece, and all denied that there was anything in it either offensive or inaccurate."³⁴ Inscoe's supposition that the film did not receive the same fanfare as the play had received in North Carolina does not deny that the press coverage of the film constructed fear for black spectators, lending support to the proposition that the press also participated in constructing horror in much the same manner as had the film.

Through the North Carolina press's overwhelming praise of the Ku Klux Klan, its laudatory commendation of white victory and defeat over the black South, and its insinuations of black inferiority, the newspaper coverage of the film's reception similarly appropriated the horror that blacks had experienced on the screen. As an example of the press reportage, when *The Birth of a Nation* was shown in Durham in 1916 at the Academy of Music, the *Durham (N.C.) Morning Herald* featured nearly a full-page story on the film, with photos accompanied by the heading: "D. W. Griffith's Great Idea and How He Worked Out Historically Accurate Battle Scenes with 18,000 Actors and 3,000 Horses."³⁵ An advertisement for the screening noted that the "gallery will be reserved for Colored People on Saturday Night Only."³⁶ (This refutes the earlier assumptions that no blacks in the South had access to the film.)

The Birth of a Nation attracted such people as the Daughters of the Confederacy, along with other southerners whose ideological views coincided with those advocated by the Reverend Charles H. Parkhurst, who claimed:

> The criticism [of the film] that it exhibits the Negro in an unfortunate light and that it is calculated to engender racial animosity is fully met by the consideration that it represents the Negro, not as he is now at all, but as he was in the days when he had just had the chains broken from him and

when he was rioting in the deliciousness of a liberty so new and untried that he had not yet learned to understand it and was as ignorant as a baby of the way to use it. It is in this respect exactly true to history, and if it reflects upon the Negro as he was then it is a compliment to the black man today.[37]

Parkhurst's doubly coded critique suggests that blacks had advanced and that the film did not represent them as they were at the time of the showing. At the same time, he implies that in the past, upon achieving their liberation, they were ignorant and riotous. On the one hand, his commentary extends praise, yet on the other, he insults blacks. Being characterized in this manner must have inflamed black spectators. Parkhurst's comments demonstrate how the press constructed horror for blacks and participated in coding blackness negatively. Equating blackness with savagery, regardless of time period, was a means of rendering blackness as horrific; the newspaper and the film committed the very same offense.

Parkhurst's views directly contrasted with those articulated by the Reverend E. T. Liddell, of the Branson Methodist Church, who prohibited his members from even seeing the film. But Liddell's more progressive stance regarding *The Birth of a Nation* and his prohibiting his church members from seeing the film could not offset the damage inflicted by Parkhurst's comments.

In Raleigh, *The Birth of a Nation* drew the same large crowds as it had in Durham. The *Raleigh News and Observer* reported that "Its fame seems to have penetrated every nook and corner of the countryside. Hardly a town in a radius of any miles but had its contingent in Raleigh yesterday." The *Raleigh News and Observer* had nothing but words of praise to bestow upon the film,[38] praise that was echoed by the *Raleigh Times*. According to John Inscoe, the *Raleigh Times* critic declared, "There has been some hostility to the picture on account of an alleged injustice to the negroes. I have not felt it; and I am one who cherishes a great affection and a profound admiration for the Negro."[39] That this critic denied seeing how the film defamed blacks is apparent in his blatant disregard for the damage that such representations inflicted and reflected a sentiment that prevailed among many in this period. Whites seemed utterly lacking in sensitivity toward blacks. And this writer touted himself as liberal. The press also appeared not to realize how they participated in fueling the horror that was bound to exist among black spectators.

Regarding the film's reception in Charlotte, the *Charlotte Daily Observer* provided thorough coverage of the film, with photos and a nearly full-page article lauding the film. This newspaper featured promotional materials written by Griffith himself entitled "*The Birth of a Nation* in Poetry, Art, and Acting."[40] Promoting the film as a cinematic spectacle, the *Observer* proclaimed, "*The Birth of a Nation* is wonderful! Ku Klux Klan! What they suffered, lost and braved! This was a brand of knights sent to make things work out as it was desired and none but these men could have accomplished it."[41] The *Observer* reported: "Often the old war shouts are heard in the audiences from the lips of veterans who momentarily forget that it is only a picture. It is hard to keep one's feet from dancing to the well-beloved tunes of the martial music. Scenes in the latter half of the picture are so skillfully managed that often the applause is practically continuous for half to three-quarters of an hour."[42] Here the screen representation of the Klan is applauded in the press as well as by spectators, and whites on screen are constructed as victims who have to be saved by the KKK, attesting to the fear that this film promulgated for blacks. It cannot be difficult to imagine the horror blacks experienced as they witnessed on screen and read in the press's coverage the greatness of the Klan, the very persecutors of blacks. In addition, the *Observer* reported that the film met sellout crowds and was described as "Overwhelming in its stupendousness, gripping in its appeal, masterful in its portraiture and profoundly thrilling in its delineation of a great historical epoch . . . [that] stirred the immense audience that thronged the Academy of Music . . . as no other play has done in years."[43] The newspaper's acceptance of the film's historical accuracy must further have inflamed black spectators. They had to be annoyed, knowing that while some of the history of the country was being unveiled, the entire history of all of its members, particularly those who had been exploited and degraded, was not being reconstructed in this dramatization. Adding insult to injury, the paper reported that those blacks who attended the film's exhibition in Charlotte were "well behaved and conservatively critical."[44] Such a statement raises the question of why these blacks remained so silent at such an inflammatory picture. Were they afraid to express their views in a theater that they shared with whites? Were they afraid that repercussions were likely to occur if they exhibited opposition to the film? Perhaps these black spectators were so stunned or terrorized by the depiction and treatment of blacks on screen that they were rendered silent. Whatever their true reaction was, it is evident that the horror that the press created in its reportage reflected the horror that they witnessed on screen.

It is of note that the *Observer*'s critique of the film differed from that of other North Carolina presses in that it assumed a more national perspective, focusing on the film's reaction in the North. The *Observer* claimed that in the North whites encouraged blacks to object to the film, implying that blacks would not have been motivated on their own accord to object to such insulting representations. The *Observer* also implied that northern whites were not operating in the best interest of blacks, as blacks in this period had so much at stake and so much to lose if they publicly expressed their objections. This source added that southern whites were more genuine than were northern whites. The *Observer* characterized southern whites as "best friends" to blacks—friends who conceivably were astute enough to *dis*courage blacks from engaging in subversive activity or behavior that would cause them trouble in their day-to-day lives and their acceptance in the American scene.

In Greensboro, *The Birth of a Nation* was exhibited at the Grand Opera House. While little is known of the film's reception, it was reported that "the historical value of the feature [was] alone enough to cause crowds of Greensboro people to rush into the Grand during the remaining... performances."[45] According to John Inscoe, "A Greensboro journalist... noted: 'it is to the advantage of the negro of today to know how some of his ancestors misbehaved and why the prejudices in his path have grown there. Surely no friend of his is to be turned into an enemy by the film and no enemy more deeply embittered.'"[46] This commentary was seemingly both laudatory and condemnatory; the review neither alleviated the fears of blacks nor assuaged the resentment that blacks held for the film.

In Asheville, when *The Birth of a Nation* was shown at the Auditorium Theatre, it was reported that "For three hours, a large crowd experienced successive thrills, several people becoming excited almost to the point of hysteria. Cheering and 'cat calls' were sustained for several minutes at various periods." However, the *Asheville Citizen* reassured audiences that "there is nothing objectionable in the picture."[47] It seems contradictory to embrace a film that features the Klan—a group that terrorized blacks—and at the same time to suggest that there was nothing objectionable in the picture. Certainly, blacks were not deceived by the press reports. White spectators' public adulation for *The Birth of a Nation* (seemingly unaware of the horrors they witnessed on screen), as well as the press's reaction to the film, show how both the white audiences and the press participated in constructing horror for black spectators.

As for the film's exhibition in Wilmington, the *Evening Dispatch* reported:

> There were times when the heart was heavy and a lumpy feeling was in the throat; times when rebellion beat fiercely within the breast; times when a laugh mounted to the lips; times when the entire being was aflame, as war lived in all its vividness upon the big screen, and then the soul of man and woman became a riotous upheaval, that found vent not only in stamping of feet and clapping of hands, but in cheers when the Ku Klux Klan, the great ghostly army that brought the South back from the pit of torture, thundered, as it were, back and forth.[48]

Again white audiences' elation with the Klan's being represented as restoring power, authority, and order to the white South created fear among blacks. In addition, the credence that the press's coverage gave to the whites' reactions horrified blacks. These elements of response add support to the position that *The Birth of a Nation* conformed to the horror film genre.

The Birth of a Nation's reception in the North Carolina press glorified the Klan, revealing the adulation that white spectators experienced in what they interpreted as an attempt to restore order to a dismantled South by subjugating blacks. The press reports actually participated in constructing black horror. As Inscoe affirms, "The increased fear of 'black beast rapists' directly inspired lynchings, riots, and other violence aimed at Southern blacks during this era. More indirectly, whites' fear of blacks combined with political efforts to bring about black disfranchisement and segregation as well,"[49] adding to the fear of blackness that was appropriated by *The Birth of a Nation* and that was amplified by the film's reception in the North Carolina press. These fears, whether imagined or real, became intertwined—reverberating on the screen as well as in the newspaper coverage of the film. Fear, the underlying tone for all horror films, is also *The Birth of a Nation*'s chief weapon, used as a visual technique (in on-screen action) and as a linguistic technique (in the newspaper coverage it received), invoking terror among whites as well as blacks.

The Birth of a Nation has woven the strands of race, sexuality, and politics into an intricate catch-all web. The pattern of the web takes as its model the coding of the horror film genre, referred to in one critique as a threat "not simply among us, but rather a part of us, caused by us."[50]

In conforming to the horror film genre, *The Birth of a Nation* constructed the white female as victim, positioned the black male as monster, created and whipped up the white males' hysterical zest for violent physical attack against the "monster," and justified the white males' lawlessness and vicious behavior. Horror has been characterized "in terms of illegitimacy: as an often shocking, spectacular, sensationalist and 'immoral' (or amoral) form which can seem to take pleasure from the fact that so many people find it disturbing, distasteful or even downright unacceptable."[51] *The Birth of a Nation*, fitting that definition in every detail, can and should be classified as a horror film, for whites and blacks alike.

NOTES

1. bell hooks, "The Oppositional Gaze: Black Female Spectators," in *Black American Cinema*, ed. Manthia Diawara (New York: Routledge, 1993), 288–302.
2. "*Birth of a Nation* Run Out of Philadelphia," *Chicago Defender*, September 25, 1915, p. 1.
3. Thomas E. Wartenberg, "Humanizing the Beast: *King Kong* and the Representation of Black Male Sexuality," in *Classic Hollywood, Classic Whiteness*, ed. Daniel Bernardi (Minneapolis: Univ. of Minnesota Press, 2001), 160–61; James Snead, "Spectatorship and Capture in *King Kong*: The Guilty Look," in *Representing Blackness: Issues in Film and Video*, ed. Valerie Smith (New Brunswick: Rutgers Univ. Press, 1997), 34; Gerald Butters Jr., *Black Manhood on the Silent Screen* (Lawrence: Univ. of Kansas Press, 2001), 73.
4. Charles Derry, "More Dark Dreams: Some Notes on the Recent Horror Film," in *American Horrors: Essays on the Modern American Horror Film*, ed. Gregory A. Waller (Urbana: Univ. of Illinois Press, 1987), 162.
5. David Cook, *A History of Narrative Film* (New York: Norton, 1981), 278.
6. David Skal, *The Monster Show* (1993; rev. ed., New York: Faber and Faber, 2001), 33.
7. Karen Hollinger, "The Monster as Woman: Two Generations of Cat People," in *The Dread of Difference: Gender and the Horror Film*, ed. Barry Keith Grant (Austin: Univ. of Texas Press, 1996), 299.
8. Adam Knee, "Gender, Genre, Argento," in Grant, ed., *Dread of Difference*, 214.
9. Linda Williams, "When the Woman Looks," in Grant, ed., *Dread of Difference*, 15–34.

10. Michael Rogin, "'The Sword Became a Flashing Vision': D. W. Griffith's *The Birth of a Nation*," in *The Birth of a Nation*, ed. Robert Lang (New Brunswick: Rutgers Univ. Press, 1994), 267.

11. Barbara Creed, "Horror and the Monstrous-Feminine: An Imaginary Abjection," in Grant, ed., *Dread of Difference*, 41.

12. Russell Merritt, "D. W. Griffith's *The Birth of a Nation*: Going after Little Sister," in *Close Viewings: An Anthology of New Film Criticism*, ed. Peter Lehman (Tallahassee: Florida State Univ. Press, 1990), 223–25.

13. Creed, "Horror and the Monstrous-Feminine," 43.

14. Jane M. Gaines, "*The Birth of a Nation* and *Within Our Gates*: Two Tales of the American South," in *Dixie Debates*, ed. Richard H. King and Helen Taylor (New York: New York Univ. Press, 1996), 187.

15. Creed, "Horror and the Monstrous-Feminine," 44.

16. Stephen Neale, *Genre* (London: British Film Institute, 1980), 44.

17. Carol J. Clover, "Her Body, Himself: Gender in the Slasher Film," in Grant, ed., *Dread of Difference*, 88.

18. Manthia Diawara, "Black Spectatorship: Problems of Identification and Resistance," in Diawara, ed., *Black American Cinema*, 217.

19. Clover, "Her Body, Himself," 97, 98.

20. Rogin, "'The Sword Became a Flashing Vision,'" 279.

21. Marie-Helene Huet, "Introduction to Monstrous Imagination," in *The Horror Reader*, ed. Ken Gelder (New York: Routledge, 2000), 86.

22. Rogin, "'The Sword Became a Flashing Vision,'" 268.

23. Hollinger, "Monster as Woman," 297.

24. Harvey Roy Greenberg, "*King Kong*: The Beast in the Boudoir—or, 'You Can't Marry that Girl, You're a Gorilla!'" in Grant, ed., *Dread of Difference*, 340.

25. Ibid., 344.

26. Gail Dines, "*King Kong* and the White Woman: Hustler Magazine and the Demonization of Black Masculinity," in *Gender, Race, and Class in Media: A Text Reader*, 2nd ed., ed. Gail Dines and Jean Humez (Thousand Oaks: Sage Publications, 2003), 453.

27. Donald Bogle, "Black Beginnings: From *Uncle Tom's Cabin* to *The Birth of a Nation*," in Smith, ed., *Representing Blackness*, 21.

28. Neale, *Genre*, 21.

29. Elizabeth Young, "Here Comes the Bride: Wedding, Gender and Race in *Bride of Frankenstein*," in Grant, ed., *Dread of Difference*, 323, 324.

30. Edward Guerrero, *Framing Blackness: The African American Image in Film* (Philadelphia: Temple Univ. Press, 1993), 14.

31. "Hate Flicker Stirs Anger of Race in N.C.," *Chicago Defender*, January 31, 1931, p. 9.

32. John C. Inscoe, "*The Clansman* on Stage and Screen: North Carolina Reacts," *North Carolina Historical Review* 64 (April 1987): 139.

33. Ibid., 148.

34. Ibid., 151.

35. "Producing a Play on a Stage Five Miles Long," *Durham (N.C.) Morning Herald*, March 10, 1916, p. 10.
36. Advertisement, Academy of Music, *The Birth of a Nation*, *Durham (N.C.) Morning Herald*, March 9, 1916, p. 8.
37. Rev. Dr. Charles H. Parkhurst, "Amusements," *Durham (N.C.) Morning Herald*, March 8, 1916, p. 6.
38. "*Birth of a Nation* Draws Big House," *Raleigh News and Observer*, November 13, 1915.
39. Inscoe, "*The Clansman* on Stage and Screen," 151.
40. D. W. Griffith, "*The Birth of a Nation* in Poetry, Art, and Acting," *Charlotte Daily Observer*, November 11, 1915, p. 1+.
41. "Country Acclaims 'The Miracle Movie,'" *Charlotte Daily Observer*, November 13, 1915, p. 8.
42. "Picture Play at Academy of Music," *Charlotte Daily Observer*, November 14, 1915, p. 20.
43. "Miracle Movie Full of Thrills," *Charlotte Daily Observer*, November 16, 1915, p. 7.
44. "Contentment for the Negro," *Charlotte Daily Observer*, November 18, 1915, p. 4.
45. "*Birth of a Nation* Is Wonderful Film," *Greensboro Daily News*, November 9, 1915, p. 8.
46. Inscoe, "*The Clansman* on Stage and Screen," 152–53.
47. "Crowd Is Thrilled by *Birth of a Nation*," *Asheville Citizen*, October 19, 1915, p. 8.
48. "*Birth of a Nation*: A Wonder Show," *Evening Dispatch*, March 30, 1916.
49. Inscoe, "*The Clansman* on Stage and Screen," 155.
50. Lianne McLarty, "'Beyond the Veil of the Flesh': Cronenberg and the Disembodiment of Horror," in Grant, ed., *Dread of Difference*, 233.
51. Gelder, ed., *Horror Reader*, 5.

Do Movies Have Rights?

LOUIS MENAND

The Birth of a Nation previewed in Riverside, California, on January 1 and 2, 1915, and then in Los Angeles on February 8. The movie was not called *The Birth of a Nation* at those screenings. It was called *The Clansman*, after the well-known and very successful play by the Reverend Thomas Dixon, which was based, in turn, on two of the novels in his Reconstruction trilogy, *The Leopard's Spots* and *The Clansman*. It was Dixon himself, after seeing the movie in Los Angeles, who decided on the name change. "The picture is better than the book!" he is supposed to have said. "This picture is—like the birth of a nation."[1]

The movie was immediately protested by the National Association for the Advancement of Colored People, which had been formed in 1909 and which by 1915 had six thousand members.[2] The NAACP succeeded in getting an injunction closing the first showing in Los Angeles on February 8, but it did not request a permanent injunction, and the movie was shown that evening to a capacity audience of twenty-five hundred people. It was a phenomenal success. That year was the fiftieth anniversary of the end of the Civil War.

The California NAACP retained Clarence Darrow to represent it in a suit to prevent the movie from being shown in Los Angeles, but the suit went nowhere. Still, the organization did not give up. It waged a national legal campaign to ban the movie completely. W.E.B. Du Bois wrote several editorials in the NAACP's journal, *The Crisis,* on the subject. He called it a "slanderous film." "The Negro [is] represented," he said, "either as an ignorant fool, a vicious racist, a venal and unscrupulous politician, or a faithful but doddering idiot."³ The NAACP advised southern blacks not to demonstrate against *The Birth of a Nation* for their own safety, but in northern cities the organization was relentless. In New York, where the movie, now renamed *The Birth of a Nation*, had its world premiere on March 3, 1915, the NAACP appealed to city officials to refuse to grant the theater a license to show it. It was unsuccessful in getting the movie banned, but it did cause a disruption in the theater. The movie ended up playing in New York City for forty-eight weeks, during which time over a million people saw it. They paid what was regarded at the time as the ridiculously high price of two dollars a ticket.

In Boston, the local NAACP chapter demonstrated against the movie and published three pamphlets, including one called "A Vicious Lie," which reprinted condemnations of the movie by prominent civic and political figures. Dixon and Griffith offered the white president of the Boston NAACP, Moorfield Storey, $10,000 if he could find a single historical inaccuracy in the movie. Storey asked them what black lieutenant governor had ever bound and gagged a white woman. The NAACP was unable to close the movie down in Boston, but it did persuade the city to create a Board of Censorship with the power to license public entertainments. The movie was banned in Minneapolis, by the mayor of the city, W. G. Nye; in Ohio, by order of the governor; and in Newark, St. Paul, Chicago, Pittsburgh, and St. Louis, among other cities. Almost all of these actions were overturned in court, and the movie was permitted to be shown. In Minneapolis, the state supreme court upheld the mayor's right to ban the movie, but Mayor Nye reversed his decision anyway, and the film was shown. *The Birth of a Nation* was not shown in Ohio, however, until 1956.

The NAACP was created for the purpose of agitating actively on African American issues, and *The Birth of a Nation* was an ideal cause, since it focused attention on what W.E.B. Du Bois regarded as the fatal weakness in Booker T. Washington's approach: the acceptance of a subservient status for African Americans, and of the demeaning stereotypes by which that status was culturally reinforced. *The Birth of a Nation* became a staple of NAACP protest. It had many occasions, because *The Birth of a Nation* was re-released regularly in the 1920s, which was also the peak period of the second Ku Klux Klan. The Klan had been restarted in 1915 by an ex-minister named William J. Simmons, who had been inspired by Dixon's book and Griffith's movie. A sound version was released in 1930, again over NAACP protests. Between 1915 and 1973, the NAACP challenged screenings of *The Birth of a Nation* more than 120 times.

There were other protesters, as well. Jane Addams, who attended a special screening of *The Birth of a Nation* in New York City a week after it opened, gave an interview afterward for the *New York Post* in which she criticized the movie for being inaccurate and unfair. Booker T. Washington himself wrote letters to the newspapers attacking the movie. These protests did have two effects. The first was to change the movie itself. The version of *The Birth of a Nation* we see today was not the version audiences saw in Riverside, California, on January 1, 1915, or even the version shown in New York City two months later. Scenes of white women being abducted by black rapists, in the riot scene in Piedmont in the second half of the movie, were cut. An epilogue showing a letter Lincoln had written stating that he did not believe in racial equality was deleted. An explicit lynching scene was removed. The so-called Gus scene, in which Walter Long, in blackface, chases Mae Marsh through the woods, was toned down, in part by adding the intertitle "I'm not going to hurt you, Missy." And the original ending, which shows blacks being deported to Africa from New York harbor—a scene introduced with the intertitle "Lincoln's solution"—was cut. Two days after Jane Addams saw the movie, Griffith cut two scenes and added the intertitle that begins "A Plea for the Art of the Motion Picture." In Boston, the entire Gus episode was removed from the picture.

The second effect of the NAACP's actions was to produce counterreactions on the part of the filmmakers. It is an indication of the context within which the movie was received that relatively little was said in the attacks about Griffith. The person identified as the author, so to speak, of *The Birth of a Nation* was Dixon, and it was Dixon who campaigned most actively on its behalf. He tended to speak of it as his picture. Dixon had, in fact, a substantial stake in the movie. He had tried to sell the rights to his novel to the producers for $25,000. This was almost a quarter of the movie's budget. When the producers refused, Dixon accepted $2,000 and what we call points—a percentage of the profits. It was the smartest thing he ever did. He received almost $1 million.

The California agitation against the movie made Dixon nervous, so he approached the White House to seek the endorsement of the president.

Woodrow Wilson was the first southerner to be elected president since the Civil War, and he and Dixon were old friends. They had been graduate students together at Johns Hopkins, and Wilson had been awarded an honorary law degree from Wake Forest, Dixon's university, on Dixon's recommendation. Wilson was happy to do his old friend a favor. He was not hostile to the view of Reconstruction presented in *The Birth of a Nation*, for some passages on Reconstruction from his popular history of the United States are used in the film. Wilson had also, as president, segregated the federal government for the first time, separating white workers from black workers in government offices and cafeterias. He even allowed Dixon to use as a blurb the famous phrase he is supposed to have uttered after seeing the film in the White House—"It is history written with lightning." The filmmakers chose not to use as a possible blurb Thorstein Veblen's response to their picture: "Never before," Veblen said, "have I seen such concise misinformation."[4]

After his success with the White House, Dixon approached the Supreme Court, where he appealed to the chief justice, Edward White. White was a formidable figure. He had never been to the movies in his life, he told Dixon, and he had no use for them. But when Dixon explained that *The Birth of a Nation* told the true story of the Ku Klux Klan, White relented and arranged a screening for members of the Court. His reason, he explained to Dixon, was that he had once been a member of the Ku Klux Klan himself, in Louisiana, after the Civil War.

Dixon's argument was that the movie was true history, and the truth is always a defense against a charge of libel. *The Birth of a Nation*, he said, "expresses the passionate faith of the entire white population of the South. If I am wrong, they are wrong. The number of white people in the South who differ from my views of the history of Reconstruction could be housed on a half-acre lot."[5] Dixon also argued that the purpose of the movie was to prevent interracial marriage by making black men odious to white women. This had always been the basis of his racism, and in the case of the controversy over *The Birth of a Nation*, he had the ideal opponent, since revocation of the laws against interracial marriage was a plank of the NAACP's platform. Dixon wrote a treatise in defense of his story with the title "The Action of the Negro Inter-Marriage Society against the Play."

Griffith adopted a different strategy. He argued that the movie should be immune from censorship on grounds that it was both a form of opinion, protected under the Constitution, and a form of artistic and moral instruction, like Shakespeare and the Bible. In 1916, Griffith published a pamphlet called *The Rise and Fall of Free Speech in America*, in which he objected to the assumption that there was a legal difference between a movie and a work of literature. Griffith's position was partly a response to Jane Addams, who had condemned the nickelodeon as a corrupter of youth, back in 1909. By the time Griffith wrote his pamphlet, seven years later, movies were the fourth-largest industry in the country, doing over $300 million worth of business a year. People *liked* the movies. It was therefore easy for Griffith to appeal to mass sentiment by implying that Addams's views were elitist. Once, he said, knowledge was purveyed in boring books to which only a select few had access. The movies brought enlightenment to millions, plus, they were fun.

On February 23, 1915, four days after the justices had their special screening of *The Birth of a Nation*, the Supreme Court handed down an opinion in a case called *Mutual Film Corporation v. Industrial Commission of Ohio*. The Mutual Film Corporation was a distribution company founded by a man who had one of the most spectacular peripeteias in Hollywood history. His name was Harry Aitken, and without him *The Birth of a Nation* would almost certainly never have been made.[6] Aitken grew up on a farm in Waukesha, Wisconsin. In 1905, he and his brother Roy, who was also his lifelong business partner, borrowed $100 from a friend and started a chain of nickelodeons in Chicago. By 1914, the Aitkens owned or had a controlling interest in two movie production companies, Majestic and Reliance; a foreign distributorship, Western Import Limited; and a distribution company, the Mutual Production Company. They were among the first filmmakers to entice Wall Street bankers to invest in movie production, and they were among the first to advertise their movies in magazines. They had on their payrolls, at one time or another, Mary Pickford, Douglas Fairbanks, Lillian and Dorothy Gish, Charlie Chaplin, Gloria Swanson, Mack Sennett, and D. W. Griffith. They also employed Raoul Walsh, who was then an actor. He plays John Wilkes Booth in *The Birth of a Nation*. The Aitken brothers lived together in a lavish New York apartment with an English butler; Roy owned three luxury cars he had imported from Europe—a Renault, a Leon Bollee, and a Rolls. They were the distributors and chief financial backers of *The Birth of a Nation*. By 1918, three years after the movie came out, they were broke and back in Wisconsin, where they spent the rest of their lives dreaming of a comeback.

The reason for the Aitkens' business failure was the same as the reason for their success: they were gamblers. When Griffith approached them to finance *The Birth of a Nation*, the typical movie was a two- to four-reeler costing between $2,000 and $10,000 to produce. *The Birth of a Nation* ran twelve reels, and it cost $110,000. No one but the Aitkens were willing to fund it. In fact, Harry Aitken could not persuade the boards of either of his companies, Majestic or Mutual, to back Griffith's picture. The boards told him that they preferred to stick to the four-reelers. So Aitken raised the money himself and created a new company, the Epoch Producing Corporation, to distribute the movie. The Aitkens personally had $59,000 in the picture. The board of Mutual responded by firing Harry Aitken as the company's president. Aitken proceeded to create a company called Triangle Films, and then made the mistake of his career. He signed Broadway stage actors, at huge salaries, to perform in his films, only to discover that stage actors tend to be older people, whose faces look fine from the fourth row, but to whom the camera is not kind. He lost his company, his Culver City studio, and his shirt. He was a mogul for a minute. On the other hand, that's a minute more than the rest of us are ever likely to enjoy.

When *The Birth of a Nation* came out, Mutual was in the midst of litigation against several states, including Ohio, that required movies and other public entertainments to be licensed by a special board.[7] Its suit against the Ohio board, which was called the Industrial Commission, went to the U.S. Supreme Court. Laws requiring licensing of public entertainments, such as theatrical productions, puppet shows, minstrel shows, and so on, had been on the books in the United States forever. Purveyors of those entertainments had sued licensing boards in the past to recover the right to put on their productions. What made the *Mutual* case different was the basis of the company's legal claim. Mutual asserted that the Ohio law was a violation of its freedom of speech under the Ohio constitution. (In 1915, there was no extension of the federal right of free speech, in the Bill of Rights, to the states;

that did not happen until 1925.) *Mutual v. Ohio* was the first case in American law involving movie censorship to be argued on free speech grounds.

Its originality did not do Mutual any good. The Supreme Court was unanimous in holding that a movie is not speech. The language of the opinion is important. "The exhibition of moving pictures," the Court said, "is a business, pure and simple, originated and conducted for profit, like other spectacles, not to be regarded, nor intended to be regarded by the Ohio Constitution, we think, as part of the press of the country, or as organs of public opinion. They are mere representations of events, of ideas and sentiments published and known; vivid, useful and entertaining, no doubt, but . . . capable of evil, having power for it, the greater because of their attractiveness and manner of exhibition. It was this capability and power, and it may be in experience of them, that induced the State of Ohio . . . to require censorship before exhibition. . . . We cannot regard this as beyond the power of government."[8]

The logic is interesting. Mutual had argued that movies are speech, and are therefore shielded from the kind of prior restraint represented by the Ohio requirement. But it also argued that movies are property, and therefore shielded from interference from the state by the contracts clause of the U.S. Constitution. Mutual tried to catch the Court on a fork: if the Court holds that movies are expression, then Mutual products are protected from prior restraint by the Ohio constitution; if it holds that movies are a business, then those products are protected by the U.S. Constitution. In order to hold that movies are not speech, the Court had to find that movies have no original power of expression, that they are, as the Court put it, only *representations* of things already known or published elsewhere. This leaves the aesthetic properties of the medium as the defining element, and the Court found that movies' aesthetic power is potent enough to engage the legitimate exercise of the state's police power. In other words, the Court justified state obstruction of the use of private property by the claim that the public good and public safety require it. This is the legal logic behind the "redeeming social value" test. It trumps the contracts clause with the police power.

Now we can see the constitutional basis for the NAACP's protests, and the reason why Dixon sought the approbation of the president and the U.S.

Supreme Court. In 1915, the Constitution did *not* protect movies from censorship. Censorship was, in fact, the norm. The possibility that *The Birth of a Nation* might be suppressed was perfectly real: nothing in the law prevented it. In 1914, the year before *The Birth of a Nation* was released, the National Board of Censorship of Motion Pictures, which was a private organization whose rulings were followed by many state censoring agencies, reviewed 5,770 films. It required changes in 522, almost 10 percent, and it condemned 79 in toto. Even after the 79 were revised and resubmitted, 27 were banned anyway. In 1915, the National Board of Censorship (by then renamed the Board of Review of Motion Pictures) approved *The Birth of a Nation*, though on a divided vote. By then, the Board was previewing virtually every film made in the United States, and it charged a fee for each film it reviewed, as did all local censorship boards. The Board's motto, incidentally, was "Selection, not censorship," which is an interesting distinction. It is estimated that the total cost to filmmakers for dealing with censorship boards across the country was half a million dollars a year.[9]

This was the motivation for Mutual's lawsuit: the cost of submitting prints for review by censorship boards, which normally charged a dollar a reel, and the interference with plans for national advertising caused by having to go up separately before independent boards in multiple jurisdictions. Mutual did not think that any of its movies were indecent or objectionable. It was perfectly willing to take its chances that, after exhibition, it would be found in violation of decency statutes. Harry Aitken was, in fact, a religious man, and he refused to distribute movies he judged to be unclean. The company only wanted to avoid the expense of the vetting. This is why it objected to the licensing process as an exercise in prior restraint. It had no intention of producing or distributing dirty pictures.

The legal context of *The Birth of a Nation* reveals something distinctive about the Progressive Era. We find a progressive group we assume to be devoted to the cause of civil liberties, the NAACP, calling for censorship, and a commercial entity we assume to be indifferent to those liberties, the Mutual Film Corporation, attempting to broaden the protections of the First Amendment. This apparent anomaly reflects the status of the idea of rights at the time of the First World War. Rights talk was understood by most people to be inherently conservative: rights were invoked by businesses and by courts in order to claim protection from regulation by the state. Progressives were hostile to rights talk because they were hostile to the argument that private commercial activities that affected the public were immune from public intervention. The chief constitutional wedge that was available to be driven into the law protecting private corporations was the police power—the power cited by the Court in *Mutual v. Ohio*, and regularly invoked by the NAACP in its efforts to censor *The Birth of a Nation*. The NAACP tried to persuade courts that the public peace would be disrupted by the exhibition of the film in its intended form. And, as we have seen, in a few places the argument had success. It was not so much sensitivity toward African Americans that prompted white mayors and governors to ban *The Birth of a Nation*; it was the fear that the movie might incite mob violence. This was the reason Mayor Nye of Minneapolis gave for his initial ban. *The Birth of a Nation* is, after all, from first to last, a justification for and celebration of vigilantism. It was only after 1917, when left-wing figures such as Eugene Debs were jailed for speaking against American intervention in the First World War, that Progressives became champions of the First Amendment. Many years later, in the civil rights era, southern segregationists would argue that enforcement of civil rights laws would cause social disturbance—that the rights of African Americans to equal protection were trumped by the police power. It was a parallel to the argument that the NAACP had used in seeking to ban *The Birth of a Nation*.

The effects of the controversy over *The Birth of a Nation* and of the *Mutual* decision were long-lasting. The *Mutual* decision was one of the things that led to the establishment of the Hays Office in 1922—an effort by Hollywood to practice self-censorship and thus avoid state regulation altogether. (The Hays Office was named for the first president of the Motion Picture Producers and Distributors Association, Will Hays, who had been a chairman of the Republican National Committee and the postmaster general. Hays's Production Code was adopted in 1930.) This is a strategy repeated in the current ratings system for movies, television, and some popular music. Self-regulation is safer than public regulation; it is also cheaper and more predictable.

Mutual was the law of the land for thirty-seven years. The case that overturned it, and that led the U.S. Supreme Court to declare movies eligible for First Amendment protection, is known as the *Miracle* case. The key figure in this story is another distributor, a man named Joseph Burstyn.[10] Burstyn was a Polish immigrant who came to New York City in 1921, when he was twenty. He worked first in the diamond business and then as a press agent for the Yiddish theater. In the 1930s, he became partners with the publicity director for Paramount, Arthur L. Mayer, and they opened the first distribution company in America that dealt exclusively in foreign films. Burstyn and Mayer managed what used to be called art houses—later known as repertory houses—in large cities around the country. Burstyn was a smart businessman, but he also knew something about the cinema. After the Second World War, he and Mayer brought to the United States, among other European films, the classics of Italian neorealism: *Open City, Paisan, Shoe-Shine,* and *The Bicycle Thief.*

Part of the appeal of European movies was that they were what we would call today unrated. They did not have to be submitted to the Motion Picture Association's internal censorship procedures for approval under the so-called Production Code, since they were not produced by studios that were members of the MPAA. Foreign films therefore acquired an aura of licentiousness that was often completely unmerited. Theater owners were not under the illusion that people came to see Italian movies for their sensitive portrayal of the human condition. In Chicago, therefore, the ads for De Sica's *The Bicycle Thief* read: "Uncut. See 'Bicycle Thief' in its entirety without a single censorship snip." The ad for Rossellini's *Open City* read: "Adults only. Savage Orgy of Lust."[11] There is no sex, of course, in either movie.

The same is true of *The Miracle*. *The Miracle* is a Roberto Rossellini movie, forty minutes long. It had been a commercial flop in Italy, where audiences found it boring. The story is by Federico Fellini. It concerns a homeless and mentally defective Italian woman, played by Anna Magnani, who meets a wanderer dressed in a cast-off American Army uniform. The wanderer, played by Fellini, believes that he is Saint Joseph, the father of Christ. Sensing an opportunity, he gets the Magnani character drunk and they have sex, off camera. The woman becomes pregnant. Having no memory of the sex, she imagines that she has been immaculately impregnated. The townspeople mock her savagely, crowning her with a washbowl for a halo, and she flees. At the end of the film, she gives birth in an abandoned church.

There is nothing remotely titillating about this movie. Anna Magnani is made into a gibbering, unkempt bag lady, and the wanderer and the townspeople are malign and abusive. There is very little that anyone would call dialogue, and the ending is disturbing. It is not a movie about religious hypocrisy; it is a movie about the wickedness of a world without spirituality. Rossellini called the film pro-Catholic—"an absolutely Catholic work," he said[12]—and although this may be taking things a little far, *The Miracle* is certainly not a satire of Catholicism.

This proved to be a distinction too fine for American audiences. In 1950, when *The Miracle* came to the United States, six states and approximately two hundred municipalities had censorship boards whose approval was required in order to exhibit a film. The industry was by then paying about $1.8 million every year in fees and other costs in order to comply with licensing requirements—although this was in an industry that, in 1950, grossed over $1.2 billion. Two movies of the time that dealt with racial relations, specifically with stories about black characters passing for white—Elia Kazan's bizarre *Pinky* and Louis de Rochmont's even more bizarre *Lost Boundaries*—were banned in many southern cities. It was common for studios themselves to cut scenes with black actors from prints sent to southern theaters—for example, Hazel Scott's performance of "The Man I Love" in *Rhapsody in Blue*, in 1945. Hazel Scott was Trinidadian; George Gershwin had been her friend; her husband was a U.S. congressman. But she was banned in Georgia.

Joseph Burstyn applied for and received a license to exhibit *The Miracle* from the New York censorship board, which was part of the Motion Picture Division of the state's Department of Education, an agency governed by the New York Board of Regents. In 1950, Burstyn combined Rossellini's movie with short films by Jean Renoir and Maurice Pagnol and released all three under the title *Ways of Love*. *Ways of Love* opened at the Paris Theatre in Manhattan on December 12, 1950. In 1950, the Paris was the leading venue in New York City, and therefore in the country, for foreign films. The theater is still there, on Fifty-Eighth Street, just off Fifth Avenue, across from the Plaza Hotel. At some point within the next two weeks, the movie was seen by a man named Edward T. McCaffrey. McCaffrey happened to be commissioner of licenses in the City of New York—a political appointee who supervised the issuance of licenses for the seventy-seven activities then requiring one in the city. McCaffrey found *The Miracle* "officially and personally blasphemous," as he put it in a letter to the owner of the Paris Theatre, and he took it upon himself unilaterally to suspend the theater's license. He had received no outside complaints and he had consulted no committee. He told reporters that "Officially, as a representative of the city government, I felt there were hundreds of thousands of citizens whose religious beliefs were assaulted by the picture." One assumes, based on his name, that McCaffrey was himself of Irish Catholic descent. McCaffrey was appointed to his post by the mayor of New York City, Vincent Impellitteri. Mayor Impellitteri stayed out of the controversy, on the time-honored New York principle that since the state never pays attention to a city problem, the city should pay no attention to anything that could be made a state problem. It was the state that licensed movies, not the city, and it was the state's politicians whose careers were in the ethnic wringer.

The National Legion of Decency, which was the Catholic Church's board of movie censorship, picked up the license commissioner's cue and condemned *The Miracle* as sacrilegious, the first movie it had ever condemned on those grounds. Joseph Burstyn went to court, and he did not have much trouble getting Commissioner McCaffrey's order rescinded on the grounds that it had been issued without due process. The movie had, after all, received a license from the state agency empowered to grant or withhold such license. As the flames were fed by controversy, the Paris Theatre started selling out. It was so crowded that there were sometimes standees. The New York City Fire Department made a habit of closing the theater down whenever, in its estimation, the crowd exceeded its legal capacity in violation of the fire code. This had not been something the New York City Fire Department had demonstrated much concern about in the past. *The Miracle* became a *cause célèbre*, and Burstyn made a lot of money.

He needed it, because the censors were not done yet. Shortly after Burstyn won his recision order, the head of the Catholic Archdiocese of New York, Francis Cardinal Spellman, decided to weigh in. On January 7, 1951, he issued a statement read at all masses that day in St. Patrick's Cathedral, in which he called on Catholics to boycott *The Miracle*, which he called "vile and harmful." The movie was blasphemous, it disrespected Italian womanhood, and it made people who saw it vulnerable to Communism. "Divide and conquer is the technique of the greatest enemy of civilization, atheistic Communism," the cardinal warned. "God forbid that these producers of racial religious mockeries should divide and demoralize Americans so that the minions of Moscow might enslave this land of liberty." Interestingly, the company that distributed Western movies to Soviet bloc countries refused to distribute *The Miracle*; they said it was "pro-Catholic propaganda."

By the time the cardinal issued his proclamation, one hundred thousand people had bought tickets to see *The Miracle* at the Paris Theatre. The theater was enjoying its highest grosses ever—despite the presence of Catholic picketers outside carrying placards, some of which read "This is the Kind of Picture the Communists Want" and "Don't be a Communist—All the Communists Are Inside." These protests may seem manifestations of righteousness and prudery, but if you think of the Catholics who picketed *The Miracle* on the analogy of the African Americans who protested *The Birth of a Nation,* you can sympathize with the motivation. It was not that they could not stomach the image of Anna Magnani made pregnant by Federico Fellini in Army boots. It was because they thought that the whole story of seduction and torment in an Italian village was bad for Catholics, which was a group then still subject to discrimination. It did not matter so much what Rossellini's "message" was. He had represented Italians as primitive and vicious and Catholicism as a superstition.

The Catholic protests stirred the New York State Board of Regents to action. It is not hard to see why. The target of the protests, ultimately, was the agency that had licensed *The Miracle* for distribution in the first place, the Motion Picture Division of the Department of Education. The department was a government agency; there were about 1.25 million Catholics in New York; and Catholics vote, often as a block. There was another reason propelling the attacks on *The Miracle*. Rossellini had famously seduced Ingrid Bergman, a great Hollywood star. Bergman was not a Catholic, of course. But she was almost an honorary Catholic. She had played Joan of Arc, and in *The Bells of St. Mary's* she had played a nun. She had abandoned her husband, Dr. Peter Lindstrom, and their daughter, Pia, when she became involved with Rossellini, and the two had a child, Robertino, out of wedlock. Robertino was born in 1950, the same year that *The Miracle* opened in New York. This made Bergman a pariah in America. She was actually denounced on the floor of the U.S. Senate as "Hollywood's apostle of degradation." Rossellini was also suspected by many people in the United States of being a Communist sympathizer—not that unusual in postwar Italy, but anathema to Americans in the early years of the Cold War. These facts help to explain why a movie as bleak and unstimulating as *The Miracle* could inspire such vehement opposition from official figures. As is often true in cases like this—as was true, for example, of protests against Martin Scorsese's adaptation of *The Last Temptation of Christ*, in 1988—most of the people who condemned the movie had never seen it.

The Regents wasted little time in unanimously rescinding the license granted to Burstyn to distribute *The Miracle,* on grounds that the movie was sacrilegious, a ban-able category under the statute authorizing the licensing board. Burstyn took his case to the state courts, which all refused to reverse the Regents' action, and in 1952, it came before the U.S. Supreme Court as *Burstyn v. Wilson*. On May 26, the Supreme Court unanimously ruled that New York's ban of *The Miracle* was an exercise of prior restraint in violation of the First Amendment of the U.S. Constitution. *Mutual v. Ohio* was overturned, and the movies became, for the first time, a constitutionally protected form of expression. According to the Court's opinion, movies are "a significant medium for the communication of ideas. . . . The importance of motion pictures as an organ of public opinion is not lessened by the fact that they are designed to entertain as well as inform."[13] This was precisely the argument that D. W. Griffith had made in his pamphlet on *The Rise and Fall of Free Speech in America,* back in 1916.

The ruling in the *Miracle* case was, in fact, a narrow one. The Court did not say that states could never ban or censor movies; it only said that they could not do so by finding them "sacrilegious," since that standard was vague and subjective. But as happens with narrow rulings, the *Miracle* decision was interpreted by subsequent Courts to prohibit censorship of movies on every ground except obscenity. *Burstyn v. Wilson* became a terrible swift sword for striking down movie censorship rulings. By 1961, only four states and fourteen municipalities—down from two hundred in 1950—still had licensing boards. All a movie had to do to defy a licensing board was to assert that it expressed an idea. Thus, in 1959, the Supreme Court unanimously struck down the state of New York's refusal to license the movie version of *Lady Chatterley's Lover*. It had not been banned because of sex scenes, the Court said. It was banned because it expressed an idea that the state of New York did not like: the idea, as Justice Potter Stewart delightfully put it in the lead opinion, was "that adultery under certain circumstances may be proper behavior."[14]

Burstyn spent between $55,000 and $75,000 of his own money to win his case against New York State. (It was, on the other hand, fully deductible as a business expense.) The American film industry was not interested in getting involved in his suit; in fact, Burstyn was discouraged by people in the industry from pursuing a legal avenue at all. The reason is not hard to understand. Since the Motion Picture Association had its own censorship regime in place, almost all the movies subject to state censorship were foreign films—in other words, the competition. No one in Hollywood lost any sleep over the thought that some French or Italian import might lose its license for American exhibition. That meant one less "uncut" adults-only foreign film for American movie audiences to spend their discretionary entertainment dollars on.

After the ruling, *The Miracle* reopened in New York City, this time in ten theaters. The ads read: "The World's Most Talked About Movie—See For Yourself—The Original Uncut Version ... Exactly as It Was Approved by the United States Supreme Court." Still, in Chicago, where *The Miracle* had previously been banned as irreligious, it was reviewed and banned again, this time as obscene. *The Miracle* was not exhibited in Chicago until 1957. (By then, Joseph Burstyn was dead. In 1953, a year after the decision in *Burstyn v. Wilson,* he had been on his way to Europe and had suffered a heart attack on the plane. Three years later, Ingrid Bergman was back in Hollywood. She was legally separated from Roberto Rossellini in 1957.)

You can see the swing in the judicial and political understanding of the right of free speech by looking at a Supreme Court case decided in the same term as the *Miracle* case. The case is *Beauharnais v. Illinois.* Joseph Beauharnais was the leader of an outfit called the White Circle League of America, Inc. He opposed housing desegregation in Chicago and was convicted by an Illinois court for distributing leaflets condemning what he called the "mongrelization" of the white race by African Americans, whom he accused of aggression, rape, robbery, drug use, and other antisocial behavior. The U.S. Supreme Court, in an opinion by Felix Frankfurter, upheld the conviction, on the theory that Beauharnais had committed the crime of what we now call "group libel"—essentially an extension of the concept of individual libel to groups. Frankfurter also said that because of Illinois' history of violent racial conflict, it was reasonable for the state to prosecute Beauharnais in the name of public safety. This had been the logic of the censors of *The Birth of a Nation,* and of the Supreme Court in the *Mutual* decision, back in 1915. The state's constitutional power to prevent harm done to a group of citizens, black Americans, overcame the protections of the First Amendment.

The *Beauharnais* decision has not stood up, largely thanks to the Court's decision in *New York Times v. Sullivan,* in 1962, which held that the *Times* was not libelous for running an advertisement that made accusations, some of them false, against certain white sheriffs in Montgomery, Alabama, at the time of civil rights protests there. The Court held that, in the interest of fostering a robust public debate, public figures, such as sheriffs, are not protected by libel laws. Robust public debate is what the First Amendment was presumably intended to protect, and plainly Beauharnais's leaflets fall into that category. So does Thomas Dixon's movie.

Still, *Beauharnais* and the concept of group libel have a continuing life in debates over hate speech and pornography. People who support codes aimed at censuring hate speech and people who advocate the suppression of pornography often use *Beauharnais,* and its legal logic, to carve out an exception from the First Amendment. They argue that racial hate speech is a libel against nonwhite people as a group, and that pornography is similarly directed at women as a group. The purpose of these types of speech, they claim, is not to foster debate, but to silence debate by intimidating nonwhites or women. It is an injury directed at a class of people.[15]

What makes the *Beauharnais* and *Mutual* arguments harder to accept today than they were in 1915 and 1952 is the general sentiment that freedom of speech is a right owned by each person individually, just by virtue of being human. We have a notion of rights as personal assets—the lone gunslinger syndrome, where each individual can shoot down anyone who ventures onto his or her designated legal turf. The Progressives, and some people today, prefer to think of rights as existing not for the good of individuals but for the good of the group. We protect political speech because it legitimizes democratic power: if dissent is suppressed, then we cannot call government decisions democratic, since some people were prevented from having their say in making them. But if dissent is permitted, and it fails to convince the majority, then the majority can legitimately impose its will on the dissenters. Respect for the rights of minorities is what gives majorities the authority, at the end of the day, to have their way.

The important point is that rights always involve a trade-off. There are always competing interests. We would not need even the idea of rights if there were not always people out there who want something which the right is intended to prevent them from doing or having. Rights are not individual goods; after all, in a state of nature, no one has a right. Coercion is the natural condition of things. Rights stand both outside of and at the center of democratic systems: they are undemocratic since they give individuals trumps against the will of the people, but they are constructed by societies for the same reason societies make any laws and rules, which is in order to further group ends. Most of the time when group ends conflict with individual rights, people are untroubled by the curtailment of the rights. This can be seen in the myriad instances in which speech is criminalized and no one has a problem with it. Perjury, false advertising, solicitation of a bribe, conspiracy to commit murder: these are all speech acts pure and simple, but they are criminalized because their threat to the public good exceeds their value as expression. So-called fighting words usually fall into this category of proscribed speech, and so does obscenity. This is why the Court was reluctant to make the *Miracle* decision a complete prohibition of state regulation of motion pictures. There are cases out there where the public interest will be seen to justify prior restraint, and no principle will determine in advance when that line has been crossed. What the majority wants, rightly or wrongly, wisely or not, the majority generally gets. When Commissioner McCaffrey was overruled in his efforts to sanction the Paris Theatre, the New York City Fire Department found another way to skin that troublesome cat.

The American Civil Liberties Union was not patient with the group libel claim—after all, claims of group libel, like speech code restrictions, tend to run both ways: the censor always rings twice—and it continually warned the NAACP that the policy of trying to ban movies was a potential boomerang. In 1942, two years after the most popular talkie ever made, *Gone with the Wind*, swept the Academy Awards (Margaret Mitchell, incidentally, sent Thomas Dixon a fan letter), the NAACP entered into an agreement with the movie industry prohibiting the use of demeaning portrayals of black characters in Hollywood movies. So far as Thomas Dixon's particular racial anxiety is concerned, the Supreme Court did not declare laws against interracial marriage unconstitutional until the case of *Loving v. Virginia*. That was in 1967.

In 1954, the phone rang in the Aitkens' house in Waukesha, Wisconsin. It was a man named Phil Ryan. He told Harry Aitken that he represented a syndicate that wanted to produce a remake of *The Birth of a Nation*. It was the call Aitken had been waiting for for almost forty years. He was still the president of Epoch Producing Corporation, a business whose sole function was to retain the rights to *The Birth of a Nation*. Aitken had already tried to get Griffith and Dixon to collaborate on a remake in the 1930s. Griffith and Dixon were by then both broken and broke. They were thrilled by the prospect of more riches descending on their heads. But Griffith needed $800,000 to make the film, and Aitken was able to raise only $100,000. Dixon died in 1946; Griffith died two years later. In 1954, Aitken was in his seventies, but he was ready to rumble. He sold Ryan's investors, a group headed by a financier named Ted Thal, an option on *The Birth of a Nation*. The remake was announced in the trades, but the money was not there, and the deal fell through. Aitken died two years later.

Suppose that *The Birth of a Nation* had been banned? Would that have been bad for art? The movie is widely regarded as one of the most important in the history of cinema. "[I]t established the motion picture once and for all as the most popular and persuasive of entertainments and compelled the acceptance of the film as art," wrote the Museum of Modern Art's founding film curator, Iris Barry, in 1940.[16] Griffith's work changed the way movies were made, and it inspired filmmakers for fifty years. *The Birth of a Nation* was as technically innovative for its time as *Citizen Kane* was for its. It is sometimes said that *The Birth of a Nation* is also intellectually simpleminded, but this seems to me to be wrong. It is a story constructed around assumptions about race that we consider false, but given those assumptions, the treatment is intelligent and reasonably complex. *The Birth of a Nation* is at least as sophisticated intellectually as *City Lights* or *Modern Times*.

On the other hand, was the Court entirely wrong in 1915 when it described the movies as "a business pure and simple"? Dixon had written a book; he had written a play. Those were not, financially, undertakings beyond the scope of most human beings. And people write and publish books to make money, too, as the Court noted in the *Miracle* decision. But Dixon could not have made his story into a movie of the size and scope of *The Birth of a Nation* without the help of Harry Aitken, and Aitken had no interest in the message of Dixon's story. He only wanted to make money. And he did make money. *The Birth of a Nation* grossed over $60 million. The same is true of Joseph Burstyn. No doubt Burstyn believed that movies are an art form deserving protection from censorship. But he had also been in films long enough to know that controversy is good for business. We do not have trouble regulating many consumer goods, like soft drinks and medications and cars. Is a big-budget commercial movie like a book or a newspaper editorial, or is it more like an advertisement or a soft drink?

Was *The Birth of a Nation* bad for black people in America? I think there is no doubt that it was. It is the most popular silent film ever made. In the first eleven years after its release, between 1915 and 1926, it was seen by more than 100 million people. "Every man who comes out of one of our theatres," Dixon once said, "is a Southern partisan for life."[17] It might be objected that one cannot prove that *The Birth of a Nation* was the cause of the suffering or death of African Americans, but one cannot prove that the art of the cinema was significantly enriched by *The Birth of a Nation*, either. The one claim seems as plausible as the other. And which is more important? Black people did suffer, and some black people were probably murdered, as a consequence of Griffith's movie and the racist passions it educated and inflamed. Was it wrong to try to suppress it?

NOTES

1. Quoted in Roy E. Aitken, as told to Al P. Nelson, *The "Birth of a Nation" Story* (Middleburg, Va.: William W. Dellinger, 1965), 46. See also Richard Schickel, *D. W. Griffith: An American Life* (1984; reprint, New York: Limelight Editions, 1996), 268.

2. See Leonard L. Archer, *Black Images in the American Theatre: NAACP Protest Campaigns—Stage, Screen, Radio, and Television* (New York: Pageant-Poseidon, 1973), and Edward de Grazia and Roger K. Newman, *Banned Films: Movies, Censors, and the First Amendment* (New York: Bowker, 1982), 3-6, 180-82.

3. Quoted in Archer, *Black Images*, 188.

4. The story of Wilson's remark is repeated in many sources; it is, of course, as reported by Dixon, and therefore impossible to confirm.

5. Quoted in Janet Staiger, "*The Birth of a Nation*: Reconsidering Its Reception," in "*The Birth of a Nation*": *D. W. Griffith, Director*, ed. Robert Lang (New Brunswick: Rutgers Univ. Press, 1994), 202.

6. See Roy E. Aitken, as told to Al P. Nelson, *The "Birth of a Nation" Story*.

7. See John W. Wertheimer, "Mutual Film Reviewed," *American Journal of Legal History* 37 (1993): 158.

8. *Mutual Film Corporation v. Industrial Commission of Ohio*, 236 U.S. 230 (1915), 244-45.

9. De Grazia and Newman, *Banned Films*, 10–13.

10. See, generally, Alan F. Westin, *The Miracle Case: The Supreme Court and the Movies*, The Inter-University Case Program, number 64 (University, Ala.: Univ. of Alabama Press, 1961).

11. See Barbara Wilensky, *Sure Seaters: The Emergence of Art House Cinema* (Minneapolis: Univ. of Minnesota Press, 2001), 122–27.

12. Quoted in Peter Bondanella, *The Films of Roberto Rossellini* (Cambridge: Cambridge Univ. Press, 1993), 16.

13. *Joseph Burstyn, Inc. v. Wilson, Commissioner of Education of New York*, 343 U.S. 495 (1952), 501.

14. *Kingsley International Pictures Corporation v. Regents of the University of the State of New York*, 360 U.S. 684 (1959), 688.

15. See, for example, Mari J. Matsudi et al., *Words That Wound: Critical Race Theory, Assaultive Speech, and the First Amendment* (Boulder, Colo.: Westview Press, 1992), and Catharine A. MacKinnon, *Only Words* (Cambridge, Mass.: Harvard Univ. Press, 1993).

16. Iris Barry, *D. W. Griffith: American Film Master*, Museum of Modern Art Film Library Series, No. 1 (New York: Museum of Modern Art, 1940), 22.

17. Quoted in Schickel, *D. W. Griffith*, 269.

Epilogue: The Enduring Worlds of Thomas Dixon

WILLIAM A. LINK

A Renaissance Man for his generation and beyond, Thomas Dixon embraced overlapping worlds of religion, print media, the spoken word, theater, movies, popular culture, and politics. With a complex personality and a restless spirit that ranged in search of fame and renown, Dixon was something of the Forrest Gump of his day. He was also a person of considerable intellectual potential who raced through Wake Forest College, apparently earning more honors than any other student before or since and trying out, if briefly, a career as a graduate student in history at the Johns Hopkins University. Subsequently, he explored an amazing variety of careers. He tinkered with acting, the law, and a political career (he was elected to the North Carolina legislature in 1885). Launching on a career as a Baptist minister, he attracted followings in Raleigh, Boston, and New York City, becoming a Social Gospeler of some prominence, even while he attracted audiences as a lecturer in the North and Midwest. Abandoning his career as a minister, Dixon successively morphed into successful novelist, playwright, and movie producer. Throughout, he exhibited abilities as a self-promoter, with a knack for attracting and keeping attention.

The authors in this volume, relying on different disciplinary perspectives, fully consider the ways in which Dixon's work reflected, embodied, and shaped vitally important cultural and political trends of Progressive Era America. Using new media that appealed to a larger national audience, he communicated an entire worldview of white supremacy. Collectively, these essays scrutinize the nature of Dixon's wide national appeal, how he marketed himself and his message, the sources of that message, its impact, and the ways in which Americans accepted or rejected it.[1]

And a powerful message it was, with a particular grip on early twentieth-century American social and cultural anxieties. Dixon is remembered for the depiction of white supremacy in his novels, especially the triumphantly racist and best-selling *The Leopard's Spots* and *The Clansman*. But he is best known for his collaboration with D. W. Griffith on *The Birth of a Nation*, at once both a breakthrough in the early movie industry and an anthem to Dixon's white supremacist ideas. Yet his appeal was not exclusively racist; a more common thread was his emphasis on gender and fetishized white womanhood. Dixon could accurately be described as a Progressive: closely associated with reformers, he was connected to anticorruption, good government, and antivice efforts in New York City in the 1890s, and he remained part of a sophisticated circle of social critics. He was also a southern Progressive who was dedicated to liberal social change, modernization of the region, and social uplift that focused on the South's intense poverty. Like most southern Progressives, however, Dixon's ideas of social progress were framed in racial terms, though his white supremacist views put him on an extreme end of the continuum. It was this combination of characteristics that revealed a sort of intellectual and social restlessness, in which, as David Stricklin puts it, he "held seemingly contradictory ideas in balance."[2]

A combination of factors explains Dixon's success, as the authors point out, and his message resonated with important tendencies in American culture. Dixon tapped into a new construction of "whiteness," the complexities of which Scott Romine so ably unveils. Jane M. Gaines finds more important Dixon's ability to develop a new cultural form, "race melodrama," that combined racism with well-known dramatic forms that came to dominate Hollywood film production. Cynthia Lynn Lyerly unpacks Dixon's appeal out of a collection of ideas, a "religious ideology," borrowing heavily from Social Gospel notions of social salvation and redemption. These themes, she points out, assumed a literary form emphasizing "larger cultural anxieties about masculinity," white heterosexual love, and a "unique gender ideology" that idealized whites and demonized blacks.[3] For Charlene Regester, the commercial success of *The Birth of a Nation* resulted from its being a horror film that defined the genre. The portrayal of blackness as evil, black males as rapists, and whiteness as heroic converged with contemporary white sensibilities in a movie that sought to exaggerate emotions and fears. These horror symbols—what she describes as the "coding of the horror film genre" —defined public responses.[4] Rejecting a psychobiographical approach, W. Fitzhugh Brundage asserts that Dixon's popularity can be explained only because he understood important tendencies resident in American culture, and his message adapted itself to a combination of Victorian morality and modernism. An "American Proteus," Dixon, according to Brundage, succeeded in aligning "himself with some of the most powerful swirling currents of his era." In Brundage's estimation, Dixon provided a kind of bridge to modernism; a transitional figure who was still wedded to Victorian models of moralism, he embraced "modern modes of cultural expression, which eventually would contribute to an emerging modernist ethos."[5]

Not all Americans accepted Dixon's racist message; his ideas stimulated opponents to sharpen the meaning of African American equality. The appearance in 1915 of *The Birth of a Nation* was highly controversial, giving rise to both spontaneous and organized opposition and an at least partly successful effort to suppress the film. As Regester correctly observes, public response to the movie became immediately polarized, and it served as a rallying symbol of racism for African Americans. The most popular silent film ever, *The Birth of a Nation* occasioned widespread protest, led by the newly created NAACP, that sought to boycott and suppress the film. As Louis Menand points out, the film became a lightning rod for more general efforts to suppress content on the big screen, and in this sense alone it had a major impact on the motion picture industry. The intensity of opposition to the Dixon-Griffith collaboration prompted Dixon to engineer the notorious White House screening. This event remains a major blight on Woodrow Wilson's contemporary reputation, and his presidency has become known as the most racist of any in the twentieth century. As John David Smith explains, African American leaders found the film disturbing, insulting, and threatening primarily because, even then, they at least partly realized the far-reaching impact of movies in American culture. He discusses how African American leaders, among them Kelly Miller, Sutton E. Griggs, and W.E.B. Du Bois, articulated a widespread outrage. These leaders poked holes, sometime gaping holes, into Dixon's racial fantasies. Both Miller and Griggs addressed Dixon's chief assumptions of African American racial inadequacy and retrogression, of the failure of emancipation and postemancipation, and of the need for radical solutions. Miller, already a critic of racial retrogression, offered a critique of *The Leopard's Spots* in 1905, while Griggs used his novels as a weapon against Dixon's views. Both offered powerful attacks on notions of innate racial inferiority, that black male sexuality threatened white women, and that aggravated racial tensions were the responsibility of African American racial inadequacy.

It thus can be said that Dixon simultaneously represented his time and led the way toward reshaping it. And in several respects he articulated a new spirit of modern America that was emerging during the Progressive Era and afterward. Most obviously, Dixon himself embodied the racial divide that had opened up in early twentieth-century America. This era was what Rayford Logan later described as the "nadir" of American race relations, a period of unprecedented racial violence, or the triumph of an ugly system of apartheid and white supremacy, and of the persistence of racial oppression at a variety of levels.[6] Behind this spirit of white supremacy lay a distinctive ideology: Dixon was one of the better articulators of what Joel Williamson calls a "Radical" approach to race relations. Appearing after the 1890s, Radicals sought basic change in race relations. According to the Radical version of history, the Civil War was a tragic occurrence in which black people played a disruptive role: first as slaves, then as freedpeople, they disrupted sectional harmony. Especially during Reconstruction, well-intentioned but deluded white northerners made the mistake of experimenting with black freedom. The result, because of blacks' underdevelopment and bestiality, was disastrous, even cataclysmic. Radicals such as Dixon favored a drastic solution to the unsettled question of the place of freedpeople in southern society. Rejecting the egalitarian traditions of Reconstruction, Dixon believed that emancipation and political empowerment for black males had been a dreadful mistake. He further believed in white supremacy and in the need to reassert white control of all aspects of southern life—not only politics, but also culture. And it was in the area of culture that Dixon's radicalism became most influential.

What are the ways in which we might understand Dixon and his influence? There has been considerable debate about Dixon's life story. In particular, how was it possible that such virulent racism could emerge from a thoughtful person? Joel Williamson, who describes Dixon's *The Leopard's Spots* as an "encyclopedia of Radicalism" and as "nearest to a codification of the Radical dogma"[7] as existed anywhere, provides one answer. According to Williamson's description in his now-classic *The Crucible of Race*, Dixon's misshapen attitudes on race resulted from a troubled youth, and his life provided one example of "how the deeply personal and largely psychic needs of an individual might impel that person to extreme racism." Describing racism as "essentially a mental condition, a disorder of the mind in which internal problems are projected upon external persons," Williamson characterizes Dixon as tortured by his mother's marriage and premenstrual sexual violation at age thirteen; his literary efforts to recast views on race, nationality, and southern history made up a "sort of ink blot," an "attempt at psychic self-cure" by a person seeking to "set himself aright with the South." Thus can we explain a person simultaneously capable of remarkable achievement and vicious racism.[8]

Whether one accepts Williamson's psycho-social explanation, Dixon undoubtedly reached so many Americans so effectively "because his work said in a total way what his audience had been thinking in fragments."[9] His most lasting legacy might well be how ideas originally southern came to achieve respectability in a wide circle, across the country. Dixon himself was one of a number of southerners who spent most of their time outside of the region, serving partly as critics of their native region, partly as interpreters. Early twentieth-century America witnessed the rise of a group of professional southerners—people such as Henry Grady and Walter Hines Page—who marketed enduring southern ideas of race, gender, class, and history to a national market. Grady proclaimed a "new South" that had abandoned traditions of slavery and rural life and embraced a new spirit of industrialism and modernization. Page, also a New South enthusiast, was unlike Grady in that he was a committed expatriate who, as an editor and publisher, became an interpreter of the South and intersectional mediator. Both Grady and Page helped to interpret the South to northern audiences; both suggested that national development depended on a sectional reunion. Sharing a common message about the New South, Dixon incorporated that message into a new construction of American nationality. Dixon's message was thus double-edged: racist and southern, it possessed profound implications for the re-creation of important qualities in American culture.[10]

A new sense of national American identity was emerging at the turn of the twentieth century that recognized regional differences but also emphasized a unified national identity. These tendencies were wrapped up in the meaning of the Civil War, and, during the late nineteenth and early twentieth centuries, history was being rewritten. In both North and South, veterans' organizations, women's groups, and many other Americans contended with the war's searing memory. Lost Cause ideology swept through the South, shaping popular memory about the war. The Lost Cause version minimized regional differences, asserted common assumptions among white Americans, and argued that the issue of states' rights was the main consideration in the Civil War's origins. In contrast, other Americans, especially former abolitionists and African Americans, stressed slavery, emancipation, and the failed if noble efforts during Reconstruction to remake the South. As David Blight shows, this struggle over memory reflected a fundamental cultural reorientation into which Dixon's ideas fit. One way of understanding Dixon might be to probe further this mixed message of white supremacy and national reunion, and how these two themes became fundamentally intertwined.[11]

Professional historians also figured prominently in the reconfiguration of historical consciousness. Beginning in the 1870s, history in the United States became professionalized. Herbert Baxter Adams's seminar at The Johns Hopkins University—in which Dixon participated—represented an attempt to apply German notions of systematic inquiry, emphasis on original sources, and the application of new social scientific methods to the study of history in the United States. The Johns Hopkins model, which came to dominate American higher education, produced a generation of professional historians who regarded the Civil War as a new turning point in national history. These scholars, however, adopted what soon became a new orthodoxy. Emphasizing the sectional crisis as a disagreement among white people, these scholars focused attention on Reconstruction's failures. Specifically, historians such as William Archibald Dunning and his students criticized a misplaced faith in African Americans' citizenship, which they believed constituted the central failure of Reconstruction. An important implication of this thinking was that renewed attempts at sectional reintegration would need to adopt radically different notions of race.

All of this above has a direct bearing on our understanding of the worlds of Thomas Dixon—and their impact during the twentieth century. A number of authors note that part of Dixon's decline and, ultimately, even his ruin can be explained by a receding of the Radical mindset. According to this explanation, the post–World War I mindset no longer accommodated the Radical worldview. Racial moderation appeared to be on the rise, and overt racism was no longer in vogue, according to this understanding. Although racial violence did decline, it did not evaporate. Nor did white supremacy—far from it. Indeed, we need not look very far in the South, and to a certain extent in the nation, to see that the benighted Jim Crow system survived, and survived very powerfully for at least five decades beyond the appearance of *The Birth of a Nation*—all of which suggests a greater continuity to American race relations from slavery, through emancipation, until the collapse of white supremacy in the 1960s. Works by Neil McMillen, writing about Mississippi, Stephen Kantrowitz, writing about South Carolina, and Leon Litwack, writing about the South as a whole, paint a portrait of unrelenting racism and despair that over time varied only slightly. These authors attempt to understand the white supremacy that Dixon championed from an African American perspective, and from that perspective white supremacy never really softened. If anything, it ossified and became less flexible with the passage of the years. Seen from this vantage point, in the end, distinctions between Dixon's Radicals and southern white moderates remain less significant.[12]

Thomas Dixon's wide appeal suggests, nonetheless, that his ideas were powerful symbols of where the twentieth century was headed. Although his ideas no longer enjoyed popularity among cultural leaders, opinion shapers, and academics after World War I, his conception of white supremacy retained a powerful hold. Much of his cultural universe and accompanying baggage survived. In popular media, African Americans remained stereotyped and despised; only recently did the film industry rid itself of most of these stereotypes. The view of history that Dixon advocated—which, in effect, argued for white supremacy and national unity while it attacked Reconstruction for unnecessary intervention in southern race relations—persisted among American historians at least until the 1930s and among the American public for many years after that. Dixon raised central questions about the meaning of race in a national context that, in many respects, remain unanswered.

NOTES

1. On the Progressive South, see William A. Link, *The Paradox of Southern Progressivism, 1880–1930* (Chapel Hill: Univ. of North Carolina Press, 1992).
2. David Stricklin, "'Ours Is a Century of Light': Dixon's Strange Consistency," in this volume.
3. Cynthia Lynn Lyerly, "Gender and Race in Dixon's Religious Ideology," in this volume.
4. Charlene Register, "The Cinematic Representation of Race in *The Birth of a Nation*: A Black Horror Film," in this volume.
5. Fitzhugh Brundage, "Thomas Dixon: American Proteus," in this volume.
6. Rayford W. Logan, *The Negro in American Life and Thought: The Nadir, 1877–1901* (New York: Dial Press, 1954).
7. Joel Williamson, *The Crucible of Race: Black-White Relations in the American South since Emancipation* (New York: Oxford Univ. Press, 1984), 140–41.
8. Ibid., 151, 165.
9. Ibid., 141.
10. John Milton Cooper Jr., *Walter Hines Page: The Southerner as American, 1855–1918* (Chapel Hill: Univ. of North Carolina Press, 1997).
11. David W. Blight, *Race and Reunion: The Civil War in American Memory* (Cambridge: Harvard Univ. Press, 2001).
12. Neil McMillen, *Dark Journey: Black Mississippians in the Age of Jim Crow* (Urbana: Univ. of Illinois Press, 1989); Stephen D. Kantrowitz, *Ben Tillman and the Reconstruction of White Supremacy* (Chapel Hill: Univ. of North Carolina Press, 2000); Leon Litwack, *Trouble in Mind: Black Southerners in the Age of Jim Crow* (New York: Knopf, 1998).

Appendix A: Thomas Dixon Jr.'s Selected Publications

(in chronological order)

Living Problems in Religion and Social Science. New York: Charles T. Dillingham, 1889.

Dixon on Ingersoll, Ten Discourses, Delivered in Association Hall, New York. New York: John B. Alden, 1892.

An Open Letter from Rev. Thomas Dixon to J. C. Beam. N.p.: self-published, 1896.

The Failure of Protestantism in New York and Its Causes. New York: Victor O. A. Strauss, 1896.

Dixon's Sermons: Delivered in the Grand Old Opera House, New York, 1898–1899. New York: F. L. Bussey, 1899.

The Leopard's Spots: A Romance of the White Man's Burden, 1865–1900. New York: Doubleday, Page, 1902.

The One Woman: A Story of Modern Utopia. New York: Doubleday, Page, 1903.

The Life Worth Living: A Personal Experience. New York: Doubleday, Page, 1905.

The Clansman: An Historical Romance of the Ku Klux Klan. New York: Doubleday, Page, 1905.

The Traitor: A Story of the Fall of the Invisible Empire. New York: Doubleday, Page, 1907.

Comrades: A Story of Social Adventure in California. New York: Grosset and Dunlap, 1909.

The Root of Evil: A Novel. Garden City, N.Y.: Doubleday, Page, 1911.

The Sins of the Father: A Romance of the South. New York: D. Appleton, 1912.

The Southerner: A Romance of the Real Lincoln. New York: D. Appleton, 1913.

The Victim: A Romance of the Real Jefferson Davis. New York: D. Appleton, 1914.

The Foolish Virgin: A Romance of Today. New York: D. Appleton, 1915.

The Fall of a Nation: A Sequel to The Birth of a Nation. New York: D. Appleton, 1916.

The Way of a Man: A Story of the New Woman. New York: D. Appleton, 1919.

The Red Dawn: A Drama of Revolution. New York: n.p., 1919.

A Man of the People: A Drama of Abraham Lincoln. New York: D. Appleton, 1920.

The Man in Gray: A Romance of North and South. New York: D. Appleton, 1921.

The Black Hood. New York: D. Appleton, 1924.

The Love Complex. New York: Boni and Liveright, 1925.

The Hope of the World: A Story of the Coming War. New York: self-published, 1925.

Wildacres in the Land of the Sky. Little Switzerland, N.C.: Wildacres Development Co., 1926.

The Rising South: An Address. Raleigh, N.C.: H.S. Storr, Printers, 1926.

The Torch: A Story of the Paranoiac Who Caused a Great War. New York: self-published, 1927.

The Sun Virgin. New York: H. Liveright, 1929.

Companions. New York: Otis Publishing Company, 1931.

H. M. Daugherty and Thomas Dixon, *The Inside Story of the Harding Tragedy*. New York: The Churchill Company, 1932.

A Dreamer in Portugal: The Story of Bernarr McFadden's Mission to Continental Europe. New York: Covici, Friede, 1934.

The Flaming Sword. Atlanta: Monarch, 1939.

Appendix B: Thomas Dixon Jr.'s Films

(in chronological order, derived from Anthony Slide, American Racist: The Life and Films of Thomas Dixon *[Lexington: Univ. Press of Kentucky, 2004], 209–12.)*

The Birth of a Nation (1915). Screenplay by D. W. Griffith and Frank E. Woods, based on *The Clansman* and the play of the same name by Thomas Dixon Jr.

The Fall of a Nation (1916). Directed by and screenplay by Thomas Dixon Jr.

The Foolish Virgin (1916). Based on the novel by Thomas Dixon Jr.

The One Woman (1918). Based on the novel by Thomas Dixon Jr.

Bolshevism on Trial (1919). Based on the novel *Comrades* by Thomas Dixon Jr.

Wing Toy (1921). Screenplay by Thomas Dixon Jr.

Where Men are Men (1921). Screenplay by Thomas Dixon Jr.

Bring Him In (1921). Screenplay by Thomas Dixon Jr., based on a story by H. H. Van Loan.

Thelma (1922). Screenplay by Thomas Dixon, based on the novel by Marie Corelli.

The Mark of the Beast (1923). Directed by and screenplay by Thomas Dixon Jr. Thomas Dixon Productions.

The Foolish Virgin (1924). Based on the novel by Thomas Dixon Jr.

The Painted Lady (1924). Screenplay by Thomas Dixon Jr., based on the *Saturday Evening Post* story by Larry Evans.

The Great Diamond Mystery (1924). Screenplay by Thomas Dixon Jr., based on a story by Shannon Fife.

The Brass Bowl (1924). Screenplay by Thomas Dixon Jr., based on the novel by Louis Joseph Vance.

Champion of Lost Causes (1925). Screenplay by Thomas Dixon Jr., based on the *Flynn's Magazine* story by Max Brand.

The Trail Rider (1925). Screenplay by Thomas Dixon Jr., based on the novel by George Washington Ogden.

The Gentle Cyclone (1926). Screenplay by Thomas Dixon Jr., based on the *Western Story Magazine* story "Peg Leg and Kidnapper" by Frank R. Buckley.

Nation Aflame (1937). Original story by Thomas Dixon Jr., in collaboration with Oliver Drake and Rex Hale.

Contributors

W. FITZHUGH BRUNDAGE is the William B. Umstead Professor of History and Director of Graduate Studies at the University of North Carolina at Chapel Hill. The author of numerous books and articles, he recently published *The Southern Past: A Clash of Race and Memory* (Harvard Univ. Press, 2005).

JANE M. GAINES is a professor of Literature and English at Duke University, where she founded and coordinates the Duke University Program in Film, Video, and Digital. She is the author of dozens of articles and three books, including *Fire and Desire: Mixed-Blood Movies in the Silent Era* (Univ. of Chicago Press, 2001) and the forthcoming *Fictioning Histories: Women Film Pioneers* (Univ. of Illinois Press).

MICHELE K. GILLESPIE is the Kahle Associate Professor of History at Wake Forest University. Her work includes *Free Labor in an Unfree World: White Artisans in Slaveholding Georgia* (Univ. of Georgia Press, 2000).

RANDAL L. HALL is acting managing editor of *The Journal of Southern History* at Rice University. He is the author of many publications, including *William Louis Poteat: A Leader of the Progressive-Era South* (Univ. Press of Kentucky, 2000).

WILLIAM A. LINK is the Richard J. Milbauer Professor of History at the University of Florida. He is the author of numerous books and articles, most recently *Roots of Secession: Slavery and Politics in Antebellum Virginia* (Univ. of North Carolina Press, 2003).

CYNTHIA LYNN LYERLY is an associate professor of history at Boston College. She is the author of several articles and *Methodism and the Southern Mind* (Oxford Univ. Press, 1998), and is currently working on a new book titled *Thomas Dixon, Jr.: Apostle of Hate*.

LOUIS MENAND is a professor of English and American Literature at Harvard University. He is a book critic and essayist for *The New Yorker*, and the author of several books, including *The Metaphysical Club* (Farrar, Strauss and Giroux, 2001), which won the 2002 Pulitzer Prize for history.

CHARLENE REGESTER is an assistant professor of African and Afro-American Studies at the University of North Carolina at Chapel Hill. She is the author of *Black Entertainers in African American Newspaper Articles* (McFarland, 2002) and the forthcoming *Black Lace and White Frills: African American Actresses in the First Fifty Years of Cinema*.

SCOTT ROMINE is Director of Undergraduate Studies and an associate professor of English at the University of North Carolina at Greensboro. He has published extensively on such authors as John Crowe Ransom, Richard Wright, Lillian Smith, A. B. Longstreet, Harry Crews, and William Alexander Percy. His forthcoming collection, coedited with Jon Smith and Kathryn McKee, is titled *Postcolonial Theory, the U.S. South, and New World Studies*.

JOHN DAVID SMITH is the Charles H. Stone Distinguished Professor of American History at the University of North Carolina at Charlotte. He is the author of numerous articles and books, and recently edited Thomas Dixon's *The Flaming Sword* (Univ. Press of Kentucky, 2005).

DAVID STRICKLIN is administrative head of the Butler Center for Arkansas Studies in Little Rock. At the time of the Dixon conference at Wake Forest, he was associate professor of history and chair of the Humanities Division at Lyon College. He is the author of *A Genealogy of Dissent: The Culture of Southern Baptist Protest in the Twentieth Century* (Univ. Press of Kentucky, 1999).

Index

"Action of the Negro Inter-Marriage Society against the Play, The" (T. Dixon), 186
Adams, Herbert Baxter, 4, 35, 208
Addams, Jane, 13, 37, 185, 187
aesthetics of spectacle, the. *See* melodrama
Aftermath of Slavery, The (W. Sinclair), 50
Aitken, Harry, 187–88, 190, 200, 201
Aitken, Roy, 187–88
Allan, Mansfield, 150n51
American Dilemma, An (Myrdal), 17
"Anglo-Saxon Alliance, The" (T. Dixon), 112–13
Armour, Philip D., 29
Arnesen, Eric, 146n10
As to the Leopard's Spots: An Open Letter to Thomas Dixon, Jr. (Miller), 53

Bakhtin, M. M., 147n14
Barry, Iris, 200
Barthes, Roland, 130
Beauharnais, Joseph, 197–98
Beauharnais v. Illinois (1952), 197–99
Beecher, Henry Ward, 110
Bell, Lilian, 148n32
Bellamy, Edward, 29
Bergman, Ingrid, 195
Berzon, Judith R., 51
Bicycle Thief, The (1948), 192
Birth of a Nation, The (1915), 11–13, 34–35, 36, 43–44n50, 44–45n63, 59, 105, 185, 200–201, 205; criticism of, 175–76; financial aspects of, 13, 185, 188, 201; first viewing of, 151–52, 183; "hoochey koochey" music and, 157–58; legal actions against by the NAACP, 183–86, 191; legal context of, 190–91; melodrama and, 154, 158–61; "Motif of Barbarism" in, 155–58, 162n15; reception of by the local press in North Carolina, 175–80; score of, 43n49, 153–55, 162n14; syncopation and, 156; screening of before the U.S. Supreme Court, 186, 187; screenplay of, 1–2. See also *Birth of a Nation, The* (1915) as a horror film
Birth of a Nation, The (1915) as a horror film, 16, 164–65, 204–5; castration as a subtext in, 168; evocation of fear in, 173–75, 179–80; females represented as victims in, 166–71; horror techniques used in, 165–66, 180; parallels with *Bride of Frankenstein* (1935), 172–73; parallels with *King Kong*, 165, 171–72
"Bishop Potter and the Saloon" (T. Dixon), 115
Black Hood, The (T. Dixon), 94, 96, 99, 104n62
Black Reconstruction in America (Du Bois), 63, 68, 69–70
Black Viper, The (1908), 33–34
Blight, David, 208

217

Bliss, W.D.P., 29
Boas, Franz, 17, 36
Boeckmann, Cathy, 124, 125, 140
Bogle, Donald, 172
Bone, Robert A., 48, 51
Braithwaite, William Stanley, 58
Breil, Joseph Carl, 2, 11, 16, 151–52, 155
Bride of Frankenstein (1935), 172–73
Brodhead, Richard, 143
Brooks, Peter, 33, 129–30, 163n23
Broughton, Len, 27
Brundage, W. Fitzhugh, 14–15, 205
Bryan, William Jennings, 107
Burgess, John W., 118
Burstyn, Joseph, 191–92, 193–94, 197, 201
Burstyn v. Wilson (1952), 196, 197
Butters, Gerald, 165

Calvinism, 121
Captain of the Gray-Horse Troop, The (Garland), 30–31, 44n59
Carnegie, Andrew, 29
Carroll, Charles, 138
Chesnutt, Charles W., 49, 54, 143, 144, 149n48
"Child Is Being Beaten, A" (Freud), 130
Choate, Joseph H., 8
Chord of Life, The (1909), 34
Christianity, 24, 39nn13, 16, 84, 85; "social," 107. *See also* evangelicalism, nineteenth-century; fundamentalism; "muscular Christianity"; Social Gospel movement, the; Southern Baptists
cinema: appeal of European, 192; censorship and, 188–90, 192–97; history of the sound track and, 153; popularity of, 187; portrayal of the Civil War in, 14
Civil Union, 28
Civil War, the, 8, 50, 206, 208; representations of in film, 14. *See also* Lost Cause, the

Clansman, The (film). See *Birth of a Nation, The*
Clansman, The (novel, T. Dixon), 7, 30, 34, 35, 46, 59, 62, 80, 95, 105, 108, 118, 151, 183, 204; mid-1960s reprint edition, 14; racism in, 48–49
Clansman, The (play, T. Dixon), 10, 11, 27, 34–35, 36, 44–45n63, 183; advertisements for, 44n54; comic elements in, 43–44n50; reception of in North Carolina, 174
Clarke, Edward Young, 62
Clover, Carol, 169
Communism, 194–95. *See also* Dixon, Thomas, Jr.: on Communism
Comrades (T. Dixon), 10, 61
Conjure Woman, The (Chesnutt), 143
Cook, Raymond A., 18, 46, 109
Cooper, James Fenimore, 139
Costigan, Edward, 77n99
Costigan-Wagner Anti-Lynching Bill (1934), 63, 77n99
Councill, William H., 66
Cox, Earnest Sevier, 59, 61
Craven, Avery O., 68
Creed, Barbara, 167–68
Crisis, The, 58, 63, 64
Crucible of Race, The (Williamson), 23, 207

Darrow, Clarence, 183
Debs, Eugene, 29, 191
Democrats, 118–19
Derry, Charles, 165–66
Diawara, Manthia, 168
"dilatory space," 130
Dines, Gail, 172
Dixon, Amanda (mother of TD), 23, 38n2
Dixon, Amzi Clarence ("A. C." [brother of TD]), 19, 25, 38n2, 102n29, 119
Dixon, Harriet (*née* Bussey [first wife of TD]), 5, 13

Dixon, Madelyn (*née* Donovan [second wife of TD]), 14
Dixon, Thomas, Jr., 39–40n17; 42n35, 57–58, 105, 123n20, 124, 148n25, 200, 203; acting career of 4–5, 25, 110, 166; African American challenges to his racist ideology, 50–59, 205–6; attacks on Tammany Hall corruption, 82; as an author, 7–11, 29–37, 88, 103n43, 151; autobiography of, 20n5, 88; as a Baptist minister, 5–6, 26, 41n27, 81–83, 84, 101n9, 106, 108, 110–12; on Catholicism, 104n62, 120; on cinema, 44n55; on Communism, 61–63, 66, 67; concern for the working poor, 83–84; critical revival of, 149n41; criticism of B. T. Washington, 69; criticism of Du Bois, 62–63, 67–69, 70; critiques of his literary works, 31–32, 41nn29, 31; 42n39 (*see also* melodrama); education of, 3–4, 25, 109–10, 120, 208; on the feminization of Protestant churches, 83–86; as film writer, 11–13, 100n1; financial stake of in *The Birth of a Nation*, 185; on gender issues and feminism, 39–40n17, 40n18, 81, 92–96, 103n41, 146n6; gift of oratory, 4, 26, 43n45; idolization of white women, 93–94; intellectual development of, 21n28; as lawyer, 5, 26–27; modernism and, 36–37; as a national lecturer, 6; on the "Negro junta," 65, 67; opposition to alcohol use, 83, 115; opposition to the Ku Klux Klan, 133, 148n21; place of in the cultural tradition of his time, 29–30, 117–18; as a playwright, 10, 34–35; posthumous influence of, 14; on race relations, 100n4, 104n62, 206; on racial assimilation (miscegenation), 49–50, 53, 63, 97–99, 104n61; racism of, 7–9, 30, 47–49, 81, 94–95, 99–100, 104n61, 108, 114, 206–7; as a reformer, 6, 28–29, 40n20, 81, 82, 110–11; relationship with the fundamentalist movement, 119–20; religious ideology of, 80–83, 109, 112, 115; responses to his critics, 38n4, 59, 60–61, 186; siblings of, 3–4; Social Gospel movement and, 26–28, 36, 39n16, 81–82, 83, 84–86, 94, 99–100, 103n53, 105–6, 108, 111–15, 119; Socialism and, 40n24, 61–62; as state representative, 5, 25, 110; success (appeal) of, 203–5, 209; transformations of, 37–38; on voting rights for blacks, 104n60, 114; on Zola, 41n28. *See also specifically listed individual works*
Dixon, Thomas, Sr. (father of TD), 38n2, 81
Domingo, Wilfred A., 61–62
Dracula (1931), 166
Dreiser, Theodore, 28–29
Du Bois, W.E.B., 9–10, 15, 17, 30, 46, 49, 52, 54, 60, 62–63, 77n96, 143, 205; criticism of *The Birth of a Nation*, 58, 183–84; criticism of Dixon, 47, 58; response to *The Flaming Sword*, 79n124
Dunning, William Archibald, 208
"Dunning School," 118

Elder, Arlene A., 75n51
Eliot, Charles, 13
Epoch Producing Corporation, 11, 188, 200
evangelicalism, nineteenth-century, 24–26
Eversley, Carlton A. G., 18

Failure of Protestantism in New York and Its Causes, The (T. Dixon), 40n24, 83, 120
Fall of a Nation, The (film, 1916), 13, 90–91; score of, 161n6
Fall of a Nation, The (novel, T. Dixon), 90; plot of, 91–92
Fatal Hour, The (1908), 34
Fellini, Federico, 192
Fiske, John, 112
Flaming Sword, The (T. Dixon), 13, 15, 60–61, 95; anti-socialist theme of, 62–63;

220 Index

Flaming Sword, The (continued)
  plot of, 63–67; portrayal of Du Bois in, 67–69, 70; reviews of, 70–71
Foner, Eric, 118
Foolish Virgin, The (T. Dixon), 88–90, 103n47
forepleasure, concept of, 129
Fossett, Judith Jackson, 146n6
Frankfurter, Felix, 197
Free Lance, The, a Monthly Magazine, 108
Freud, Sigmund, 130
"Friendly Warning to the Negro, A" (T. Dixon), 114
Fulton, Justin D., 5
fundamentalism, 102n29, 119–20

Gaines, Jane M., 16, 43n49, 140, 168, 204
Garland, Hamlin, 30–31, 37, 42n35, 44n59
Garvey, Amy Jacques, 76n79
Garvey, Marcus, 59–60, 61–62
gender, 39–40n17, 40n18, 81, 86, 92–96, 100, 103n41, 146n6; feminization of Protestant churches, 83–86; plight of women workers, 83–84. See also *Birth of a Nation, The* (1915) as a horror film: females represented as victims in; Dixon, Thomas, Jr.: idolization of white women; "muscular Christianity"; *Way of a Man, The: A Story of the New Woman* (T. Dixon, Jr.)
Gershwin, George, 193
Gilbert, M. W., 9
Gillman, Susan, 54
Gilman, Charlotte Perkins, 36
Gilmore, Glenda Elizabeth, 52
Gladden, Washington, 113
Glasgow, Ellen, 37, 44n59
Gloster, Hugh M., 54
Gone With the Wind (1939), 199
Gorbman, Claudia, 155
Grady, Henry, 30, 207
Graves, John Temple, 66

Greenberg, Harvey Roy, 171–72
Griffith, D. W., 1–2, 11, 33–34, 158, 164–65, 183, 184, 196, 200. See also *Birth of a Nation, The* (1915)
Griggs, Sutton E., 15, 52, 53–56, 75nn49, 51, 205–6; criticism of Dixon, 55–56, 57; works of, 54
group libel, concept of, 197–98, 199
Guerrero, Edward, 173
Gunning, Sandra, 132, 136, 146n11

Hackett, Francis, 154, 157–58
Hale, Grace Elizabeth, 124
Handy, Robert, 113–14
Harper, Lucius C., 51
Harris, Joel Chandler, 7
Harris, Trudier, 135
Hays Office, the, 191
Hendler, Glenn, 140
Herbert, Victor, 162n6
Higham, John, 32
Hill, Samuel S., 19
Hindered Hand, The (Griggs), 15, 54, 55, 57
History of the American People (W. Wilson), 118
Hoffman, Frederick L., 53
Hollinger, Karen, 166–67
Holsey, Lucius, 66
Howard, Anna, 86
Hunt, Michael, 80–81

Imperium in Imperio (Griggs), 54–55
industrialization, 109, 110
Ingersoll, Robert, 110, 119
Inscoe, John, 44–45n63, 149n47, 174–75, 178, 179
Ivanhoe (W. Scott), 139

J. Johnson or "The Unknown Man" (Walker), 51–52
Jameson, Fredric, 126
Jim Crow system, 47, 119, 209

Johnson, James Weldon, 36, 61, 64
Jungle, The (U. Sinclair), 44n59

Kantrowitz, Stephen, 209
Kazan, Elia, 193
King, Richard H., 17
King Kong (1933), 165, 171–72
Kinney, James, 63
Kristeva, Julia, 167
Ku Klux Klan, 8, 13, 104n62, 133, 146n6, 147n15, 184; as represented in *The Birth of a Nation*, 175, 177, 179, 186; romanticization of, 30. *See also* Dixon, Thomas, Jr.: opposition to the Ku Klux Klan

Lady Chatterley's Lover (film, 1955), 196
Lang, Robert, 33
Last Temptation of Christ, The (1988), 196
Lears, Jackson, 32
Lease, Mary Elizabeth, 29
Leopard's Spots, The (T. Dixon), 7, 10, 34, 46, 72n12, 80, 93–94, 95, 130–31, 151, 183, 204, 206–7; criticism of, 47, 58, 38n4; history and white identity in, 137–40; literary genres and whiteness in, 135–45; racist narrative in, 125–26, 142–43; regressionist theme of, 48, 148n25; reviews of, 47–48, 124, 144, 149n39; whiteness and nationhood in, 128–29, 132–34; whiteness and racial identities in, 125–28, 130, 134–35, 147n12. *See also* forepleasure, concept of
Lerner, Neil, 155
Lewis, David Levering, 58
Liberal Congress of Religion, 86, 108
Liddell, E. T., 176
Lincoln, Abraham, 49
Lindsay, Vachel, 154, 157
Lindstrom, Peter, 195
Link, William A., 17, 19
Litwack, Leon, 209
Logan, Rayford W., 47–48

Long, Huey, 143
Lost Boundaries (1949), 193
Lost Cause, the, 81, 114, 138, 208
Love Complex, The (T. Dixon), 103n52
Loving v. Virginia (1967), 199
Lubin, David, 16–17
Lucas, Sean, 43n45
Lukács, Georg, 139–40
Lumpkin, Katharine Du Pre, 12
Lyerly, Cynthia Lynn, 15, 42n36, 204
lynching, 132, 135–36, 137–38, 172–73, 179. *See also* Costigan-Wagner Anti-Lynching Bill (1934)

Magnani, Anna, 192
Magowan, Kim, 145, 146n6
manhood/manliness, 7–8, 84–85, 125, 146n11. *See also* "muscular Christianity"
Marks, Martin, 153
Marrow of Tradition, The (Chesnutt), 144
Mayer, Arthur L., 192
McCaffrey, Edward T., 193–94
McKinley, William, 107, 112
McMillen, Neil, 209
Meekins, Isaac M., 62
melodrama, 14–15, 16, 32–34, 36, 43n49, 151, 158–60; race and, 161, 163n21; "whiteness" and, 125
Melodramatic Imagination, The (Brooks), 163n23
Menand, Louis, 17, 18
Michaels, Walter Benn, 124, 147n15
Micheaux, Oscar, 18, 161n1
Miller, Kelly, 9, 15, 17, 49, 52–53, 144, 205–6; criticism of Dixon, 53, 55–56; on slavery, 53
Miller, Paul D., 1–2
Miracle, The (Rossellini), 17; court case involving, 192–97, 201
miscegenation, 52, 56, 97–99. *See also* Dixon, Thomas, Jr.: on racial assimilation (miscegenation)

modernism, 36–37, 44–45n63, 205
Moody, Dwight, 27
Motion Pictures Association of America (MPAA), 192, 197
"muscular Christianity," 27, 39n16, 85–86
Mutual Film Corporation, 187, 188, 189, 190
Mutual Film Corporation v. Industrial Commission of Ohio (1915), 187, 189, 191, 196, 198
Myrdal, Gunnar, 17

National Association for the Advancement of Colored People (NAACP), 15, 17, 59–60, 61, 63, 65, 77n99, 205; agreement with movie industry over portrayals of blacks in films, 199–200; legal actions against *The Birth of a Nation* by, 183–86, 191
National Board of Censorship of Motion Pictures, 190
National League of Decency, 194
Neale, Stephen, 168, 172
"Negro problem" the, 47, 48, 150n51
New York City Fire Department, 194, 198
New York State Board of Regents, 195–96
New York Times v. Sullivan (1962), 198
Niagara Movement, 9–10, 54
Nigger, The (Sheldon), 43n48
Nye, W. G., 184, 191

Ogden, Robert C., 8, 51
Oliver, Lawrence J., 63, 65, 78n112
One Great Question: A Study of Southern Conditions at Close Range (Griggs), 55
One Woman, The (T. Dixon), 7, 10, 61, 80; plot of, 86–88; republication of under another title, 103n52
Open City (1945), 192
Our Country (Strong), 112

Page, Thomas Nelson, 7, 30
Page, Walter Hines, 7, 46, 72n3, 144–45, 207

Parkhurst, Charles H., 175–76
Pillsbury, Albert E., 65
Pinky (1949), 193
Plague of Fantasies, The (Žižek), 131–32
political speech, and dissent, 198–99
Populist movement, the (Populism), 107–8, 118–19, 121
Poteat, Edwin M., 4
Poteat, William L., 109
Powderly, Terence, 115
Progressives/Progressive Era, 82–83, 84, 198, 203, 206
"prooftexting," 115–16
Protestantism. *See* Christianity
Public Sentiments (Hendler), 140
Puritans/Puritan commonwealth, 121

racial essentialism, 147n13
racism, 7–8, 15–16, 17, 30–31; genteel, 145. *See also* Dixon, Thomas, Jr.: racism of
Radicals/political Radicalism, 10
Rauschenbusch, Walter, 85, 105
Rawick, George, 143
Rebirth of a Nation (2004/2005), 2
Reconstruction, 8, 50, 118, 138, 186, 206, 208
Red Rock (Page), 30
"Redeemers," 2
Regester, Charlene, 16, 18, 204–5
Riis, Jacob, 83, 94
Riley, Denise, 125
Rise and Fall of Free Speech in America (Griffith), 187, 196
Roberts, Samuel K., 53
Rochmont, Louis de, 193
Rockefeller, John D., 6, 29
Roediger, David, 126
Rogin, Michael, 167, 171
Roman Catholicism, 121, 193, 194–95. *See also* Dixon, Thomas, Jr.: on Catholicism
romance/romantic love, 81–82, 93; juxtaposition of white/black romantic love, 97–99; southern tradition of, 8

Romine, Scott, 16, 43n45
Roosevelt, Eleanor, 61
Roosevelt, Franklin D., 61
"Roosevelt, the Heroic Hero" (T. Dixon), 115
Roosevelt, Theodore, 6, 28, 37, 42n35, 85, 115, 117, 141
"Roosevelt's Personality" (T. Dixon), 115
Root of Evil, The (T. Dixon), 10, 61, 94
Rossellini, Roberto, 17, 192, 193, 195
Rotundo, Anthony, 85
Royall, William, 109
Ryan, Phil, 200

Scenting a Terrible Crime (1913), 166
Schmidt, Peter, 139, 140
Scorsese, Martin, 196
Scott, Hazel, 193
Scott, Walter, 139
Sheldon, Edward, 43n48
Shelton, Robert, 14
Simkins, Francis Butler, 47
Simmons, William, J., 184–85
Sinclair, Upton, 44n59
Sinclair, William A., 50
Singer, Ben, 34
Sins of the Father (T. Dixon), 10, 97–99
Sister Carrie (Dreiser), 28
Skal, David, 166
slavery, 53, 56, 81, 114; legacy of, 54
Smethurst, Frank, 70
Smith, J. Howell, 19
Smith, John David, 15, 18
Snead, James, 165
Social Gospel movement, the, 15, 26–27, 29, 81–82, 84–86, 99–100, 121; and Populism, 107–8; progressive proponents of in the North, 106–7; and the subject of race, 113–14; tenets of according to Dixon, 105–6. *See also* Dixon, Thomas, Jr.: Social Gospel movement and
Socialism, 86–87

Souls of Black Folk, The (Du Bois), 68, 79n120
Southern Baptists, 108, 109, 116–17, 123n31
Southern Horizons (T. Dixon), 152, 160–61
Spellman, Francis Cardinal, 194
Spencer, Herbert, 112, 115
Spingarn, Joel E., 65
Spooky, Dj. *See* Miller, Paul D.
Stevens, Thaddeus, 35
Stewart, Potter, 196
Stokes, Mason, 54, 124, 133
Storey, Moorfield, 59, 65, 184
Stowe, Harriet Beecher, 7, 136, 140, 141, 158–59
Stricklin, David, 15–16, 39n13, 41n27
Strong, Josiah, 112, 114
"Studies of Contemporary Celebrities" (Dreiser), 29
Survey, The, 58

Tempter of Eve, The (Carroll), 138, 148n31
Thal, Ted, 200
Thomas, William Hannibal, 65
Tillman, Ben ("Pitchfork Ben"), 60, 114, 117
Tourgée, Albion, 30
Towards the Abolition of Whiteness (Roediger), 126
Traitor, The (T. Dixon), 7, 10, 96, 104n62, 133
Triangle Films, 188
Trotter, William Monroe, 17, 50
Turner, Henry McNeal, 50, 66
Turner, Ted, 14
Twain, Mark, 8

Uncle Tom's Cabin (Stowe), 7, 95, 140, 159
Up From Slavery (Washington), 46

Veblen, Thorstein, 186
Villard, Oswald Garrison, 65

Wagner, Robert, 77n99
Wake Forest University, 21n27. *See also* Dixon, Thomas, Jr.: education of

Walker, Thomas H. B., 51–52
Walsh, Raoul, 187
Wartenberg, Thomas, 165
Washington, Booker T., 8, 13, 37, 49, 51, 72n12, 114, 117, 184, 185
Watts, Sarah L., 19
Way of a Man, The: A Story of the New Woman (T. Dixon, Jr.), 92–93
Ways of Love (1950), 193
White, Edward, 186
White, Walter, 58–59
White Circle League of America, Inc., 197
White Man, Listen! (Wright), 142
white studies, 146n10
white supremacy, 138, 146n10, 167, 204, 206; melodrama of, 37–38; modes of, 136
white witch (temptress), the, 65, 78n112
"White Witch, The" (Johnson), 64, 65

Williams, Linda, 43n49, 158, 167
Williams, Raymond, 36
Williamson, Joel, 18, 23, 24, 48, 50, 93, 124, 145, 206–7
Wilson, Edwin G., 19
Wilson, Woodrow, 4, 11–12, 42n35, 90–91, 118, 186, 201n4, 205
Within Our Gates (Micheaux), 18
women. *See* gender
Woodward, C. Vann, 47
Words of Selves, The (Riley), 125
Wright, James Zebulon, 64
Wright, Richard, 142

Young, Elizabeth, 172

Žižek, Slavoj, 131–32, 134, 144, 145
Zola, Emile, 41n28

www.ingramcontent.com/pod-product-compliance
Lightning Source LLC
Chambersburg PA
CBHW060949230426
43665CB00015B/2131